METALITERACY
IN PRACTICE

METALITERACY IN PRACTICE

TRUDI E. JACOBSON
and
THOMAS P. MACKEY

An imprint of the American Library Association

CHICAGO 2016

Extensive effort has gone into ensuring the reliability of the information in this book; however, the publisher makes no warranty, express or implied, with respect to the material contained herein.

ISBNs
978-0-8389-1379-6 (paper)
978-0-8389-1387-1 (PDF)
978-0-8389-1388-8 (ePub)
978-0-8389-1389-5 (Kindle)

Library of Congress Cataloging-in-Publication Data

Names: Jacobson, Trudi E., 1957- editor. | Mackey, Thomas P., editor.
Title: Metaliteracy in practice / edited by Trudi E. Jacobson and Thomas P. Mackey.
Description: Chicago : ALA Neal-Schuman, an imprint of the American Library Association, 2016. | Includes bibliographical references and index.
Identifiers: LCCN 2015029948| ISBN 9780838913796 (print : alk. paper) | ISBN 9780838913888 (epub) | ISBN 9780838913871 (pdf) | ISBN 9780838913895 (kindle)
Subjects: LCSH: Information literacy—Study and teaching (Higher)—United States. | Electronic information resource literacy—Study and teaching (Higher)—United States. | Academic libraries—Relations with faculty and curriculum—United States. | Library orientation for college students—United States. | Media literacy—Study and teaching (Higher)—United States. | Critical thinking—Study and teaching (Higher)—United States. | Social media. | User generated content. | Metacognition. | Educational change—United States.
Classification: LCC ZA3075 .M48 2016 | DDC 028.7071/173—dc23 LC record available at http://lccn.loc.gov/2015029948

Cover design by Kim Thornton. Cover images ©agsandrew/Shutterstock, Inc. and ktsdesign/ Shutterstock, Inc.

Text design in the Chaparral, Gotham, and Bell Gothic typefaces.

♾ This paper meets the requirements of ANSI/NISO Z39.48-1992 (Permanence of Paper).

Printed in the United States of America

20 19 18 17 16   5 4 3 2 1

The editors would like to express their deep appreciation
for the hard work, creativity, and camaraderie of the Metaliteracy
Learning Collaborative. Working with all of you has been a sheer
pleasure, and we look forward to future projects.

Trudi would also like to thank her parents, Reva and
Herbert Jacobson, for serving as outstanding role models.

Tom thanks his family, friends, and colleagues for ongoing
inspiration and support.

Theory surely leads to practice. But practice also leads to theory. And teaching, at its best, shapes both research and practice. Viewed from this perspective, a more comprehensive, more dynamic understanding of scholarship can be considered, one in which the rigid categories of teaching, research, and service are broadened and more flexibly defined.

ERNEST L. BOYER
Scholarship Reconsidered: Priorities of the Professoriate
(Princeton, NJ: Carnegie Foundation
for the Advancement of Teaching, 1990, 16)

Contents

Figures and Tables

FIGURES

TABLES

Foreword

THE CONCEPT OF INFORMATION LITERACY IS NOT NEW. FOR decades, educators—particularly academic and school librarians—have devoted tremendous effort and resources to teaching students how to navigate increasingly complex information systems in the digital age. Their task is to teach students how to be discriminating information seekers and consumers as well as ethical content producers. Their overarching goal is to help students succeed in school and society, so that they remain self-directed, effective, and motivated learners long after graduation.

Despite these widespread efforts, something surprising has *not* occurred: Few have thought to ask what happens to college students once they graduate. For instance, what are the outcomes of training and curricula aimed at producing more-information-literate adults? What critical thinking and information competencies learned and developed in college are adapted and applied by graduates when they join the workplace and continue on the journey of their lives?

These are the types of challenging research questions that Project Information Literacy (PIL) addresses. Our latest research tackled some of these questions when we conducted a two-year federal study of relatively recent graduates from ten US colleges and universities. Our survey results tell us most young graduates do credit college with teaching them how to sort through large amounts of content and synthesize key points. Many also reported picking up the finer competencies of evaluation, especially determining bias and establishing the authority and credibility of Web sources.

While these are essential competencies for the digital age, we also found this generation's information-finding savvy may be masking some deep and troubling shortcomings. In particular, fewer than one in three of the graduates we surveyed believed they had developed the ability to formulate questions during college. As one graduate we interviewed as part of the study recalled, "I don't even remember being in any classes ever where I saw students asking professors questions in front of the entire class—but wouldn't that be good if students did? It bugs me every day now—why did I rush to get through college, why didn't I take the time to develop questions of my own?"

This and related findings underscore a gap between the critical thinking and information literacy competencies colleges may be teaching students and the work skills they may need at their first job and to remain competitive in the workplace. One recent study from the Association of American Colleges and Universities (AAC&U) confirms our suspicions: Critical thinking competencies matter to employers that are hiring today's graduates. When more than 300 executives in US companies and nonprofits were surveyed, nine out of ten agreed that the ability to "think critically, communicate clearly, and solve complex problems" mattered more than the major of a potential hire right out of college.

Moreover, these findings raise serious questions about the nature of higher education that today's students may be receiving. Are colleges and universities turning out curious question-askers who are equipped to solve information problems? Or are they churning out an abundance of "strategic learners" among the digital generation? These are the students who chase the highest grade rather than self-reflection and deep learning, according to Ken Bain, acclaimed educator and author of *What the Best College Students Do.*

Regardless of what you may be thinking as you read these words, one thing is certain. As we face the challenges of educating today's students, we need more class discussions, assignments, and faculty-student and librarian-student interactions that nurture individual discovery and curiosity while fostering students' ability to formulate and ask their own questions. With this approach, graduates are more likely to become what Ken Bain calls "adaptive experts"—those who can tackle unusual problems and generate new solutions, which, few would disagree, are needed in an increasingly complex world. They are also likely to be lifelong learners, an essential ingredient in a democratic society and for living a full and rich life.

This call for improving higher education curricula and pedagogy is a mandate of the highest order. It applies to librarians as much as it does to faculty. But how do academic and school librarians, often working in close collaboration with faculty, pick up the strands of this inevitable educational shift and participate actively in their daily work with students? What new curricular ideas exist for helping students think about their own learning styles? What classroom exercises help students understand the information practices they may use every day as collaborative consumers and producers of all kinds of information that enters their lives, whether a book chapter, a *Wikipedia* entry, or a Pinterest board?

Look no further. If you are in need of up-to-date and thought-provoking information literacy curricula and instructional approaches you can use in your teaching, then keep reading. Trudi Jacobson and Tom Mackey, two respected leaders in distance education and library instruction, have brought readers *Metaliteracy in Practice*. As a follow-up to their acclaimed book *Metaliteracy: Reinventing Information Literacy to Empower Learners*, *Metaliteracy in Practice* delivers a compilation of innovative and practical teaching ideas from some of the leading thinkers in library and information literacy instruction today.

What makes this collection different from other curricular guides is this book's focus on *metaliteracy*, which is a powerful reframing of information literacy from its 2000 ACRL (Association of College and Research Libraries) standards. According to Trudi and Tom, metaliteracy retrofits the concept of information literacy so it works better in the Web 2.0 era where information can jump its boundaries and become as transient, free-flowing, and participatory as a Facebook post or a tweet. Moreover, their concept of metaliteracy provides an inclusive and self-referential framework that encompasses, rather than excludes, all the "other" newer literacies, such as digital, visual, cyber, and media literacy.

Each chapter in *Metaliteracy in Practice* takes readers through the process of using the metaliteracy framework in new and exciting ways that easily transfer to the classroom and to work with students. These ideas are grounded in teaching traditional information literacy competencies yet are brought into the twenty-first century with the addition of methods for teaching and learning about metacognition, information creation, and participation in learning communities, too.

Readers will benefit from this collection's practical ideas for teaching students about the importance of format choice, assessing user feedback, creating information as teachers, evaluating dynamic content critically and effectively, and sharing information in collaborative environments. Plus, the case studies contained in *Metaliteracy in Practice* detail the hows and whys of curricular design for metaliteracy, fitting for both beginners and seasoned experts.

Taken together, this collection has some of the most innovative teaching ideas for inspiring librarians and faculty to revise lessons on critical thinking and information literacy, so that their students will graduate from college with the ability to formulate and ask their own questions. The great contribution that a book like *Metaliteracy in Practice* makes is that it gives today's students a better chance at becoming adaptive experts; Ken Bain's phrase for describing individuals who, in his words, "understand the conventional routines, but also have the capacity to recognize and even relish the opportunity and necessity for invention."[1]

Alison J. Head

Alison Head founded and directs Project Information Literacy, a national study about today's college students and their research habits.

NOTE

1. Ken Bain, "Deep Learning: Pursuing Questions That Are Important, Intriguing, or Just Beautiful," *Project Information Literacy Smart Talk*, no. 13 (October 10, 2012). http://projectinfolit.org/smart-talks/item/105-ken-bain.

BIBLIOGRAPHY

Bain, Ken. *What the Best College Students Do.* Cambridge, MA: Harvard University Press, 2012.

Hart Research Associates. "It Takes More Than a Major: Employer Priorities for College Learning and Student Success." *Liberal Education* 99, no. 2 (Spring 2013). www.aacu.org/publications-research/periodicals/it-takes-more-major-employer-priorities-college-learning-and.

Head, Alison J. *Staying Smart: How Today's Graduates Continue Learning Once They Complete College.* Seattle, WA: Project Information Literacy Research Report, University of Washington Information School, November 2015.

Mackey, Thomas P., and Trudi Jacobson. *Metaliteracy: Reinventing Information Literacy to Empower Learners.* Chicago: Neal-Schuman, 2014.

Preface

THIS BOOK SHARES INNOVATIVE AND EMERGING PRACTICES that represent the influence of metaliteracy in teaching and learning. As we completed our coauthored book, *Metaliteracy: Reinventing Information Literacy to Empower Learners*,[1] we knew that our next project would be a return to editing to engage with faculty and librarians in the field about ways they have started to apply these ideas. The title of this book, *Metaliteracy in Practice*, initially appeared as a heading in our first article introducing this concept, "Reframing Information Literacy as a Metaliteracy,"[2] reinforcing the ongoing intersection between theory and practice. Our own work has reflected the interrelated nature of both approaches: writing and presenting about these concepts while working with colleagues in the Metaliteracy Learning Collaborative on multiple projects. This expanded team led to the development of comprehensive metaliteracy learning goals and objectives, our Metaliteracy .org blog, three massive open online courses (MOOCs), a metaliteracy digital-badging system, and additional open educational resources (OERs) available at our Metaliteracy Learning Collaborative YouTube channel (see http://metaliteracy.org/youtube-channel).

Metaliteracy applies to all stages and facets of an individual's life. It is not limited to the academic realm, nor is it something learned once and for all. Indeed, metaliteracy focuses on adaptability as information environments change and the critical reflection necessary to recognize new and evolving needs in order to remain adept. As we know from the groundbreaking work of Dr. Alison J. Head, Director and Principal Investigator for Project Information Literacy (PIL) and author of this book's foreword, the relationship between information literacy and lifelong learning is continuously intertwined in both theory and practice. These connections extend from prior learning and knowledge, to undergraduate education and graduate school, to local communities and workplace settings. Alison's contributions to the field through PIL have been informed by data-driven research, publications, conversations among colleagues, and resources for teachers and learners. The PIL findings and the insights of students who have participated in PIL projects have immeasurably enriched our knowledge and enhanced our effectiveness in advocating for richer, more nuanced opportunities for student learning connected with information literacy. Our own work with metaliteracy is similarly focused on engaging colleagues in the field to think in novel ways about how to involve learners in applying critical thinking across a wide spectrum of scholarly and lifelong learning activities as informed participants in dynamic collaborative spaces. Metaliteracy emphasizes the metacognitive dimension of learning and the active roles we play as producers of original and repurposed information. At times, this takes place through emerging technologies and social media spaces and in the classroom, online, or in community and employment settings. Today's learning environments are networked and collaborative, requiring an understanding of how to connect with others in meaningful ways and to contribute as critical and independent thinkers. In doing so, our learners are also teachers who are empowered to instruct, partner with, and assess peers, and to teach us in the process.

While working on this book we were engaged in our own version of *metaliteracy in practice* with colleagues at the University at Albany, Empire State College, and the University of Buffalo, all within the SUNY system. The metaliteracy model and related learning goals and objectives informed the design of several metaliteracy-inspired learning spaces we have created with colleagues. Recently, we developed two MOOCs that integrated our codeveloped, competency-based, digital-badging content in distinct ways. We developed a Coursera MOOC titled Metaliteracy: Empowering Yourself in a Connected World (www.coursera.org/course/metaliteracy) and a Canvas MOOC called Empowering Yourself as a Digital Citizen (https://learn.canvas .net/courses/591). These projects built on our previous work with the Metaliteracy Learning Collaborative to develop our first connectivist Metaliteracy MOOC (http://metaliteracy.cdlprojects.com) and a metaliteracy digital-badging system that applies these concepts in a competency-based environment and maps the learning goals and objectives in a gamified learning space. These collaborative initiatives were supported with two top-tier Innovative Instruction Technology Grants (IITGs) funded by the State University of New York

(SUNY) and continue to impact our own thinking about the role of metaliteracy in learning.

This book expands beyond our application of metaliteracy in several interrelated projects to metaliteracy practices developed by our esteemed colleagues in the field. Based on our conversations with librarians and faculty at keynote presentations, conferences, workshops, and webinars, we know that these chapters represent broader changes that are taking place in how information literacy instruction is envisioned and designed through metaliteracy.

While all of this metaliteracy-related activity has been moving forward, we have seen significant changes in the field through the work of the Association of College and Research Libraries (ACRL) Information Literacy Competency Standards for Higher Education Task Force. This group, which completed its work in January 2015, was cochaired by one of this book's editors, Trudi E. Jacobson. She and Craig Gibson of the Ohio State University worked with a very strong team to develop what became the ACRL *Framework for Information Literacy for Higher Education* (www.ala.org/acrl/standards/ilframework).

The approach taken by the *Framework* differs significantly from that of the *Information Literacy Competency Standards for Higher Education*, which was adopted by ACRL in 2000 (www.ala.org/acrl/standards/informationliteracy competency). This is immediately apparent in the new definition of information literacy written for the *Framework*:

> Information literacy is the set of integrated abilities encompassing the reflective discovery of information, the understanding of how information is produced and valued, and the use of information in creating new knowledge and participating ethically in communities of learning.[3]

The similarities to metaliteracy are striking: metacognition, information creation, and participation in learning communities all reflect elements espoused by metaliteracy when it was originally developed to significantly broaden the conception of information literacy that was commonly accepted, at least in the United States, due to the definition in the ACRL *Information Literacy Standards*:

> An information literate individual is able to:
>
> - Determine the extent of information needed
>
> - Access the needed information effectively and efficiently
>
> - Evaluate information and its sources critically
>
> - Incorporate selected information into one's knowledge base
>
> - Use information effectively to accomplish a specific purpose
>
> - Understand the economic, legal, and social issues surrounding the use of information, and access and use information ethically and legally[4]

With this new definition, information literacy has moved much closer to metaliteracy on the spectrum of information-related literacy models.

Metaliteracy's inclusion of the affective domain has its counterpart in the *Framework*'s section of dispositions for each frame. This element has long been noted as an important factor in information literacy, particularly in the seminal work of Carol Kuhlthau[5] and also in the more recent AASL (American Association of School Librarians) *Standards for the 21st-Century Learner*,[6] though it was noticeably absent in the ACRL *Information Literacy Standards*.

Readers interested in the evolution from the *Standards* to the *Framework* might explore a thematic 2013 issue of *Communications in Information Literacy* (http://comminfolit.org/index.php?journal=cil&page=issue&op=view&path[]=14), *Reflecting on the Standards*. The issue was released prior to the completion of the *Framework*, and hence authors were not yet aware of its final form or contents. However, several articles make the connection between metaliteracy and the *Framework*, either implicitly or explicitly. Foremost among these is our lead article, "Proposing a Metaliteracy Model to Redefine Information Literacy."[7] However, metaliteracy is also noted in Marcus Banks's "Time for a Paradigm Shift."[8] Speaking to the need for affective elements are Carol Kuhlthau[9] and Ellysa Stern Cahoy,[10] as well as the concluding piece, "Moving Forward,"[11] based on the work of an earlier task force considering the fate of the *Standards*. Lesley Farmer, a member of the Framework Task Force, contributed "How AASL Learning Standards Inform ACRL Information Literacy Standards,"[12] which provides more detail on this impact.

A second strand of inquiry in the field strongly influences the *Framework*: threshold concepts. Lori Townsend, who, with several colleagues, has researched and written on threshold concepts for information literacy (including one article in the special issue of *Communications in Information Literacy*[13]), was a member of the Task Force. While the Task Force members, informed by an extraordinary response by members of the profession to several drafts, crafted the contents and direction of the six threshold concepts that inform the *Framework*, the work of her research team was an important influence. The integration of threshold concepts marked a distinct shift from the skills-based approach found in the ACRL *Information Literacy Competency Standards for Higher Education*. According to Jan Meyer and Raymond Land, "A threshold concept can be considered as akin to a portal, opening up a new and previously inaccessible way of thinking about something. It represents a transformed way of understanding, or interpreting, or viewing something without which the learner cannot progress."[14] The threshold concepts underpinning the *Framework* align very well with metaliteracy, as those who are moving from novice toward expert for each concept will undergo transformations that encompass the same domains as found in metaliteracy: behavioral, cognitive, affective, and metacognitive.

All of the chapters in this volume examine issues relevant to the ACRL *Framework* in relation to metaliteracy. Both are having a transformative effect on the field of information literacy. The chapter authors show why we needed to reframe and reinvent information literacy as a metaliteracy and why a new definition of information literacy was required at this pivotal time in higher education. They all raise issues that reflect today's dynamic information environment and exemplify a shared commitment to learner success in these spaces. This work continues to evolve through the metacognitive reflection of our learners and peers, as we all try to mediate collaborative social environments through active and informed participation.

We have appreciated this opportunity to work with the authors of this text because they are at the forefront of applying the metaliteracy framework in their teaching. This process has had significant impact on their learners and has supported the vital connections between theory and practice. During this past year, the enthusiasm of each author to pioneer such engaging and innovative metaliteracy practices has been an inspiration to us. We have been enriched, informed, and challenged by the ideas articulated here to continuously reflect and think in new ways about the framework we first introduced. We are confident that you will be similarly inspired as you read through each chapter and consider all of the insights and innovations presented in this volume.

BOOK ORGANIZATION

This book starts with a scenario most instructors have faced as they prepared for the first day of class. Donna Witek and Teresa Grettano, both from the University of Scranton, provide us with a real-world teaching situation that reflects the iterative nature of curriculum development, especially in today's dynamic social media world. This first chapter, "Revising for Metaliteracy: Flexible Course Design to Support Social Media Pedagogy," features a collaboration between an information literacy librarian and a professor of rhetoric and composition to develop and teach a 200-level, writing-intensive course, Rhetoric and Social Media, based on metaliteracy. This collaborative process required revisions over time and thoughtful reflections about teaching and learning with social media. The authors effectively demonstrate how theory and practice are interrelated and that metaliteracy is about more than any particular technology because it encourages adaptation to new environments, flexibility, metacognition, and collaboration.

The second chapter, by Lauren Wallis and Andrew Battista, "The Politics of Information: Students as Creators in a Metaliteracy Context," describes their experience teaching an information literacy course at the University of

Montevallo in Alabama. The course was structured such that it interrogated many of the accepted constructs of higher education teaching. Weaving metaliteracy throughout the course, an emphasis was placed on empowering students and recognizing their roles as creators of information and as teachers.

Chapter 3, "Metaliteracy Learning of RN to BSN Students: A Fusion of Disciplinary Values and Discourses," by Barbara J. D'Angelo and Barry M. Maid, documents an undergraduate research and writing course designed for nursing students at Arizona State University. The authors chronicle course development and detail points of alignment with metaliteracy by connecting the learning objectives of both disciplinary writing and metaliteracy. To be effective in their nursing responsibilities, it is critical that these individuals draw upon relevant resources and share information using ePortfolios and digital media. This chapter includes a strong emphasis on the metacognitive dimension of metaliteracy and models how to revise the curriculum in a way that encourages students to reflect on their learning.

Next, in chapter 4, "Where Collections and Metaliteracy Meet: Incorporating Library-Owned Platforms into Open and Collaborative Library Instruction," Amanda Scull explores metaliteracy in the context of collections and teaching about collections, and she does so specifically related to library-owned content platforms. She delves into the open and collaborative nature of institutional repositories and research guide software that allow students to become content creators and curators. Her chapter illuminates not only the opportunities to engage students to enhance their metaliteracy but also the benefits of enhancing and promoting information owned by the institution.

In chapter 5, "Empowering Learners to Become Metaliterate in a Digital and Multimodal Age," Sandra K. Cimbricz and Logan Rath describe the process of moving from the use of multiliteracies to metaliteracy as the organizing framework in a graduate education course. The course focused on how to teach students in fifth through twelfth grades to be critical, empowered, metacognitive users of digital texts, but the chapter highlights the increasing resonance of the metaliteracy model with the authors and the graduate students in the course as they worked through newly developed assignments. Two of these assignments are examined in detail, illustrating their role in developing metaliterate learners.

Chapter 6, "Metacognition Meets Research-Based Learning in the Undergraduate Renaissance Drama Classroom," by librarian Michele R. Santamaria and professor Kathryn M. Moncrief of Washington College, chronicles the experiences of undergraduate students who were invited in a Renaissance Drama course to work collaboratively with their classmates and their instructors. The project was a digital open access endeavor called the Map of Early Modern London (MoEML). The students therefore took on a role of information producer, rather than just information consumer. They each also wrote a research narrative, encouraging metacognition. Between the contribution to the map and review of the research narratives, the chapter authors were able to gauge their students' development as metaliterate learners. A particularly interesting observation in this chapter was that students were using subscription-based library resources to find the information that informed their suggested change to this open access resource.

Student empowerment is a key theme in several chapters in this volume, reflecting the importance of this theme in metaliteracy. In chapter 7, Kristine N. Stewart and David M. Broussard describe a major shift in an established credit-bearing course, Information Use and Student Success. The curriculum was originally based on the ACRL *Information Literacy Standards*, but the authors argue that using material from 2000 is insufficient for a radically altered information environment. "Promoting Empowerment through Metaliteracy: A Case Study of Undergraduate Learning Outcomes" explores changes that focus on understanding the difference between information and knowledge, the integration of multimedia exercises and working in groups, exploring social media sources, and an introduction to online information management.

Chapter 8, "Developing Agency in Metaliterate Learners: Empowerment through Digital Identity and Participation," features the work of Irene McGarrity, coinstructor of a credit-bearing course, Digital Identity and Participatory Culture, at Keene State College, and details the student-centered, collaborative, metaliterate nature of the course. She provides the background on the instructors' efforts to have students develop a sense of agency through the enhanced roles they played in the course. Rather than being the recipients of instructor-selected content and assignments, the students themselves created these key components of the course. The chapter provides details about the successes and challenges of developing a learning experience of this type and clearly ties individual course elements with the metaliteracy goals and learning objectives.

Chapter 9, "Metaliteracy, Networks, Agency, and Praxis: An Exploration," closes the book with an engaging and thoughtful investigation from Paul Prinsloo, who is the research professor in open distance learning (ODL) in the College of Economic and Management Sciences, University of South Africa (Unisa). In this closing chapter, the author situates metaliteracy within a larger theoretical context of literacy itself, while exploring the relationship to praxis, agency, and many distinct theoretical perspectives, including Paulo Freire and Pierre Bourdieu, among others. Prinsloo intentionally opens up the conversation by challenging assumptions and expanding the scope of what we mean by metaliteracy *in praxis*. He contextualizes metaliteracy as agency in networked social spaces that requires more than the development of discrete skills to include the ability to make choices. By doing so, the author opens the unlimited possibilities for metaliteracy in both theory and practice, as the model continues to evolve.

This volume is a complement to our *Metaliteracy* book with nine new chapters that apply the metaliteracy framework in creative and inventive ways. We closed our last book with two case studies about metaliteracy in practice based on our teaching, and now we expand the dialogue with contributions from our colleagues in the field. The chapter authors are from multiple disciplines and explore diverse pedagogical issues within higher education related to the theory and practice of this model. Collectively, the chapters represent the exciting work that is happening in the field and are certain to inspire new innovations among readers.

As always, we welcome your thoughts and insights about these ideas and approaches to teaching and learning at our Metaliteracy.org blog, the central hub for all things metaliteracy.

NOTES

1. Thomas P. Mackey and Trudi Jacobson, *Metaliteracy: Reinventing Information Literacy to Empower Learners* (Chicago: Neal-Schuman, 2014).\\i Meta-literacy: Reinventing Information Literacy to Empower Learners\\i0{} (Chicago: Neal-Schuman, an imprint of the American Library Association, 2014.

2. Thomas P. Mackey and Trudi E. Jacobson, "Reframing Information Literacy as a Metaliteracy," *College and Research Libraries* 72, no. 1 (January 1, 2011): 62–78, doi:10.5860/crl-76r1.

3. Association of College and Research Libraries, *Framework for Information Literacy in Higher Education* (Chicago: American Library Association, 2015), www.ala.org/acrl/standards/ilframework.

4. Association of College and Research Libraries, *Information Literacy Competency Standards for Higher Education* (Chicago: American Library Association, 2000), www.ala.org/acrl/standards/informationliteracy competency.

5. Carol Collier Kuhlthau, *Seeking Meaning: A Process Approach to Library and Information Services*, 2nd ed. (Westport, CT: Libraries Unlimited, 2004).

6. American Association of School Librarians, *Standards for the 21st-Learner* (Chicago: American Library Association, 2007).

7. Trudi E. Jacobson and Thomas P. Mackey, "Proposing a Metaliteracy Model to Redefine Information Literacy," *Communications in Information Literacy* 7, no. 2 (January 10, 2013): 84–91, doi:10.7548/cil.v7i2.255.\\uc0\\u8220{} Proposing a Metaliteracy Model to Redefine Information Literacy,\\uc0\\u8221{} \\i Communications in Information Literacy\\i0{} 7, no. 2 (January 10, 2013.

8. Marcus Banks, "Time for a Paradigm Shift: The New ACRL Information Literacy Competency Standards for Higher Education," *Communications in Information Literacy* 7, no. 2 (September 12, 2013): 184–88, doi:10.7548/cil.v7i2.256.

9. Carol C. Kuhlthau, "Rethinking the 2000 ACRL Standards: Some Things to Consider," *Communications in Information Literacy* 7, no. 2 (January 10, 2013): 92–97, doi:10.7548/cil.v7i2.232.

10. Ellysa Stern Cahoy, "Affective Learning and Personal Information Management: Essential Components of Information Literacy," *Communications in Information Literacy* 7, no. 2 (May 12, 2013): 146–49, doi:10.7548/cil.v7i2.267.

11. Ellysa Stern Cahoy, Craig Gibson, and Trudi E. Jacobson, "Moving Forward: A Discussion on the Revision of the ACRL Information Literacy Standards for Higher Education," *Communications in Information Literacy* 7, no. 2 (October 12, 2013): 189–201, doi:10.7548/cil.v7i2.273.

12. Lesley S. J. Farmer, "How AASL Learning Standards Inform ACRL Information Literacy Standards," *Communications in Information Literacy* 7, no. 2 (July 12, 2013): 171–76, doi:10.7548/cil.v7i2.266.

13. Amy R. Hofer, Korey Brunetti, and Lori Townsend, "A Threshold Concepts Approach to the Standards Revision," *Communications in Information Literacy* 7, no. 2 (February 12, 2013): 108–13, doi:10.7548/cil.v7i2.262.

14. Jan Meyer and Ray Land, "Threshold Concepts and Troublesome Knowledge: Linkages to Ways of Thinking and Practising within the Disciplines" (Occasional Report 4, ETL Project, Universities of Edinburgh, Coventry, and Durham, 2003), 1, www.etl.tla.ed.ac.uk/docs/ETLreport4.pdf.

BIBLIOGRAPHY

Association of College and Research Libraries. *Framework for Information Literacy in Higher Education.* Chicago: American Library Association, 2015. www.ala.org/acrl/standards/ilframework.

———. *Information Literacy Competency Standards for Higher Education.* Chicago: American Library Association, 2000. www.ala.org/acrl/standards/informationliteracycompetency.

Banks, Marcus. "Time for a Paradigm Shift: The New ACRL Information Literacy Competency Standards for Higher Education." *Communications in Information Literacy* 7, no. 2 (September 12, 2013): 184–88. doi:10.7548/cil.v7i2.256.

Cahoy, Ellysa Stern. "Affective Learning and Personal Information Management: Essential Components of Information Literacy." *Communications in Information Literacy* 7, no. 2 (May 12, 2013): 146–49. doi:10.7548/cil.v7i2.267.

Cahoy, Ellysa Stern, Craig Gibson, and Trudi E. Jacobson. "Moving Forward: A Discussion on the Revision of the ACRL Information Literacy Standards for Higher Education." *Communications in Information Literacy* 7, no. 2 (October 12, 2013): 189–201. doi:10.7548/cil.v7i2.273.

Farmer, Lesley S. J. "How AASL Learning Standards Inform ACRL Information Literacy Standards." *Communications in Information Literacy* 7, no. 2 (July 12, 2013): 171–76. doi:10.7548/cil.v7i2.266.

Head, Alison J. "Project Information Literacy: What Can Be Learned about the Information-Seeking Behavior of Today's College Students?" In *Association of College and Research Libraries (ACRL) Proceedings 2013*, 472–82. Chicago: American Library Association, 2013. www.ala.org/acrl/sites/ala.org.acrl/files/content/conferences/confsandpreconfs/2013/papers/Head_Project.pdf.

Hofer, Amy R., Korey Brunetti, and Lori Townsend. "A Threshold Concepts Approach to the Standards Revision." *Communications in Information Literacy* 7, no. 2 (February 12, 2013): 108–13. doi:10.7548/cil.v7i2.262.

Jacobson, Trudi E., and Thomas P. Mackey. "Proposing a Metaliteracy Model to Redefine Information Literacy." *Communications in Information Literacy* 7, no. 2 (January 10, 2013): 84–91. doi:10.7548/cil.v7i2.255.

Kuhlthau, Carol C. "Rethinking the 2000 ACRL Standards: Some Things to Consider." *Communications in Information Literacy* 7, no. 2 (January 10, 2013): 92–97. doi:10.7548/cil.v7i2.232.

Kuhlthau, Carol Collier. *Seeking Meaning: A Process Approach to Library and Information Services*. 2nd ed. Westport, CT: Libraries Unlimited, 2004.

Mackey, Thomas P., and Trudi Jacobson. *Metaliteracy: Reinventing Information Literacy to Empower Learners*. Chicago: Neal-Schuman, 2014.

———. "Reframing Information Literacy as a Metaliteracy." *College and Research Libraries* 72, no. 1 (January 1, 2011): 62–78. doi:10.5860/crl-76r1.

Meyer, Jan, and Ray Land. "Threshold Concepts and Troublesome Knowledge: Linkages to Ways of Thinking and Practising within the Disciplines." Occasional Report 4, ETL Project, Universities of Edinburgh, Coventry, and Durham, 2003. www.etl.tla.ed.ac.uk/docs/ETLreport4.pdf.

Acknowledgments

WE ACKNOWLEDGE THE DEDICATED AND INNOVATIVE WORK of all of our chapter authors as this book progressed during the past year. This has been an important opportunity for us to read and edit your chapters since each one focuses on applying metaliteracy in diverse teaching and learning situations. We also appreciate Rachel Chance, Acquisitions Editor at ALA Neal-Schuman and ALA Editions, who was interested in this book idea from the start and offered excellent advice and support throughout the project. As always we recognize the creative and professional work of our copy editor Amy L. Knauer and everyone from the ALA Neal-Schuman team!

Special thanks to Alison J. Head, PhD, Executive Director, Project Information Literacy (PIL), Principal Research Scientist, the Information School, University of Washington, and Faculty Associate, Berkman Center for Internet and Society, Harvard University. Alison wrote the exceptional foreword to this book, providing a critical context based on PIL findings and situating the chapters into the essential issues related to learners, higher education, and their postgraduation lives.

We acknowledge our colleagues in the Metaliteracy Learning Collaborative because they allowed us to envision metaliteracy in practice through several innovative projects, including a competency-based digital badging system, a Coursera MOOC, and a Canvas MOOC, all within the same year. The current members of this group include Kathleen Stone, Kelsey O'Brien,

Jenna Pitera, Allison Hosier, Michele Forte, and Amy McQuigge. Thanks as well to Sam Abramovich, Assistant Professor at the University at Buffalo, for joining this group and helping us to design a research strategy for our related metaliteracy projects. We are also grateful to Lisa Stephens, Senior Strategist for Academic Innovation, Academic Technology and Instructional Services at the Office of the SUNY Provost, for her support and guidance throughout the development and implementation phases of our two Innovative Instruction Technology Grants (IITGs) and related Coursera MOOC.

During the editing of this manuscript we also took on another project for ALA Editions, the design of an e-course based on our previous *Metaliteracy* book. We acknowledge the support we received from Dan Freeman and Samantha Imburgia to develop and present this online course and especially want to thank all of the librarians and faculty who participated in the weekly sessions. We valued the chance to interact with you about your approaches to applying metaliteracy in teaching and learning.

Deep appreciation goes to John Vallely for his patience when "I have to work on the book" was a common refrain. Thanks go as well to James Kellerhouse for being such a great sounding board for ideas.

As always, we appreciate this chance to work together on another metaliteracy project with the support of colleagues and our publisher.

DONNA WITEK and
TERESA GRETTANO

1

Revising for Metaliteracy

Flexible Course Design to Support
Social Media Pedagogy

I T IS TWO WEEKS BEFORE CLASSES BEGIN AND TIME TO REFRESH
your information literacy instruction lessons for the coming semester. You
pull out your notes, including syllabi and assignment prompts for the courses
you support with information literacy instruction every semester, as well as
your learning outcomes and outlines of how you typically use the fifty to sev-
enty-five minutes you will have with the students. An assignment that asks
students to find journal articles means you've built into your instruction a
demonstration of how to search for, evaluate, select, and access information
through the use of one of the library's online databases. When you open that
database to prepare, however, you realize the vendor has just rolled out an
interface upgrade that has repositioned all of the functionality for the user,
rendering your "Search Tips and Strategies for X Database" resource for students out of date and more likely to confuse than assist. It also means having
to reconceive how you will demonstrate the search process within this database, because now you are in the position of having to learn the ins and outs
of this new upgrade yourself, prior to being capable of teaching it to your students. Suddenly two weeks until the start of the semester feels much shorter
than it did when you sat down to prepare.

Instruction librarians, as well as faculty who teach students to engage with library resources or collaborate with librarians to do so, likely relate to this scenario, which points to the constant state of revision in which our instruction materials—and our relationships to those materials—must necessarily exist in the digital information environments in which we all teach. It is offered as an analog to the metaliteracy case study that follows. If information literacy instruction situated within traditional research environments like databases and library catalogs must consistently be revisited, revised, and refreshed, it then follows that instruction which situates the development in students of information literacy knowledge, behaviors, and dispositions within environments that are dynamic and ever-changing—that is, social media platforms, networks, and communities—must be in a constant state of revision as well.

The metaliteracy framework for information literacy invites instructors to bring these dynamic environments into the teaching and learning experience.[1] In this case study, we—an information literacy librarian and a rhetoric/composition professor—offer concrete examples of integrating social media tools and platforms into a 3.0-credit course we codesigned and coteach each spring at our institution. In this 200-level writing-intensive (W) course, called Rhetoric and Social Media, students "investigate rhetoric *through* and the rhetoric *of* social media."

In its first offering in spring 2011, the course focused on the social media platform Facebook as both the primary object of analysis and the vehicle for learning in the course.[2] By 2013, it became clear to us that a course intentionally designed to develop both information literacy and rhetorical and critical practice in students *on* social media needed to address more platforms than Facebook, and it needed to be structured less around the tools themselves and more around the conceptual learning goals the tools are meant to support. This approach would allow for flexibility in how the course could be continually updated moving forward and would support the development of metaliteracy in students that can in turn be transferred across contexts and environments.

To this end, we significantly revised the course in time for the spring 2013 semester to include Twitter, Instagram, and Pinterest, in addition to Facebook, with new learning exercises and assignments developed to take advantage of this expansion in scope. The case study offered in this chapter shares with readers this revision process: what the revisions were, our pedagogical rationale for the revisions made, reflection on the outcomes of the revisions, and the relationship between the revision process and the development of metaliteracy in all involved—students and instructors alike.

We also use this case study as an opportunity to reflect metacognitively and metaliterately on the experience of designing learning opportunities for metaliteracy situated within participatory information environments that are always changing. Because in many ways these environments are a "moving target," the need for metaliteracy that enables learners to transition between and among these environments becomes essential.

RELATED LITERATURE

The term *metaliteracy* first appeared in the library and information science literature in Mackey and Jacobson's "Reframing Information Literacy as a Metaliteracy,"[3] where it is described as "an overarching and self-referential framework that integrates emerging technologies and unifies multiple literacy types."[4] This early conception of the metaliteracy framework is significant in how it describes social media environments as "transient, collaborative, and free-flowing, requiring a comprehensive understanding of information to critically evaluate, share, and produce content in multiple forms."[5] Mackey and Jacobson argue that although there is a plethora of literacies, such as media, visual, digital, and cyber, that proliferated after the emergence of social media on the Web, it is *information* literacy—conceptualized as early as 1974[6]—whose goals and concepts hold the greatest potential to sustainably support learning in information environments that are constantly changing.

As Mackey and Jacobson introduced to the profession their vision for information literacy as a metaliteracy, we began our first offering of the Rhetoric and Social Media course, grappling with these same questions in the pedagogical lab that is the writing and information literacy classroom. Out of that first offering of the course in 2011 came our own conception of "metaliteracy" as a foundation for information literacy in participatory, networked environments: "information literacy in the age of social media requires a kind of 'meta-literacy' that previous understandings of information literacy did not: educators must teach themselves and their students to be critically aware of why they do what they do with information, otherwise the tools will make decisions for them."[7]

Two elements of this early conception of "meta-literacy" are significant to this present case study: (1) it was social media that provided the catalyst for us to become aware of the complex relationships between researchers, information tools, and agency in and through the research process; and (2) from the beginning of this exploration, the development of metaliteracy in *instructors* was of equal import to facilitating the development of the same in *students*. We experienced this firsthand when the need to significantly revise our Rhetoric and Social Media course became clear, resulting in the course revision described in this chapter's case study.

Both Mackey and Jacobson and we, the authors of this case study, had occasion to develop further our conceptions of metaliteracy in later work, where the latter pair took the opportunity to intentionally situate their own work within that of the former. In "Teaching Metaliteracy: A New Paradigm in Action," we offer "a model of information literacy instruction that utilizes social media to teach metaliteracy—defined . . . as a critical awareness of why we do what we do with information—as the foundation of what it means to be information literate today."[8] More specifically, that study offers extensive data from the 2011 offering of the Rhetoric and Social Media course as evidence for the effects of social media use on students' information literacy practices and behaviors.[9] These effects highlight the significance of expanding information literacy in both breadth and depth so it is understood, now and moving forward, as a metaliteracy, a point we emphasize by presenting our findings through the lens of Mackey and Jacobson's emerging metaliteracy framework.[10]

Mackey and Jacobson also more fully flesh out their framework with a focus on the metacognitive learning domain as essential to mastery of the behavioral, cognitive, and affective metaliteracy goals and objectives, both in their book *Metaliteracy: Reinventing Information Literacy to Empower Learners*[11] and in their work with the Metaliteracy Learning Collaborative on multiple projects, including the development of the "Goals and Learning Objectives" first published at Metaliteracy.org.[12] While all four of the learning domains addressed in the metaliteracy learning objectives are touched on in the case study that follows,[13] the objectives that are developed in the metacognitive domain resonate most strongly with our work on the Rhetoric and Social Media course, as will be made clear through the concrete examples offered in this chapter.

In addition to the aforementioned literature, which has been foundational to our developing understanding of metaliteracy within our own work in the classroom, a survey of the literature indexed in Library, Information Science and Technology Abstracts (LISTA) related to the specific work that we do in our Rhetoric and Social Media course reveals several related studies and commentaries. The goal of conducting this survey was to uncover articles about information literacy instruction that are related in some way to any of the four social media platforms we revised and expanded our course to include, or to social media and/or networks more generally. What follows is a brief review of the literature that was found through this process.

The library and information science literature connects information literacy—conceptually and pedagogically—to Facebook and Twitter far more than it does to Instagram and Pinterest.[14] This is likely because Instagram and Pinterest are image-based platforms that communicate information in ways less obviously connected to traditional conceptions of information literacy than do the text-based platforms Facebook and Twitter. Several other studies connect information literacy learning to social and networked technologies more broadly, alternating between arguments in favor of social technologies as potentially powerful tools to develop ideas and research[15] and warnings of the consequences of personalized networked environments on learners' critical thinking and information literacy processes.[16]

There are also several thoughtful commentaries that reflect on the relationship between information literacy and the complex information environment in which it is now taught, developed, and practiced.[17] Two case studies of significance offer examples of information literacy instruction using social media platforms that are similar to the case study offered previously by us in "Teaching Metaliteracy: A New Paradigm in Action";[18] one focuses on a course that taught information literacy intentionally "from a socio-technical perspective" using social technologies,[19] and the other describes the critical gaps identified in information literacy learning for students in a political science course who used new media to gather and evaluate information about the congressional races of the 2010 election season.[20]

Finally, a literature review and discussion of a debate that occurred at the UNESCO Training the Trainers in Information Literacy (TTT) Workshop in 2008 is directly related to Mackey and Jacobson's goal for metaliteracy as a unifying framework for multiple literacies.[21] The debate focused on the question of whether information literacy and media literacy are complementarily connected or conceptually independent of each other; the author of that piece finds in favor of complementarity and argues that educators must develop both types of literacy in order to successfully teach and develop the same in their students.[22] The absolute necessity that educators understand themselves as both instructors and learners in these complex, networked, participatory information environments, in order to successfully teach students within these same environments, is clearly on the minds of many researchers, including us.

METALITERACY IN THE CATHOLIC JESUIT INSTITUTIONAL CONTEXT

We work at the University of Scranton, a private, master's, comprehensive, liberal arts university in an urban Northeast Pennsylvania city. The majority of the university's roughly 5,000 students are traditionally matriculated (eighteen to twenty-two years old), geographically from the surrounding areas (New York, New Jersey, and Pennsylvania), ethnically white, and economically middle-class to upper-middle-class.

The university is a Catholic, Jesuit school and, as such, is run by the Society of Jesus founded by St. Ignatius Loyola. The Ignatian pedagogical paradigm,[23] first articulated in 1599 in the *Ratio Studiorum*,[24] consists of five elements: context, through which the material conditions of the student's learning are considered, as well as the predispositions of the student; experience, through which students move beyond rote learning to something more active and personal; reflection, during which students apply the subject matter to their own lives and processes, and where meaning is said to be made in this paradigm; action, which involves the changes in students' attitudes and behaviors through the application of and reflection upon knowledge; and evaluation, through which students assess their own learning and set new learning needs. Each element in this paradigm contributes to the development of metaliteracy in general; but in the Rhetoric and Social Media course, this link between Ignatian pedagogy and the development of metaliteracy is evident in the fact that instruction in information literacy and rhetorical theory is situated within the context of students' own participatory networked environments, that students are enacting their learning in these environments through their coursework, and that through reflection and evaluation students' dispositions toward information and social media undergo a change.

After the course was first developed, but within the timing of the revision shared in this case study, the university's undergraduate core curriculum underwent a partial revision in which the literacy or "skills" courses became housed under the umbrella program Eloquentia Perfecta. Teresa has been instrumental in the design of this curriculum, and Donna has been embedded in some of its first-level courses. The mission of the program states, "The Jesuit pedagogical goal of Eloquentia Perfecta aims to develop students' abilities to generate topics of inquiry; to gather, evaluate, and disseminate information and ideas; and to communicate in varied modes within appropriate contexts and disciplines, so that they are empowered to excel as professionals and citizens to serve more fully the common good." The aims of the program are "to prepare students to speak, write, and communicate effectively in varied modes and media" and to develop excellence in communication "as students produce a variety of discourse and master the associated arts of reading, listening, observing, inquiring, analyzing, and thinking critically." In all, the program houses and defines the Oral, Digital, and Writing designations in the core curriculum, and information literacy is embedded in the outcomes for each of these designations. We offer this overview of Eloquentia Perfecta in order to indicate that though the program is still in the early stages, there is institutional support for student learning initiatives that bridge the academic and the digital and that embed information literacy into classroom instruction.

CONNECTION TO RHETORICAL THEORY AND PRACTICE

The rhetorical tradition through which Eloquentia Perfecta is developed is the discipline in which Teresa situates her professional identity. Rhetoric (and Rhetoric and Composition) as an academic discipline is multifaceted and complex. Put simply, the discipline studies how meaning is made through language—or, more politically, how language constructs reality—and it is through this lens that Teresa first conceived of the Rhetoric and Social Media course. Teresa's Facebook activity had become complicated by the expansion of her network into different and multiple audiences, and she realized the platform was fertile ground through which to teach rhetorical theories to students. Both the developing cultures and shifting functions on Facebook implored rhetorical explorations into identity construction through language and text,[25] persuasion and motivation,[26] poststructural theories about power and agency,[27] and concerns with audience and purpose.[28] In essence, Teresa's conception of the course arose from her own metaliteracy, though she would have never labeled the process as such then.

Teresa arrived at the university with the desire to design the course and, through an internal stipend program, found an opportunity to collaborate with Donna.[29] By bringing the ACRL *Information Literacy Competency Standards for Higher Education* and Donna's disciplinary expertise into the course design,[30] "literacy" as a specific pedagogical goal and instructional method was introduced, and the functional computer literacy work of Selber was added to the rhetorical theory course material and readings cited earlier.[31]

The course we designed carries a WRTG prefix, meaning it is offered through the Department of English and Theatre and counts toward the Writing minor; in the core curriculum, it is designated a writing-intensive (W) course and more than likely will soon be folded into the Eloquentia Perfecta program. While most of the students enrolled in the course have been English and Communication majors or Writing minors, some have also come from Marketing, Computer Science, and Counseling. The course cap for seminar courses like Rhetoric and Social Media is eighteen students.

REVISING WRTG 224: RHETORIC AND SOCIAL MEDIA

A CASE STUDY

We approached the revision of the Rhetoric and Social Media course with the following goals in mind: to expand the course scope to add Twitter, Instagram, and Pinterest to Facebook as the objects of analysis as well as vehicles of learning within the course; to reconfigure the course schedule around conceptual units and goals instead of specific readings or types of assignments; and to simplify and streamline the "moving parts" of the course so that we, the instructors, would have flexibility regarding the extent to which the course is cotaught.

The last goal was especially important because we codesigned the first iteration of the course around Donna's availability as an information literacy librarian capable of being present in every class meeting; the complexities of the course components for its first run in spring 2011 attest to this. In spring 2012, however, Donna was unable to commit as much time to the course, though she still participated in instruction related to the assignments and readings she led in designing. Through reflection, we agreed that the second semester felt more piecemeal than the first time the course ran. Revising the course for flexibility became our modus operandi between spring 2012 and spring 2013, and the need to expand the course scope from one to four social media platforms provided the perfect pedagogical opportunity through which to make this revision.

Already our approach to the revision process can be understood in light of the metaliteracy learning objectives.[32] In "Goal 4: Demonstrate ability to connect learning and research strategies with lifelong learning processes and personal, academic, and professional goals," two metacognitive learning objectives are evidenced by our approach to revising the course. The overarching goal of making Rhetoric and Social Media more flexible as a course demonstrates that we "value persistence, adaptability, and flexibility," not only in our own learning processes but also in designing learning opportunities for students. We also used the course revision process as an occasion to "recognize that learning is a process and that reflecting on errors or mistakes leads to new insights and discoveries." The complexity of the initial course design was not a mistake or error in and of itself because it created the space to approach the classroom as a lab in which to test pedagogical uses and applications of social media with students. That initial complexity, however, was not a sustainable model for a course that we were submitting for curriculum review as a permanent offering at the same time that we were undertaking the course revision for flexibility and expansion in scope.

While this may seem counterintuitive, to put the prerevision course through curriculum review while simultaneously revising the course in the ways described in this case study, the course goals as well as the foundational texts that are the theoretical underpinnings for the course went through the least amount of revision. In many ways, the revision focused more on the pedagogy within the course, rather than the course itself, though anyone who studies the theory and praxis of pedagogy understands that course "content" cannot truly be separated from the pedagogy through which it is taught. That the course successfully passed through curriculum review and was permanently added to the course catalog by the spring 2013 offering was all the more reason the course revision was essential, because it in turn made the course flexible and sustainable moving forward.

Course Goals

The simplest way to share the concrete changes made to the course between spring 2012 and spring 2013 is to offer elements of the syllabus side by side for the reader's comparison. In figure 1.1, on the left are the course goals in spring 2012 and on the right are the course goals in spring 2013. The first two goals in both lists—"Analyze a rhetorical situation in terms of audience, purpose, and style" and "Determine options for communication and make

COURSE GOALS, SPRING 2012	COURSE GOALS, SPRING 2013
By the end of the course, you should be able to	By the end of the course, you should be able to
1. Analyze a rhetorical situation in terms of audience, purpose, and style 2. Determine options for communication and make effective choices based on a rhetorical situation 3. Understand the difference between thesis-driven, academic arguments and visual-driven arguments, and be able to compose both effectively 4. Incorporate others' ideas/outside information into your own arguments effectively and ethically 5. Become aware of your online behavior, its reasoning and effects 6. Develop more purposeful and effective practices in social network environments	1. Analyze a rhetorical situation in terms of audience, purpose, and style 2. Determine options for communication and make effective choices based on a rhetorical situation 3. Understand the differences among various genres and modes of communication 4. Become aware of your online behavior, its reasoning and effects 5. Develop more purposeful and effective practices in social network environments

NOTE: Goals are numbered to facilitate discussion in the chapter; in the syllabi they are bulleted.

FIGURE 1.1

Course Goals Compared

effective choices based on a rhetorical situation"—are related to rhetorical theory and practice, while the last two goals in both lists—"Become aware of your online behavior, its reasoning and effects" and "Develop more purposeful and effective practices in social network environments"—are explicitly tied to metaliteracy, of which more will be shared in the following. The middle two goals for spring 2012 are the ones that were revised and simplified into one corresponding goal for spring 2013. The reasons for this change were twofold.

First, the construction of the revised spring 2013 goal—"Understand the differences among various genres and modes of communication"—is simpler because it relies on complex concepts (*genres* and *modes of communication*) that would be taught in the course, instead of relying on concrete yet arbitrary descriptors such as *thesis-driven*, *academic*, and *visual-driven*, as does the corresponding spring 2012 goal—"Understand the difference between thesis-driven, academic arguments and visual-driven arguments, and be able to compose both effectively." The benefit of this change was that mapping the new course goal to specific learning exercises became easier and more intuitive because the goal itself was revised to be more flexible in the ways in which it could be practiced and reached.

Second, the fourth course goal in the spring 2012 list—"Incorporate others' ideas/outside information into your own arguments effectively and ethically"—was eliminated for spring 2013 because we believed this was something 100-level courses should have targeted, and that while this goal and activity would be practiced repeatedly within the Rhetoric and Social Media course, it was not necessary to characterize the course as a whole by including it as a primary goal. In addition, five course goals are easier to assess than six, and since assessments are in turn tied to assignments, eliminating this course goal once again made the process of designing and mapping new assignments for the course more flexible.

Assignments

Another instructive side-by-side comparison from the syllabus before and after the revision is the list of assignments and their weights within the course. In figure 1.2, on the left are the assignment names and weights for spring 2012 and on the right are the assignment names and weights for spring 2013. The first three assignments and learning tasks—Participation, Reading Responses, and User Log—remain the same before and after the revision but bear mentioning because of their connection to the metaliteracy learning objectives.[33]

Participation in the course requires more than coming to class on time both prepared and willing to discuss the readings and homework tasks assigned. In addition, there is a course Facebook group (set to "secret" so it is only visible to course participants) through which we, the instructors, engage students outside of the physical classroom about the course content. We do this by encouraging students' analysis *of* the platform—and of their behaviors *on* the platform—all while working *within* the platform itself (via the group). A significant part of students' participation grade comes from their engagement

ASSIGNMENTS, SPRING 2012		ASSIGNMENTS, SPRING 2013	
Participation	10%	Participation	10%
Reading Responses	10%	Reading Responses	10%
User Log	20%	User Log	20%
Mini-Assignments	15%	Identity Lesson	15%
Rhetorical Analysis	15%	Literacy Lesson	15%
Presence Construction	30%	Inquiry Lesson	15%
		Privacy Lesson	15%

FIGURE 1.2

Assignments Compared

in the course Facebook group, and this engagement facilitates the practice of several metaliteracy learning objectives.[34] In "Goal 3: Share information and collaborate in a variety of participatory environments," participation in the course Facebook group directly leads learners to "participate conscientiously in collaborative environments." This required participation on Facebook also ties to the learning objective under metaliteracy goal 4 in which learners "communicate effectively with collaborators in shared spaces and learn from multiple points of view." One of the purposes of the course Facebook group is to bring diverse learners together in a shared digital space, so that the rapport developed during in-person class meetings might extend into the very spaces being studied. In this way, participation in the course as a whole, and in the course Facebook group specifically, also maps to course goals 2, 4, and 5 from spring 2013 (see figure 1.1), where course goal 4, "Become aware of your online behavior, its reasoning and effects," and course goal 5, "Develop more purposeful and effective practices in social network environments," are the two course goals through which metaliteracy is deeply and intentionally woven into the fiber of the course. The course Facebook group is one of the primary vehicles through which these two goals are addressed.

The Reading Responses also remain consistent as assignments (see figure 1.2) before and after the course revision, though the readings themselves vary somewhat between semesters. This is because the subject matter that half of the readings address—social media—is always changing and evolving, which in turn means the readings that provide commentary and analysis on social media topics always need to be updated. More specific to metaliteracy, though, is the fact that these readings are curated by us, the instructors, from blogs and other online publishing platforms. We do this intentionally because it is in these spaces that up-to-date, public discourse about social media is occurring. This means that several metaliteracy learning objectives are addressed through this regular course activity.[35] In "Goal 1: Evaluate content critically, including dynamic, online content that changes and evolves, such as article preprints, blogs, and wikis," learners in the course are offered regular opportunities to "distinguish between editorial commentary and information presented from a more research-based perspective, recognizing that values and beliefs are embedded in all information." This learning objective in particular is reflected in the diversity of course readings, since the other half of the readings are intentionally theoretical in orientation and academically situated.

An example of this intentional diversity of reading types and formats can be found in the Identity unit of the revised course. This first unit of the course opens with two readings from Ramage's *Rhetoric: A User's Guide*[36] to theoretically orient the students to rhetoric as a discipline and to theories of identity within that discipline. These readings are followed by three blog posts that, in the latest iteration of the course, have been commentaries on a controversial statement made by Mark Zuckerberg, cofounder and CEO of Facebook, in 2009: "You have one identity. . . . The days of you having a different image for your work friends or co-workers and for the other people you know are probably coming to an end pretty quickly. . . . Having two identities for yourself is an example of a lack of integrity."[37] Zuckerberg made this comment about identity in the context of speaking about the presence (or absence) of privacy on Facebook. Students are tasked with reading three blog posts that respond to Zuckerberg's position published by writers filling three different roles: a political science professor,[38] a technology researcher,[39] and a journalist.[40] The final reading of the unit is a rhetorical theory reading by Burke called "Terministic Screens."[41] Thus, over the first four weeks of the course, students engage and respond to writing on the same complex concept—identity—written in modes that are academic, practical, theoretical, editorial, researched, or a combination of these characteristics, depending on which reading, in which format, students are engaging with at any given time. The written Reading Responses as well as the in-class/on-Facebook discussions about these readings enable learners to "demonstrate the ability to translate information presented in one manner to another in order to best meet the need of particular audiences [and] integrate information from multiple sources into coherent new forms,"[42] one of the learning objectives in metaliteracy goal 3. These Reading Responses, assigned regularly throughout the course, also map to course goal 1, "Analyze a rhetorical situation in terms of audience, purpose, and style," and course goal 3, "Understand the differences among various genres and modes of communication," from spring 2013 (see figure 1.1), illustrating another way in which the goals for this Rhetoric and Social Media course are shared with the goals for metaliteracy.

The final assignment that was not substantially revised is the User Log of students' activity on social media platforms (see figure 1.2). The only significant revision to this assignment was to expand the number of social media platforms that students may log their activity on, from only Facebook in spring 2012 to Facebook, Twitter, Instagram, and Pinterest in spring 2013. From the syllabus, this assignment tasks students with the following: "You will keep a log of 3 hours of your social media activity per week. This log will be descriptive, analytical, and reflective—meaning you will identify the moves you made on social media platforms, explain your motives for doing so, and evaluate the outcomes. Logs will be submitted for grading at scheduled intervals throughout the semester." This ongoing assignment, which spans the entire semester and is meant to get more detailed and reflective as the course progresses, is the primary site for the development of course goal 4, "Become aware of your online behavior, its reasoning and effects," and course goal 5, "Develop more purposeful and effective practices in social network environments," from spring 2013 (see figure 1.1); these two course goals *are* metaliteracy.

The User Log assignment is directly tied to metaliteracy goal 4,[43] offering opportunities for students to demonstrate several learning objectives within that goal. Through the User Log activity students "use self-reflection to assess one's own learning and knowledge of the learning process," "demonstrate the ability to think critically in context and to transfer critical thinking to new learning," and "engage in informed, self-directed learning that encourages a broader worldview through the global reach of today's information technology." The User Log activity is designed to shift learners' activity in social media environments from what Burke theorizes as the difference between "motion" and "action,"[44] from automated to personal activity and behavior. Learners who shift metacognitively from motion to action in their interactions with information, whether this happens on social media platforms or in other information systems, in so doing are demonstrating and practicing metaliteracy. The goals for the User Log activity may have originated in rhetorical theory, but it is clear that rhetorical theory shares many of the same concerns, goals, and mind-sets with metaliteracy, making a course focusing explicitly on Rhetoric and Social Media fertile ground for integrating metaliteracy into instruction.

From a Task-Based to a Concept-Based Course Schedule

One of the primary aims of revising the Rhetoric and Social Media course was to orient the learning units less around specific capstone assignment tasks and more around the complex conceptual understandings we, the instructors, aim for students to develop through those assignments. The side-by-side comparison of assignments from spring 2012 and spring 2013 in figure 1.2 illustrates the manner in which this aim was accomplished.

In spring 2012, there were three Mini-Assignments, a Rhetorical Analysis that occurred at midterm, and a Presence Construction that served as the final capstone experience for the course. The Mini-Assignments were originally conceived as opportunities to target the development of specific practices and habits on social media through homework activities designed to be both practical and fun. The Rhetorical Analysis and Presence Construction assignments required students to both write and act in social media platforms in ways that demonstrated the full matrix of knowledge, skills, and dispositions represented in the course goals (see figure 1.1). These assignments all experienced success in both the spring 2011 and spring 2012 runs of the course, when Facebook was the only object of detailed analysis; however, in expanding the scope of the course to include three additional social media platforms, it became clear that the course learning goals needed to be scaffolded in a more flexible manner, rather than anchored to specific, discrete assignments, each with its own set of requirements to track.

The solution lay in the specific complex concepts the various assignments had been originally designed to explore. One of the Mini-Assignments

COURSE UNITS AND ASSIGNMENTS, SPRING 2013 (short descriptions from original course syllabus)	COURSE GOALS, SPRING 2013	METALITERACY LEARNING OBJECTIVES (LOS)*
Identity Assignment (15%) You have two choices for this assignment: you will either write a rhetorical analysis of a social media identity (on any platform) or write a process narrative on the creation of your own NEW identity on one of the platforms studied in this course. Final papers should be 4–5 pages.	1, 2, 3, 4, 5	Goal 1, LO 1 Goal 2, LO 3 Goal 3, LO 8
Literacy Assignment (15%) You will analyze the information literacy functions and practices of two of the social media platforms studied in this course, then write a compare/contrast analysis drawing conclusions about how the culture and functions of the platforms foster or hinder the development of information literacy skills. Final papers should be 4–5 pages.	1, 2, 4, 5	Goal 1, LO 5 Goal 2, LOs 6, 7 Goal 3, LOs 1, 3, 8 Goal 4, LOs 1, 2, 3

Revision made during the run of the course

Compose a 4–5-page analysis of one of the social media platforms studied in this course (Facebook, Twitter, Pinterest, or Instagram) in which you identify ways that literacy is present or absent (or both) on the platform chosen. To do this you will analyze the functions (i.e., tools) and practices (i.e., user behaviors) of the platform by connecting them to the different forms of literacy (information literacy, functional computer literacy, writing program literacies) studied in this unit. You will then draw conclusions about how the culture and functions of the platform foster and/ or hinder the development of literacy skills.

	COURSE GOALS, SPRING 2013	METALITERACY LEARNING OBJECTIVES (LOS)*
Inquiry Assignment (15%) You will follow a discussion on Instagram or Twitter using #hashtags for a current news event and write an analysis of how the culture and functions of the platform affect users' understanding of the topic. Final papers should be 4–5 pages.	1, 3, 5	Goal 1, LOs 2, 5 Goal 3, LO 9 Goal 4, LO 9
Privacy Assignment (15%) You will analyze the privacy functions and agreements for two platforms and write a compare/contrast analysis of user agency, awareness, and practice. Final papers should be 4–5 pages.	1, 2, 4, 5	Goal 2, LOs 2, 3, 5, 6, 7 Goal 4, LOs 1, 2, 3

Revision made during the run of the course

You will compose an argument in which you will contribute to a current conversation about privacy and social media, using as evidence information found through both traditional (library databases, consulting an expert) and nontraditional (social media platforms, web-based publishing platforms) tools and sources. Final papers should be 4–5 pages.

*See Metaliteracy.org, "Goals and Learning Objectives."

FIGURE 1.3

Revised Assignments Mapped to Course Goals and Metaliteracy Learning Objectives focused on privacy settings, and with Foucault's "Panopticism" chapter serving as the theoretical anchor for explorations of privacy and surveillance,[45] it made sense to expand this topic into its own unit within the course. Another Mini-Assignment focused on using tools and functions on social media platforms to practice information and functional computer literacy,[46] and so in the revised course a conceptual unit focusing on literacies was born. Both the Rhetorical Analysis and the Presence Construction assignments dealt explicitly with questions of identity, so this became the third conceptual unit in the revised course. And, in expanding to include both Twitter and Instagram as objects of analysis as well as vehicles for learning, the hashtag entered the repertoire of social media tools that could be incorporated into the course pedagogy. At this point in the revision process, we discovered that we needed to flex our own metaliteracy muscles to determine what conceptual tasks or processes learners practice when they use hashtags to discover information, participate in discourse, and make meaning in networked environments. We landed on "inquiry" as the best way to describe these processes, and so the fourth conceptual unit of the revised course was born.

Rather than offer a detailed analysis of the specific readings, activities, and written work students were tasked with in each of the four revised course units, we provide an overview; figure 1.3 describes the culminating assignment for each unit and maps these assignments to both the course goals (see figure 1.1) and to the metaliteracy learning objectives at both the goal and the learning objective (LO) levels.[47]

As the chart indicates, all four revised course units map comprehensively to both of the revised course goals (see figure 1.1) and to the metaliteracy learning objectives.[48] The short descriptions offered from the original course syllabus for spring 2013 explain the tasks through which students' metaliteracy learning develops. In addition, this revised course structure enabled us, the instructors, to evenly distribute the four complex concepts (and the readings and tasks that accompany them) across the fifteen-week semester. Dividing the time evenly also meant the amount of writing assigned for each unit could be uniform as well, making the tasks of grading and assessment easier to streamline.

Revising the Revisions

Of particular relevance to this metaliteracy case study, besides the presence of metaliteracy in the learning outcomes for the course units themselves, is the fact that two of the unit-level assignments were revised even as the course was running (see figure 1.3). We identified a need to develop new assignment prompts for both the Literacy assignment and the Privacy assignment in response to the learning the students in the course were exhibiting. For the Literacy assignment, the number of platforms students were asked to analyze was decreased from two to one; the reason for this was that the level of detail at which the students were practicing analyzing social media tools and functions leading up to this assignment was so high that asking students to analyze two platforms would have required twice as many pages of written work than the assignment calls for. In addition, the readings for the literacy unit were dense and detailed, coming from composition studies,[49] writing program administration,[50] and the field of information literacy,[51] which meant students were already doing a high volume of reading and responding leading up to the Literacy assignment paper. These factors were good problems to have, and the learning outcomes for this unit were better served by simplifying the task students were asked to do in the final Literacy assignment paper.

A similar process occurred for the Privacy assignment, though in this case it was less due to level of detail of analysis and more due to a desire to see students synthesize their learning into a developed argument related to this final (and controversial) concept covered in the course. The original Privacy assignment description called upon the same kinds of functional analysis skills required in earlier assignments, and by this point in the semester the students were exhibiting fatigue at this kind of work, valuable though it is. It made better sense to ask students to do a broader synthesis, requiring all of the muscles that were exercised in previous units, and encourage students to follow their curiosity to choose a topic related to privacy and social media that was of interest to them. This assignment revision is an interesting example of the instructional collaboration coming full circle and returning to a more traditionally structured researched paper—something we had initially designed our pedagogy to avoid—but with the added layers and depth offered by the students' critical engagement with social media platforms and information environments that preceded it.

REFLECTION AND NEXT STEPS

In the Ignatian pedagogical paradigm, it is in and through reflection—during which learners apply the material being learned to their own lives and processes—that meaning is said to be made.[52] In the learning objectives for metaliteracy goal 4, metaliterate learners "use self-reflection to assess one's own learning and knowledge of the learning process."[53] And in the revised Rhetoric and Social Media course, the four conceptual units each concluded with a one- to two-page single-spaced reflection, in which students analyzed what they learned by working through the readings and responses, in-class/on-Facebook discussions and activities, and the culminating paper for the unit. Reflection has occurred at every stage of the process of initially designing and then revising the Rhetoric and Social Media course; for us, this present moment in the course's evolution is no exception.

This case study was written in spring 2015, during which the revised course is running for the first time since its first run in spring 2013. In preparing to teach the course again this semester, we reflected on the revisions made for spring 2013 to determine what was successful and what could be improved upon. There is no doubt that we achieved our aims in revising the course. The addition of three social media platforms to the original one the course was designed for has only improved student engagement within the course; for instance, Instagram is turning out to be the platform of the four that the majority of students in the course gravitate toward in their everyday lives, making it a valuable addition to the course repertoire. The assignments and learning tasks are far more manageable, with four unit papers of equal weight complementing the various Reading Responses, User Logs, and Participation tasks that remain the backbone of the course. And the course is more flexible as a whole, which is evidenced by the freedom to experiment with learning activities that we feel this second time around teaching the revised course.

An example of an exciting tweak we were able to make for spring 2015, as a result of the spring 2013 revision of the course schedule into four conceptual units, is the inclusion of the *Framework for Information Literacy for Higher Education*,[54] the *Framework for Success in Postsecondary Writing*,[55] and the first chapter of *Metaliteracy: Reinventing Information Literacy to Empower Learners*[56] as readings in the Literacy unit, all of which complement Selber's "Reimagining the Functional Side of Computer Literacy" article that remains from previous versions of the course.[57] Two of these new readings did not yet exist in spring 2013,[58] but because the course was revised to be oriented around complex concepts instead of specific assignments or readings, it was simple to replace the *Information Literacy Competency Standards for Higher Education* and the "WPA Outcomes Statement for First-Year Composition" with these new, dynamic conceptions of information and writing program literacies.[59]

We were able to update the course for spring 2015 with exciting new material without having to give it a complete overhaul (as we did for spring 2013). And we will be able to make similar updates to the course again the next time it is offered, because the course as a whole is now more flexible and we are metacognitively aware of that flexibility because we intentionally designed for it. This is a sustainable, flexible, metaliterate approach to course design, for a course that is intentionally situated on social media platforms that are always changing, which can serve as a model for how to successfully approach teaching and learning, and curricular and course design, with metaliteracy.

NOTES

1. Thomas P. Mackey and Trudi E. Jacobson, *Metaliteracy: Reinventing Information Literacy to Empower Learners* (Chicago: Neal-Schuman, 2014), 23. See figure 1.1, Metaliteracy Model, for a visualization of the relationship

between these dynamic environments (e.g., social media, mobile, online, OER [open educational resource]) and the expanded learning activities these environments facilitate in learners (e.g., share, participate, use, incorporate, produce, collaborate).

2. Donna Witek and Teresa Grettano, "Information Literacy on Facebook: An Analysis," *Reference Services Review* 40, no. 2 (2012): 242–57; Donna Witek and Teresa Grettano, "Teaching Metaliteracy: A New Paradigm in Action," *Reference Services Review* 42, no. 2 (2014): 188–208.

3. Thomas P. Mackey and Trudi E. Jacobson, "Reframing Information Literacy as a Metaliteracy," *College and Research Libraries* 72, no. 1 (2011): 62–78. doi:10.5860/crl-76r1.

4. Ibid., 62.

5. Ibid.

6. Paul G. Zurkowski, "The Information Service Environment Relationship and Priorities" (Related Paper No. 5, National Commission on Libraries and Information Science, National Program for Library and Information Services, November 1974), http://files.eric.ed.gov/fulltext/ED100391.pdf.

7. Witek and Grettano, "Information Literacy on Facebook," 255.

8. Witek and Grettano, "Teaching Metaliteracy," 190.

9. Witek and Grettano, "Teaching Metaliteracy."

10. Mackey and Jacobson, "Reframing Information Literacy."

11. Mackey and Jacobson, *Metaliteracy*.

12. Metaliteracy.org, "Goals and Learning Objectives" (updated September 11, 2014), http://metaliteracy.org/learning-objectives/.

13. Ibid.

14. Paige Alfonzo, "Using Twitter Hashtags for Information Literacy Instruction," *Computers in Libraries* 34, no. 7 (2014): 19–22; Amanda Click and Joan Petit, "Social Networking and Web 2.0 in Information Literacy," *International Information and Library Review* 42, no. 2 (2010): 137–42; Donna Witek, "Information Literacy Gets Social," *Pennsylvania Library Association Bulletin* 67, no. 4 (2012): 24–26.

15. Kara Jones, "Connecting Social Technologies with Information Literacy," *Journal of Web Librarianship* 1, no. 4 (2007): 67–80.

16. Frank Menchaca, "The Future Is in Doubt: Librarians, Publishers, and Networked Learning in the 21st Century," *Journal of Library Administration* 52, no. 5 (2012): 396–410.

17. Peter Godwin, "Information Literacy and the Internet Generation," *Library and Information Update* 6, no. 3 (2007): 36–39; Cory Laverty, "Our Information Literacy Heritage: From Evolution to Revolution," *Feliciter* 55, no. 3 (2009): 88–91; Meredith Farkas, "Information Literacy 2.0," *American Libraries* 42, no. 11/12 (2011): 32.

18. Witek and Grettano, "Teaching Metaliteracy."

19. Erik T. Mitchell and Susan Sharpless Smith, "Bringing Information Literacy into the Social Sphere: A Case Study Using Social Software to Teach

Information Literacy at WFU," *Journal of Web Librarianship* 3, no. 3 (2009): 183–97.

20. Jonathan Cope and Richard Flanagan, "Information Literacy in the Study of American Politics: Using New Media to Teach Information Literacy in the Political Science Classroom," *Behavioral and Social Sciences Librarian* 32, no. 1 (2013): 3–23.

21. Nieves González Fernandez-Villavicencio, "Helping Students Become Literate in a Digital, Networking-Based Society: A Literature Review and Discussion," *International Information and Library Review* 42, no. 2 (2010): 124–36.

22. Ibid.

23. Jesuit Institute, "Ignatian Pedagogy: A Practical Approach" (Jesuit Institute, Society of Jesus, [1993] 2013), http://jesuitinstitute.org/Resources/ Ignatian%20Pedagogy%20(JI%20Edition%202013).pdf.

24. *Ratio Studiorum*, trans. Allan P. Farrell (Conference of Major Superiors of Jesuits, [1599] 1970), www.bc.edu/sites/libraries/ratio/ratio1599.pdf.

25. John D. Ramage, *Rhetoric: A User's Guide* (New York: Pearson Longman, 2006); Kenneth Burke, *Language as Symbolic Action: Essays on Life, Literature, and Method* (Berkeley: University of California Press, 1966).

26. Burke, *Language as Symbolic Action*. See "Terministic Screens" chapter.

27. Michel Foucault, *Discipline and Punish: The Birth of the Prison*, trans. Alan Sheridan (New York: Pantheon Books, 1977). See "Panopticism" chapter.

28. Ramage, *Rhetoric*; Burke, *Language as Symbolic Action*.

29. Witek and Grettano, "Information literacy on Facebook"; Witek and Grettano, "Teaching Metaliteracy."

30. Association of College and Research Libraries (ACRL), *Information Literacy Competency Standards for Higher Education* (Chicago: American Library Association, 2000), www.ala.org/acrl/standards/informationliteracycom petency.

31. Stuart A. Selber, "Reimagining the Functional Side of Computer Literacy," *College Composition and Communication* 55, no. 3 (2004): 470–503.

32. Metaliteracy.org, "Goals and Learning Objectives."

33. Ibid.

34. Ibid.

35. Ibid.

36. Ramage, *Rhetoric*.

37. David Kirkpatrick, *The Facebook Effect: The Inside Story of the Company That Is Connecting the World* (New York: Simon and Schuster Paperbacks, 2011), 199.

38. Henry Farrell, "An Internet Where Everyone Knows You're a Dog," *Crooked Timber* (blog), May 14, 2010, http://crookedtimber.org/2010/05/14/ an-internet-where-everyone-knows-youre-a-dog.

39. danah boyd, "Facebook and 'Radical Transparency' (a Rant)," *Apophenia* (blog), May 14, 2010, www.zephoria.org/thoughts/archives/2010/05/14/ facebook-and-radical-transparency-a-rant.html.

40. Dara Lind, "Mark Zuckerberg's Silver-Spoon Vanguardism," *ThinkProgress*, May 28, 2010, http://thinkprogress.org/yglesias/2010/05/28/197384/mark-zuckerbergs-silver-spoon-vanguardism.
41. Burke, *Language as Symbolic Action*, 44–62.
42. Metaliteracy.org, "Goals and Learning Objectives."
43. Ibid.
44. Burke, *Language as Symbolic Action*.
45. Foucault, *Discipline and Punish*.
46. ACRL, *Information Literacy Competency Standards*; Selber, "Reimagining Computer Literacy."
47. Metaliteracy.org, "Goals and Learning Objectives."
48. Ibid.
49. Selber, "Reimagining Computer Literacy."
50. Council of Writing Program Administrators (CWPA), "WPA Outcomes Statement for First-Year Composition (3.0)" (approved July 17, [2000, 2008] 2014), http://wpacouncil.org/positions/outcomes.html.
51. ACRL, *Information Literacy Competency Standards*.
52. Jesuit Institute, "Ignatian Pedagogy."
53. Metaliteracy.org, "Goals and Learning Objectives."
54. Association of College and Research Libraries (ACRL), *Framework for Information Literacy for Higher Education* (Chicago: American Library Association, 2015), www.ala.org/acrl/standards/ilframework.
55. Council of Writing Program Administrators (CWPA), National Council of Teachers of English (NCTE), and National Writing Project (NWP), *Framework for Success in Postsecondary Writing* (January 2011), http://wpacouncil.org/files/framework-for-success-postsecondary-writing.pdf.
56. Mackey and Jacobson, *Metaliteracy*, 1–31.
57. Selber, "Reimagining Computer Literacy."
58. ACRL, *Framework for Information Literacy*; Mackey and Jacobson, *Metaliteracy*, 1–31.
59. ACRL, *Information Literacy Competency Standards*; CWPA, "WPA Outcomes Statement."

BIBLIOGRAPHY

Alfonzo, Paige. "Using Twitter Hashtags for Information Literacy Instruction." *Computers in Libraries* 34, no. 7 (2014): 19–22.

Association of College and Research Libraries (ACRL). "*Framework for Information Literacy for Higher Education*." Chicago: American Library Association, 2015. www.ala.org/acrl/standards/ilframework.

———. *Information Literacy Competency Standards for Higher Education*. Chicago: American Library Association, 2000. www.ala.org/acrl/standards/informationliteracycompetency.

boyd, danah. "Facebook and 'Radical Transparency' (a Rant)." *Apophenia* (blog), May 14, 2010. www.zephoria.org/thoughts/archives/2010/05/14/facebook-and -radical-transparency-a-rant.html.

Burke, Kenneth. *Language as Symbolic Action: Essays on Life, Literature, and Method.* Berkeley: University of California Press, 1966.

Click, Amanda, and Joan Petit. "Social Networking and Web 2.0 in Information Literacy." *International Information and Library Review* 42, no. 2 (2010): 137–42.

Cope, Jonathan, and Richard Flanagan. "Information Literacy in the Study of American Politics: Using New Media to Teach Information Literacy in the Political Science Classroom." *Behavioral and Social Sciences Librarian* 32, no. 1 (2013): 3–23.

Council of Writing Program Administrators (CWPA). "WPA Outcomes Statement for First-Year Composition (3.0)." Approved July 17, (2000, 2008) 2014. http:// wpacouncil.org/positions/outcomes.html.

Council of Writing Program Administrators (CWPA), National Council of Teachers of English (NCTE), and National Writing Project (NWP). *Framework for Success in Postsecondary Writing.* January 2011. http://wpacouncil.org/files/framework -for-success-postsecondary-writing.pdf.

Farkas, Meredith. "Information Literacy 2.0." *American Libraries* 42, no. 11/12 (2011): 32.

Farrell, Henry. "An Internet Where Everyone Knows You're a Dog." *Crooked Timber* (blog), May 14, 2010. http://crookedtimber.org/2010/05/14/an-internet-where -everyone-knows-youre-a-dog/.

Fernandez-Villavicencio, Nieves González. "Helping Students Become Literate in a Digital, Networking-Based Society: A Literature Review and Discussion." *International Information and Library Review* 42, no. 2 (2010): 124–36.

Foucault, Michel. *Discipline and Punish: The Birth of the Prison.* Translated by Alan Sheridan. New York: Pantheon Books, 1977.

Godwin, Peter. "Information Literacy and the Internet Generation." *Library and Information Update* 6, no. 3 (2007): 36–39.

Jesuit Institute. "Ignatian Pedagogy: A Practical Approach." Jesuit Institute, Society of Jesus, (1993) 2013. http://jesuitinstitute.org/Resources/Ignatian%20 Pedagogy%20(JI%20Edition%202013).pdf.

Jones, Kara. "Connecting Social Technologies with Information Literacy." *Journal of Web Librarianship* 1, no. 4 (2007): 67–80.

Kirkpatrick, David. *The Facebook Effect: The Inside Story of the Company That Is Connecting the World.* New York: Simon and Schuster Paperbacks, 2011.

Laverty, Cory. "Our Information Literacy Heritage: From Evolution to Revolution." *Feliciter* 55, no. 3 (2009): 88–91.

Lind, Dara. "Mark Zuckerberg's Silver-Spoon Vanguardism." *ThinkProgress*, May 28, 2010. http://thinkprogress.org/yglesias/2010/05/28/197384/mark -zuckerbergs-silver-spoon-vanguardism/.

Mackey, Thomas P., and Trudi E. Jacobson. *Metaliteracy: Reinventing Information Literacy to Empower Learners.* Chicago: Neal-Schuman, 2014.

————. "Reframing Information Literacy as a Metaliteracy." *College and Research Libraries* 72, no. 1 (2011): 62–78. doi:10.5860/crl-76r1.

Menchaca, Frank. "The Future Is in Doubt: Librarians, Publishers, and Networked Learning in the 21st Century." *Journal of Library Administration* 52, no. 5 (2012): 396–410.

Metaliteracy.org. "Goals and Learning Objectives." Updated September 11, 2014. http://metaliteracy.org/learning-objectives/.

Mitchell, Erik T., and Susan Sharpless Smith. "Bringing Information Literacy into the Social Sphere: A Case Study Using Social Software to Teach Information Literacy at WFU." *Journal of Web Librarianship* 3, no. 3 (2009): 183–97.

Ramage, John D. *Rhetoric: A User's Guide.* New York: Pearson Longman, 2006.

Ratio Studiorum. Translated by Allan P. Farrell. Conference of Major Superiors of Jesuits, (1599) 1970. www.bc.edu/sites/libraries/ratio/rati01599.pdf.

Selber, Stuart A. "Reimagining the Functional Side of Computer Literacy." *College Composition and Communication* 55, no. 3 (2004): 470–503.

Witek, Donna. "Information Literacy Gets Social." *Pennsylvania Library Association Bulletin* 67, no. 4 (2012): 24–26.

Witek, Donna, and Teresa Grettano. "Information Literacy on Facebook: An Analysis." *Reference Services Review* 40, no. 2 (2012): 242–57.

————. "Teaching Metaliteracy: A New Paradigm in Action." *Reference Services Review* 42, no. 2 (2014): 188–208.

Zurkowski, Paul G. "The Information Service Environment Relationship and Priorities." Related Paper No. 5. National Commission on Libraries and Information Science, National Program for Library and Information Services, November 1974. http://files.eric.ed.gov/fulltext/ED100391.pdf.

LAUREN WALLIS and
ANDREW BATTISTA

2
The Politics of Information

Students as Creators in a Metaliteracy Context

INFORMATION LITERACY IS OFTEN DIFFUSE AND DISASSOCI-
ated from undergraduate learning, a challenge compounded by one-shot
library instruction sessions in which students learn about research in a vac-
uum, with little connection to their existing information practices. Recent
developments, including the turn toward metaliteracy and the adoption of
the *Framework for Information Literacy for Higher Education*, position students
as active creators of information, rather than passive consumers. Librarians
and other educators must move beyond the one-shot model in order to help
students develop critical practices for creating information in participatory
online environments.[1] In this chapter, we explore these developments in the
context of undergraduate information literacy instruction at the University of Montevallo, Alabama. In the spring 2014 semester, we taught a one-
credit class called the Politics of Information, an interactive seminar based
on metacognitive, participatory information literacy learning principles.[2] We
designed the class as an alternative to traditional skills-based information literacy instruction that often takes place in one-shot classes. In such sessions,
it is difficult to have students conceptualize information and research on a
scale any larger than their individual assignment at hand, and it is equally
challenging to help them reflect critically on their position as information

consumers and creators. Constructing a semester-long class allowed us to expand students' conception of information as a social construct rather than a static, amorphous entity that reifies academic authority. In what follows, we outline the Politics of Information course in the context of metaliteracy-based pedagogy, evaluate how our students responded as empowered information creators, and suggest future directions for metaliteracy courses that disrupt traditional ideas about scholarly production.

RELATED LITERATURE

The self-reflexive approach to information implied by metaliteracy has multiple precedents, within and beyond the library instruction community. Thomas Mackey and Trudi Jacobson unite and extend these conversations with their discussion of metaliteracy as an "overarching, self-referential, and comprehensive framework" that incorporates multiple existing literacies into our understanding of information literacy.[3] One of these related literacies is James Elmborg's idea of critical information literacy, which applies critical pedagogy methods to library instruction.[4] Elmborg resists an overt instruction model in which teachers "become conservative protectors of traditional, authoritative knowledge and cease to respect students as people capable of agency and meaning-making in their own right."[5] Instead, he believes that the project of information literacy should be to help students conceptualize, critique, and resist the capitalist functions of information systems in society. Similarly, Howard Rheingold encourages students to engage in an ongoing process of questioning communication practices in order to become more deliberate stewards of information. His conception of literacies like attention management, mindfulness, network awareness, and collaboration encourage a process of metacognition that is akin to metaliterate thinking.[6] Char Booth connects intentionality to the unique classroom environment of library instruction, suggesting that metacognition on the part of teachers is a precursor to the kind of learning that eventually fosters metaliteracy in students.[7] Inherent in the concept of metaliteracy is the imperative that we as librarians will think metacognitively about the content of our instruction in order to reenvision the ways we ask students to engage with information.

We have also drawn from feminist pedagogy, which encourages collaborative learning environments where students—especially those from marginalized groups—are heard, valued, and enabled to question traditional power structures, inside and outside of the classroom.[8] We tried to mitigate instructor authority, even though the usefulness and feasibility of this practice is debated by feminist teachers.[9] For our class, the practice of destabilizing our own authority related directly to another key feature of this pedagogical approach: our study of texts that would not be traditionally valued as authoritative. Maria Accardi is one of the first to write about applying feminist pedagogy in library instruction. She sees this pedagogical perspective as integral to one-shot library instruction "because it equips students with the skills and knowledge to navigate and transform the dominant culture of knowledge production,"[10] but her approach is equally relevant to semester-long courses. Accardi notes that while there are definite obstacles to developing feminist teaching methods, including institutional cultures that value easily quantifiable representations of student learning, it is imperative to engage in teaching that helps students question dominant information systems. In our course, we wanted to embark on a meditation on information in which no form of written, oral, or digital media would be excluded from consideration as a form of evidence or an object of critique.

Finally, our class should be considered in the context of the existing conversation about credit-bearing information literacy classes. Innovative classes taught by librarians are not a new development in our field, but they are also not a normal part of undergraduate curricula at most universities. This is due to a litany of institutional challenges, including administrative resistance to teaching roles for librarians as well as concerns about staffing and compensation models.[11] Credit-bearing information literacy classes run the gamut from "skills-based" overviews of library search strategies to open, exploratory investigations of information in our fluid, digital landscape. For instance, Anne Leonard and Maura Smale structure their credit-bearing class around the idea of user-generated content. They make a sharp distinction between "library skills" classes, which seek to train students to think like librarians, and their approach, which places focus on social media and collaborative publishing technologies as the locus of a participatory culture of creating and consuming information.[12] Their model proved to be valuable as we positioned our class within our university context.

INSTITUTIONAL OR OTHER ASSOCIATED CONTEXT

The Politics of Information course emerged out of several initiatives at the University of Montevallo, a public liberal arts college in Alabama. The first was a five-year focus on information literacy as the theme of a Quality Enhancement Plan (QEP), an accrediting affirmation process for the Southern Association of Colleges and Schools (SACS).[13] The goal of this initiative is to establish classes that have a specific information literacy (IL) component at every phase of an undergraduate major. In such IL-designated classes, assignments are identified, implemented, and assessed with at least one learning outcome closely derived from the ACRL *Information Literacy Competency Standards for Higher Education*.[14] Because the QEP also stipulates that the efforts of the initiative should leave a lasting impact on the curriculum, we pushed to have one-credit information literacy classes become a fixture within Montevallo's course catalog. The second and related context is an institution-wide effort to revise the university's general education curriculum. Montevallo has had a distributive model for its general education courses and wanted to move toward a more integrative curriculum, in which classes are clustered around higher-order thinking skills instead of traditional disciplinary silos. The Politics of Information was a proposed pilot for a one-credit course, which would serve as a general education elective in the revised curriculum. As it stands, credit-bearing classes on information literacy at Montevallo would fall within the rubric of Personal Development, a miscellaneous category of classes that are designed to reinforce the general education learning outcome related to personal and social responsibility.

Additionally, we taught the Politics of Information while discussions were still in progress about integrating an information literacy class in the general education curriculum, so the only place the class could be listed was within the Honors Program. This meant that it was open to only a small group of students and did not fulfill a specific requirement for students who took it. As a result of these limitations, only four students enrolled in the course. This context in particular is indicative of the need for credit-bearing information literacy courses to become truly integrated into a curriculum.

OVERVIEW OF THE COURSE

As we designed the Politics of Information, we wanted to share classroom power in order to signal to students that their ideas and experiences as information creators and consumers were as valid as ours. We engaged in an ongoing, collective metacognitive process of questioning information and authority inside and outside of school. The questioning began before our first class meeting, when we asked our students to "purchase" our textbook, which carried a price of zero dollars, at the campus bookstore. Our text, a zine we made called *Authorize This!* included personal narratives in our own hand-writing about childhood memories of questioning information.[15] Our additional readings for the first class session were a few short blog posts about the corporatization of college bookstores. These readings about unjust pricing strategies for college textbooks naturally resonated with students. They were elated to pay nothing for a textbook, and the trip to the bookstore ultimately encouraged them to think about textbook adoption as an exercise of academic authority. We meant for this to be a surprising experience for students, one that would situate our class as distinct from other encounters with traditional academic forms of information in their discipline-based classes.

The class blog was designed to facilitate discussion and allow learners to experiment with writing in a variety of blog genres. We wanted the blog to be organic and distinct from the writing students often do for online discussion boards on learning management systems, such as Blackboard. Instead, we established the blog as a public, front-facing community, in which students became aware that the process of class participation was tantamount to the creation of information for an open, online audience.[16] Students wrote posts in five blogging genres: Reflection, Q&A, Links Roundup, Review, and Current Events.

Metaliteracy has a goal of student empowerment, achieved through metacognitive processes that help students take control of their learning.[17] In keeping with this idea, we encouraged students to take ownership of the blog and the class itself by giving them control over content. In addition to their regular posting in five blogging genres, they each selected two weeks to be Class Blogger, and we used their posts as discussion material alongside the other readings. We also built two open weeks into the syllabus, leaving space for pairs of students to choose the topic, select the readings, and lead class discussion. As instructors, we held ourselves to the same requirements, which gave us a chance to model our own metacognitive processes about our interactions with information and our positions within academia.

We also asked students to make five "creations" throughout the semester: writing a BuzzFeed article, editing *Wikipedia*, engaging with a blogosphere, producing a Bizarro Research "Paper," and devising a way to effectively spread the message of that "paper."[18] We called these pieces "creations" rather than assignments in order to emphasize a departure from traditional forms of academic information, and as with the blog posts, we produced creations alongside students. The creations are outlined in table 2.1.

TABLE 2.1
Creations

CREATION	DESCRIPTION
Edit Wikipedia	Select a *Wikipedia* page to edit or create. While you may choose any topic, consider these approaches: researching and adding citations, revising the conceptual structure of the article, balancing overt or implicit bias, adding the viewpoints of underrepresented people or groups.
Enter a Blogosphere	Explore the activist blogosphere and select a social issue that you find interesting. Find, organize, and monitor a collection of blogs and Twitter feeds throughout the semester.
Write for BuzzFeed	Write a BuzzFeed article about any topic.
Bizarro Research "Paper"	Perform research about a topic and make anything except a text-based essay in response.
Spread a Message	Develop and implement a strategy for communicating your ideas from the Bizarro Research "Paper" to an audience beyond the classroom.

Collectively, the creations were opportunities for students to engage with familiar media and gain firsthand knowledge about the way information originates and circulates on such platforms.

APPLICATION OF METALITERACY LEARNING OBJECTIVES

Mackey and Jacobson developed their concept of metaliteracy to critique and revise library instruction methods that were based on an outdated understanding of information literacy. The significant changes in technology and information-sharing practices that have occurred since the ACRL *Standards* were established in 2000 became a point of departure for a new ACRL task force, which revisited the standards to account for a "dynamic and uncertain information ecosystem" that now exists.[19] After several drafts, the task force released a final version that posits six frames, each focused around a threshold concept that can be used to reposition information literacy within existing curricula.[20] Metaliteracy, as a foundational concept for this movement, "challenges a reliance on skills-based information literacy instruction and shifts the focus to knowledge acquisition in collaboration with others."[21] By putting learners in a position to engage in dialogue and create information online, metaliteracy "promotes critical thinking and collaboration in a digital age."[22] Metaliteracy moves library instruction away from a focus on text-based information, produced by and for academic communities, and instead recognizes the value in a proliferation of information formats and viewpoints.

A turn toward metaliteracy and an unconditional acceptance of the *Framework* will give us language to express the necessity of a move beyond the skills-based one-shot as the standard for information literacy instruction. Because of its capaciousness as a concept, metaliteracy can be used to develop learning goals that are highly relevant to course content in any discipline. The metaliteracy learning objectives, outlined in the following as they relate to our course, give a cohesive, but flexible way to describe goals for student learning in our class. They allow us to outline specific topics and competencies that students will learn in a way that is assessable, while simultaneously foregrounding students' metacognitive and affective experiences.

The metaliteracy learning goals relate to four domains: behavioral and cognitive, which correspond to skills and knowledge gained through learning activities, and affective and metacognitive, which emphasize emotional or attitudinal responses to learning and critical reflections on one's own learning process.[23] The second set can be difficult to quantify and assess—and nearly impossible to address in traditional one-shot library instruction. Nevertheless, it is imperative to prioritize these modes of thinking when designing instruction that requires students to engage with both traditional print-based and participatory online forms of information. Hegemonic systems control the production and use of information, especially in the contexts of academia, government, and corporations. Students who are growing as metaliterate learners should develop awareness of how information affects their lives and influences society as a whole. Emotional reactions and major attitudinal shifts are signs that metaliterate learning is taking place. Mackey and Jacobson establish a connection between affective and metacognitive domains, showing that "the way learners think or feel about something allows for a meta-cognitive experience."[24] To be effective users and creators of information in rapidly changing online environments, students must develop metacognitive habits of interacting with information that will last throughout their lives.

Our learning outcomes for the Politics of Information course are as follows:

1. Challenge conceptions of expertise and authority
2. Identify ways in which societal power and injustice affect access to information
3. Interrogate the conventions of writing and teaching in academia
4. Describe the relationships between production of information in personal, corporate, and governmental spheres

We will relate these learning outcomes in the course to the metaliteracy goals developed by Mackey and Jacobson:

1. Evaluate content critically, including dynamic, online content that changes and evolves, such as article preprints, blogs, and wikis
2. Understand personal privacy, information ethics, and intellectual property issues in changing technology environments
3. Share information and collaborate in a variety of participatory environments
4. Demonstrate ability to connect learning and research strategies with lifelong learning processes and personal, academic, and professional goals[25]

COURSE LEARNING OUTCOME 1
Challenge conceptions of expertise and authority

Our overarching goal for the class was to challenge traditional conceptions of expertise and authority, which relates directly to metaliteracy goal 1. We began the class by discussing the cycle of power in academic publishing and classroom environments, which created context for our focus on creating and using information in participatory online spaces. We also included a week on radical librarians that encouraged students to question the hegemonic system of the library itself. While many of the creations that students and instructors completed throughout the course took place in participatory online environments like BuzzFeed and *Wikipedia*, our final project was called a Bizarro Research "Paper," which required students to present their ideas in any form other than a text-based argumentative paper. Through these types of content and assignments, we encouraged students to engage with both traditional and emerging forms of information, placing emphasis on metacognitive interactions with information in open and closed formats.

COURSE LEARNING OUTCOME 2
Identify ways in which societal power and injustice affect access to information

Our focus on critical information literacy and our use of feminist pedagogical methods influenced our concern with power and justice in the second course learning outcome, which relates to metaliteracy goals 2 and 4. Goal 2 involves understanding intellectual property, information ethics, and personal privacy in changing technology environments,[26] while goal 4 emphasizes the metacognitive process of developing lifelong learning strategies for interacting with information in personal, professional, and academic contexts.[27] Our weekly topics emphasized the implications of information access, use, and creation in terms of race, gender, and class. We discussed the digital divide, political activism on social media, and national security. We also spent one week discussing copyright and intellectual property in terms of rapidly changing online environments. As we discuss later, student performance on the creations demonstrated that they developed ideas they would take beyond the classroom and apply in personal and professional contexts in the future.

COURSE LEARNING OUTCOME 3
Interrogate the conventions of writing and teaching in academia

We wanted students to practice evaluating all modes of information critically (metaliteracy goal 1), but we started with the cycle of knowledge production in academic publications and classrooms because it was relevant to college students' experience. Destabilizing students' preconceived notions that academic, peer-reviewed sources are always the absolute highest authority helped establish the importance of considering information in all forms. Throughout the class, we had students write blog posts and make creations that departed from traditional forms of academic information and were designed in a variety of open, online spaces. Creating information in participatory online environments (metaliteracy goal 3) encouraged students to appreciate and critically evaluate other user-generated content, which helped them realize that they had valuable contributions to make in these digital spaces.

COURSE LEARNING OUTCOME 4
Describe the relationships between production of information in personal, corporate, and governmental spheres

As we discussed ethical use of information in personal, corporate, and governmental spheres (metaliteracy goal 2), we aimed to help students conceptualize production and use of information on a variety of systemic levels. We wanted to engage in a collective metacognitive process of critiquing hegemonic information systems while simultaneously considering our own participation in them. This last objective represents a magnitude of material, more than we could possibly cover in one semester. One of the strengths of a metaliteracy approach, though, is the inherent expectation that students will use metacognitive skills to "fill in the gaps in learning and develop strategies for understanding more than what we, as teachers, present or discuss."[28] Our class introduced students to large-scale systems of information, and as teachers we modeled strategies for learning more about these systems and critiquing them in terms of class, gender, and race. In turn, students used blog posts, creations, and their turns as class leaders to delve deeper into topics that they found most engaging, and, as we discuss later, they identified specific practices that they would continue once the semester ended (metaliteracy goal 4). We found that these methods, grounded in feminist and critical pedagogies, fit the metaliteracy model in which "the learner is also a teacher and each individual is a collaborative partner in the learning experience."[29]

METALITERACY CASE STUDY

In keeping with metaliteracy's emphasis on learner-generated information in participatory online spaces, our case study focuses on the ideas and content shared on our class blog and in digital environments like *Wikipedia* and Buzz-Feed. Learners (including ourselves as instructors) used the course blog as a place for metacognitive reflection on information experiences. Often, these reflections involved an emotional reaction to new ideas about major systems of information in the academic, corporate, and governmental spheres. Through blog posts and creations, learners took on many of the active roles outlined by Mackey and Jacobson in their Metaliterate Learner figure, including collaborator, researcher, author, teacher, and translator.[30] As the course progressed, we saw incremental shifts in students' attitudes about the value, use, and production of information in its varied forms.

As students wrote and assembled BuzzFeed articles, edited *Wikipedia* entries, and curated a blogosphere, they expressed surprise at the difficulties they encountered, which in turn led them to articulate the skills needed to effectively create and engage with information. These acts of creating unique, new online content helped them gain a more nuanced view about the value of information in online formats as compared to traditional print-based and academic products. Although students engaged with the behavioral domain of metaliteracy as they learned skills required to produce content on specific online platforms, our course was mostly focused on building knowledge (cognitive domain) through metacognition about our affective experiences with course content.

Through blog posts, learners discussed and reflected on their emotional reactions to new ideas about information. When we started the class by talking about the cycle of academic research and publication, students expressed surprise about the system of academic tenure, promotion, and review that generates the scholarly journal articles they used so extensively in other classes. The information skills that subject faculty deem important for their students to learn in one-shot sessions and apply in research assignments are often limited to traditional academic forms of information like journal articles and print books. In fact, subject faculty often expressly forbid students from citing websites and user-generated online content as sources for research.[31] This stipulation suggests that sources not filtered through the process of academic approval have no value and denies students the opportunity to explore and create information in participatory online spaces. In comments responding to a post by Andrew, "Universities Pay Twice for Information," students engaged in a dialogue in which they questioned their experiences with traditional academic sources.[32] One student, Hannah, says she would always choose articles from print, peer-reviewed journals rather than open access, online journals: "Most of my professors are more traditional (even preferring that their students use physical journals and books to online databases), and as a student I'm not going to put my grade on the line to use non-traditional sources."[33] Hannah reflected on her past research experiences and realized that her position as a student meant that she had no choice but to use traditional academic sources. In the same conversation, another student, Rachael, notes, "Until this class I was never aware of this issue, nor have I ever heard a professor mention [the cycle of academic publishing]."[34] Like Hannah, Rachael critiqued the complicity of her professors by hypothesizing, "Perhaps professors maintain a perspective that these journals are vital to their careers instead of recognizing the obvious power they have over [academic journals] as scholars."[35] Initiating the class by discussing the cycle of academic publishing allowed students to practice metacognition about their previous experiences in college classes, in which they had been taught that scholarly sources were the most authoritative and, in many cases, the only acceptable evidence to use in research. While we wanted to foreground nontraditional information produced in online spaces throughout the course, we also needed to understand and critique traditional academic formats.

The open class sessions built into the syllabus allowed pairs of students to choose the topic, select the readings, and lead class discussion. Both groups chose topics related to K–12 education, showing us that they valued the space to reflect on how they had been taught to understand information in their previous educational experiences. This aspect allowed students to take on the metaliteracy role of teacher, both in blog posts they wrote and in the class discussions they facilitated. To prepare for this role, they also had to take on the role of researcher. Rachael and Hannah chose the topic "Critical Thinking and Education," and Rachael wrote a Links Roundup blog post that outlined the practices of standardized testing in public education in the United States.[36] The pair posed questions that encouraged their fellow students to reflect on their experiences with learning critical thinking practices in a public school environment focused heavily on standardized testing. Their questions included the following:

- Do you think being 'digital natives' helps us or hurts us?
- What does standardized testing suggest about information?
- When is accessing information not enough? What good is information if you have it but don't know how to use it?
- Can you reflect on an instance in which a teacher taught you how to truly understand a subject matter, as opposed to just the facts and data surrounding the matter?[37]

Building student-chosen topics into the syllabus demonstrated to the class members that their ideas and reflections were important, and the students' choices gave us insight into their experiences with information. Katie and Kayla chose "Education and Poverty" as their topic, which extended a theme of economic class that had been developing throughout the course. They asked questions that encouraged us to think about the digital divide and how information is controlled in society, including "Do you think information and the sharing of it can challenge inequality?" and "Why do you think people have the need to control information?"[38] In her reflection at the end of the semester, Katie discussed her affective experience of reading and discussing the digital divide. She writes, "The week we talked about the digital divide, something hit close to home," and then she goes on to explain her personal position of having attended high school in a school district that had recently made national news for purchasing iPads for all students while also cancelling school bus services.[39] As she worked toward leading her class session and her Bizarro Research "Paper" and Spread a Message creations, Katie began to understand the digital divide and to help others learn about it. This is one example of how a metaliteracy approach, which allows room for affective and metacognitive experiences as students learn about information systems, can give students the tools they need to extend their learning. We found that the content of the course, designed with student input, allowed students to make personal, emotional connections that helped them better understand systems of information, feel equipped to participate, and gain confidence in their ability to make quality contributions.

Throughout the course, we engaged in a continual process of evaluating sources of information. This included both traditional academic sources and online content, but the Q&A blog posts also allowed students to think critically about the value and use of information from their peers and friends. Producing this information in the form of a blog post for an open online audience helped students apply a variety of viewpoints, inside and outside of academia, to our course topics. While we were discussing the corporatization of college bookstores and the academic publication cycle, Kayla interviewed one of her professors and one of her friends, a freshman at Montevallo, asking each about her attitudes toward traditional academic forms of information.[40] Their responses are an excellent illustration of how disconnected the information attitudes and practices of faculty and students can be. The faculty member discusses how her department carefully selected a textbook for an introductory class because they thought the way the material was presented would be most beneficial for students, and the student notes that she only uses the textbook for homework problems and considers it "a huge waste of money."[41] Similarly, the faculty member notes how she expects students' research projects to contain only traditional academic sources but also describes how she uses Internet searching extensively in both personal and academic contexts. The student expresses a less nuanced approach, noting that when information is needed in an academic context, "I go straight to Google."[42] While the ideas of the professor would generally be considered much more authoritative, Kayla recognized the value in presenting two viewpoints together and used the voice of a beginning undergraduate to highlight a stark contrast in information practices.

Katie used this same approach to present multiple sides of an issue. She asked a high school student, a high school teacher, and a recent college graduate to imagine their lives with no Internet access, especially in terms of how it would affect their access to education or employment. By asking her interview subjects to imagine their lives on the low-tech side of the digital divide, Katie was able to encourage them to take a metacognitive stance toward their information use, and their responses highlighted a high degree of perceived difficulty from three different perspectives.[43]

The other students conducted interviews with friends who had experience related to our topics of discussion but at the same time, as undergraduate college students, would still be seen as lacking authority in a traditional academic context. Rachael interviewed a friend whom she labeled "feminist extraordinaire."[44] She asked her about personal experiences that led her to consider herself a feminist and to engage in feminist activism. Introducing her interview subject as "a self-identified feminist and an Asian American woman," Rachael recognized the authority that personal experience can have. As she explains, "I thought it would be pertinent to get her perspective on some issues we read about this week." Hannah interviewed a friend who had completed a McNair Scholars research project about social media and volunteerism and had published a traditional academic article in the campus's undergraduate research journal.[45] This was a particularly interesting choice, since the interviewee was researching participatory online content but writing about it in a traditional academic format. Hannah's Q&A blog post allowed her to act as a translator between formats, moving information from her friend's academic study and journal article into a jargon-free blog post that would be accessible to a larger audience. Translator is one of several roles metaliterate learners can take on, and Hannah's ability to engage in this role shows how metaliteracy-based learning helped her recognize the value of information presented in multiple formats.[46]

The course included continual opportunities for students to produce information in participatory online environments, on the class blog, and through digital platforms, including BuzzFeed, *Wikipedia*, and a blogosphere related to a social issue. The creations gave students experience in making and organizing information online, practices that they learned were much more difficult than they had expected. Students expressed feelings of frustration, particularly with the *Wikipedia* editing interface and with the process of entering a blogosphere, which involved selecting and organizing blogs, Twitter feeds, and other forms of online content in order to learn more about a social justice topic. As the students produced their creations, they went through a cyclical process of learning the discrete skills they needed to create something in a digital space and reflecting on the value of information in participatory online environments.

In a blog post introducing her *Wikipedia* creation, Hannah notes, "I have a new found [sic] respect for Wikipedia contributors."[47] She describes her attitude going into the assignment, writing, "I honestly thought that I could just copy, paste, and cite right onto Wikipedia, and immediately see my polished new article. Wrong."[48] She goes on to describe the complicated steps involved in her frustrating process of creating a new article, which ends with the article landing in "Wikipedia purgatory," where it could be waiting for approval for up to three weeks.[49] In her final reflection blog post at the end of the course, she discusses the challenge of writing a *Wikipedia* article and realizes, "This just makes Wikipedia seem more and more reliable . . . people have to go through a lot to get articles published."[50]

In reaction to the BuzzFeed creation, Hannah drew related conclusions about the potential authority and usefulness of BuzzFeed articles. Students noted that they often read BuzzFeed articles for fun, but none of them had ever created an article. Going through the process of choosing a topic and writing about it within the conventions of BuzzFeed, which relies heavily on graphics like memes and GIFs, helped them think about how the relevance of information has to be evaluated in terms of the needs of the audience. For example, Hannah notes, "Condensing things into short lists and including popular memes is great for frivolous information, but it can also work for more serious matters."[51] She recognized that BuzzFeed can provide quality information about a variety of subject matters even though it looks so different from traditional print-based media or academic sources.

The Enter a Blogosphere creation asked students to organize and manage user-generated content, instead of creating it themselves. We asked students to choose a social issue they cared about and collect blogs, Twitter feeds, and other online content to follow for the second half of the semester. Students found the blogosphere creation challenging because we did not give them a clear entry point by assigning topics, requiring them to follow a certain number of blogs, or asking them to use specific tools for organization. The blogosphere creation reflected the postmodern state of information addressed by metaliteracy, in which information is nonlinear and comes from a multiplicity of voices.[52] Reflecting on her process of entering a blogosphere, Katie says, "Once I finally understood what a blogosphere actually was, trying to find information was crazy overwhelming. There was SO much to look at!"[53] Students' affective experiences of being frustrated and overwhelmed by the magnitude of user-generated content available through blogs helped them reflect on the value of organizing this content as they learned specific skills like using Feedly and Twitter lists to learn about a social issue through multiple viewpoints.

Because of this broad approach, we saw students use a variety of methods for entering a blogosphere. Katie wrote about how she struggled with this creation until a current event, played out on Twitter, gave her an idea for a relevant topic. Already a Twitter user, Katie noticed #photoshopfail being used in response to Target's editing of teen models' bathing suit pictures to accentuate their "thigh gaps" artificially. Katie describes a turning point, when "social media and Twitter were buzzing about the negative portrayal of women in the media and once I got all my information organized . . . I was hooked."[54] Hannah had a specific idea for following a blogosphere based on French language education advocacy, an interest she had because of her major. While Hannah found that there were very few blogs or posts specifically about advocacy, she was able to cultivate a collection of blogs about related topics, including French teaching resources, French language learning blogs, and generalist blogs about foreign language education.[55] These two examples of blogospheres look quite different from each other; the first originates from a specific incident and grows out of a Twitter hashtag, while the second is inspired by Hannah's academic interests. These differences speak to the effectiveness of open assignments that allow students to experience the flexibility inherent in participatory online spaces.

While instructors often view students of traditional college age as digital natives, naturally able to navigate and create in online environments, our experience in the Politics of Information course dictated otherwise.[56] Students were adept at using BuzzFeed and *Wikipedia* to find information, but the act of creating information in these familiar participatory online spaces required them to learn a new set of skills. And although students were skilled at Internet searching to find information about specific topics, they struggled with the idea of organizing a set of blogs to monitor a topic for an extended period of time. Once they developed the needed skills, students were able to organize and create information effectively. However, this experience suggests that college students can benefit from metaliteracy-based teaching methods that ask them to move beyond simply consuming information in online formats.

ASSESSMENT

Assessment for a course like the Politics of Information can serve at least two purposes: to monitor students' progress toward metaliteracy goals and to provide data that proves the worth of nontraditional information literacy instruction to stakeholders inside and outside of the library. For the purpose of understanding students' engagement with learning goals, we asked them to engage in an ongoing process of self-assessment through reflective blog posts. In these posts and in their final reflections at the end of the course, we saw them articulate the evolution of their information practices. Hannah notes that the topics of our class interconnected and extended throughout the semester,[57] to which Katie adds, "We have covered so many topics in class that have truly changed how I think about something that I once thought was so simple: information. I had never realized how information and the dissemination of it was such a large social issue. I now understand how privileged I am to have the ability to access information."[58] While the course was successful at helping our students think metacognitively, our assessment process could be improved by using a rubric based on affective learning outcomes, such as Carol Kuhlthau's Information Search Process.[59] Affective learning outcomes, which parallel metaliteracy's goals, are designed to measure how students feel as they navigate the information-seeking process.[60] An established rubric such as Kuhlthau's could help us better understand and describe students' metacognitive learning processes.

Since a goal of metaliteracy is to integrate courses like ours into the curriculum, it is also necessary to consider assessment methods that will resonate with administrators and subject faculty, who may be wary of teaching that blurs disciplinary boundaries and questions traditional information formats. One of the best ways to do this might be through a standardized, established assessment tool, such as SAILS (Standardized Assessment of Information Literacy Skills; www.projectsails.org)—even though our course did not focus on traditional information literacy skills. For example, the performance of students in a credit-bearing metaliteracy course could be compared to that of a random sample of students who did not take the course. While SAILS would not address any of the metaliteracy goals of the Politics of Information, we believe that students would still perform well on this *Standards*-based assessment. Many of the questions on the SAILS cohort test measure students' ability to understand the matrices of information they encounter in scholarly settings, even if that measure is done in an ontologically impoverished manner. One sample question asks test takers to select the appropriate source of information if one needed to learn about an event that took place two days ago. Students can choose between "book, dissertation, journal article, magazine, or newspaper."[61] The Politics of Information course positions students to learn strategies for conceptualizing and using traditional information sources and resources *as they critique them*. Thus, our students would likely select "newspaper," based on our discussions and readings on the cycle of scholarly publishing. This kind of assessment could even lead to a teaching moment, as students could be asked to reflect on the content of the standardized assessment tool in contrast to the content of the course.

CONTRIBUTIONS AND CONCLUSION

As librarians work to integrate metaliteracy learning into the curriculum, individual courses like the Politics of Information demonstrate the value of sustained, critical information literacy instruction—as well as challenges we will face in advocating for more meaningful, integrative teaching roles. Without a home that falls within the established disciplinary structure of the university and without regular teaching responsibilities, librarians exist on the margin of the academy. This position, compounded and reproduced by the pervasiveness of one-shot sessions, makes it challenging for librarians to build enough rapport and trust with students that would allow us to focus on affective and metacognitive domains of learning. Subject faculty tend to see us as helpers and service providers rather than as educators with the authority to teach beyond basic information skills. The Politics of Information gave us a space to examine that problematic structure alongside students—and, in the process, to subvert it by taking on credit-bearing teaching responsibilities. Still, as we discussed earlier, our impact was limited because we could teach only through the Honors Program. While the course was successful, there would be many more steps to take for it to truly be integrated into the curriculum. At most institutions, acceptance of metaliteracy learning into the established curricular structure will likely be slow, which is all the more frustrating because metaliteracy emphasizes the rapidly changing nature of the information environment outside of academia.

Because of these challenges, librarians are in a unique position to act as leaders and innovators in advocating for metaliteracy learning. From our position outside of the disciplines, we have a broad-scale view of students' research experiences in a variety of subjects throughout their academic careers. Subject faculty are not likely to question the system of scholarly knowledge production because they are thoroughly invested in it. As a result, they develop assignments that ask students to reproduce traditional text-based forms of information, and they often frame online information as off limits or even dangerous. As we saw in the small community of our course, metaliteracy teaching helps students develop as critical creators and users of both digital and traditional forms of information. This kind of teaching will be most effective when it reaches the most students, ideally through a combination of courses, like ours, that are taught by librarians and deal with information as the subject and through courses in the disciplines. For either case, our course provides a model for taking a critical stance toward traditional forms of academic information, foregrounding the relevance and importance of information outside of academia and positioning students as active, metacognitive creators of information in participatory online environments.

NOTES

1. On metaliteracy as a reinvention of information literacy instruction, see Thomas P. Mackey and Trudi E. Jacobson, "Reframing Information Literacy as Metaliteracy," *College and Research Libraries* 72, no. 1 (2011): 62–78, doi:10.5860/crl-76r1; their following book, *Metaliteracy: Reinventing Information Literacy to Empower Learners* (Chicago: Neal-Schuman, 2014); and the Metaliteracy.org website (http://metaliteracy.org). For the final version of the ACRL *Standards* revision, see Association of College and Research Libraries, *Framework for Information Literacy for Higher Education* (Chicago: American Library Association, 2015), www.ala.org/acrl/standards/ilframework.

2. All course documents, including the syllabus and student projects, are available online. See the Politics of Information website at www.carmichaeldigitalprojects.org/politicsofinfo.

3. Mackey and Jacobson, "Reframing Information Literacy," 70. We talk about the principles of metaliteracy and connect them to our learning outcomes in the Politics of Information in the Application section of this chapter.

4. James Elmborg, "Critical Information Literacy: Implications for Instructional Practice," *Journal of Academic Librarianship* 32, no. 2 (2006): 192–99.

5. Ibid., 194.

6. Rheingold's theory is not one that Mackey and Jacobson specifically identify as being encompassed by metaliteracy, but its clear relationship to metaliteracy concepts demonstrates the flexibility of a metaliteracy model. See Howard Rheingold, *Net Smart: How to Thrive Online* (Cambridge, MA: MIT Press, 2012).

7. Char Booth, *Reflective Teaching, Effective Learning: Instructional Literacy for Library Educators* (Chicago: American Library Association), 19.

8. Robbin Crabtree, David Alan Sapp, and Adela C. Licona, eds., *Feminist Pedagogy: Looking Back to Move Forward* (Baltimore, MD: Johns Hopkins University Press, 2009), 5.

9. Ellen Carillo, "'Feminist' Teaching/Teaching 'Feminism,'" *Feminist Teacher* 18, no. 1 (2007): 33.

10. Maria T. Accardi, *Feminist Library Pedagogy* (Duluth, MN: Library Juice Press), 67.

11. Christopher V. Hollister, ed., *Best Practices for Credit-Bearing Information Literacy Courses* (Chicago: Association of College and Research Libraries, 2010).

12. Anne Leonard and Maura A. Smale, "The Three-Credit Solution: Social Justice in an Information Literacy Course," in *Information Literacy and Social Justice: Radical Professional Praxis*, ed. Lua Gregory and Shana Higgins (Duluth, MN: Library Juice Press, 2013), 150–51.

13. University of Montevallo, *Building Information Literacy Brick by Brick: QEP 2011–2016* (Montevallo, AL: University of Montevallo, 2011), https://legacy.montevallo.edu/QEP/Documentation/QEP%20SACS%20DOC_Revised%20with%20cover_1-25-11_MMW.pdf.

14. Association of College and Research Libraries, *Information Literacy Competency Standards for Higher Education* (Chicago: American Library Association, 2000), www.ala.org/acrl/standards/informationliteracycompetency.

15. Lauren Wallis and Andrew Battista, *Authorize This!* (zine), accessed March 15, 2015, www.joomag.com/en/newsstand/authorize-this/0220614001388692589?ref=ib.

16. Many instructors worry about privacy and student work online. We emphasized in our course description that public creation online was a prerequisite of the class, and students agreed to this by registering. This practice is in keeping with metaliteracy's emphasis on open learning resources and environments.

17. Mackey and Jacobson, *Metaliteracy*, 9.

18. This Spread a Message component of the class coalesces with the justice-oriented information circulation strategies described in Melissa Morrone, ed., *Informed Agitation: Library and Information Skills in Social Justice Movements and Beyond* (Duluth, MN: Library Juice Press, 2014).

19. For the final version of the *Framework*, see Association of College and Research Libraries, *Framework for Information Literacy for Higher Education* (Chicago: American Library Association, 2015), www.ala.org/acrl/standards/ilframework.

20. Ibid.

21. Mackey and Jacobson, *Metaliteracy*, 2.

22. Ibid., 5.

23. Ibid., 86–87.

24. Ibid., 86.

25. These goals were developed by collaborators in the SUNY Innovative Instruction Technology Grant. See Metaliteracy.org, "Goals and Learning Objectives" (updated September 11, 2014), http://metaliteracy.org/learning-objectives.

26. Mackey and Jacobson, *Metaliteracy*, 88.

27. Ibid., 90.

28. Ibid., 13.

29. Ibid.

30. Ibid, 92.

31. This is a common problem for instruction librarians. See Meredith Farkas, "'I Need Three Peer-Reviewed Articles' or the Freshman Research Paper," *Information Wants to Be Free* (blog), October 27, 2011, http://meredith.wolfwater.com/wordpress/2011/10/27/i-need-three-peer-reviewed-articles-or-the-freshman-research-paper.

32. Andrew Battista, "Universities Pay Twice for Information," *The Politics of Information* (blog), January 21, 2014, http://carmichaeldigitalprojects.org/politicsofinfo/?p=199.

33. Ibid.

34. Ibid.

35. Ibid.

36. Rachael Swokowski, "Test Scores May Not Have All the Answers: Understanding as a New Educational Approach," *The Politics of Information* (blog), February 11, 2014, http://carmichaeldigitalprojects.org/politicsofinfo/?p=300.

37. For the first three questions, see Hannah Gentry, "Critical Thinking and Education: Questions to Consider," *The Politics of Information* (blog), February 11, 2014, http://carmichaeldigitalprojects.org/politicsofinfo/?p=308; for the final questions, see Swokowski, "Test Scores."

38. Katie Saunders, "Questions to Consider," *The Politics of Information* (blog), March 19, 2014, http://carmichaeldigitalprojects.org/politicsofinfo/?p=414.

39. Katie Saunders, "How Do I Spread a Message of the Digital Divide?" *The Politics of Information* (blog), April 22, 2014, http://carmichaeldigitalprojects.org/politicsofinfo/?p=561.

40. Kayla Pilkington, "Interview with Dr. Matthews and Anonymous Student," *The Politics of Information* (blog), January 21, 2014, http://carmichaeldigitalprojects.org/politicsofinfo/?p=225.

41. Ibid.

42. Ibid.

43. Katie Saunders, "Q and A: How Not Having Internet Access Would Affect Our Everyday Lives," *The Politics of Information* (blog), February 19, 2014, http://carmichaeldigitalprojects.org/politicsofinfo/?p=331.

44. Rachel Swokowski, "Interview with Feminist Extraordinaire: Tanya Hoang," *The Politics of Information* (blog), February 4, 2014, http://carmichaeldigitalprojects.org/politicsofinfo/?p=270.

45. Hannah Gentry, "Social Media and Volunteerism," *The Politics of Information* (blog), February 4, 2014, http://carmichaeldigitalprojects.org/politicsofinfo/?p=286.

46. Mackey and Jacobson, *Metaliteracy*, 92.

47. Hannah Gentry, "Writing for Wikipedia or: How I Learned to Stop Worrying and Love Coding," *The Politics of Information* (blog), April 15, 2014, http://carmichaeldigitalprojects.org/politicsofinfo/?p=492.

48. Ibid.

49. Ibid.

50. Ibid.

51. Hannah Gentry, "Peace Out," *The Politics of Information* (blog), April 22, 2014, http://carmichaeldigitalprojects.org/politicsofinfo/?p=538.

52. Mackey and Jacobson, *Metaliteracy*, 7.

53. Katie Saunders, "The End: Final Reflection," *The Politics of Information* (blog), April 22, 2014, http://carmichaeldigitalprojects.org/politicsofinfo/?p=549.

54. Ibid.

55. Gentry, "Peace Out."

56. The assumption that "digital natives" are inherently fluid participants in online environments has persisted among educators for some time. For a collection of essays that challenges common assumptions about digital natives, see Michael Thomas, ed., *Deconstructing Digital Natives: Young People, Technology, and the New Literacies* (New York: Routledge, 2011).

57. Gentry, "Peace Out."

58. Saunders, "The End: Final Reflection."

59. Carol C. Kuhlthau, "Inside the Search Process: Information Seeking from the User's Perspective," *Journal of the American Society for Information Science* 42, no. 5 (1991): 361–71. For a discussion of using affective learning outcomes in library instruction based on Kuhlthau's model and others, see Ellysa Cahoy and Robert Schroeder, "Embedding Affective Learning Outcomes in Library Instruction," *Communications in Information Literacy* 6, no. 1 (2012): 73–90.

60. Ibid.
61. Project SAILS, "Sample Questions from Our Information Literacy Assessment" (last modified September 4, 2012), www.projectsails.org/SampleQuestions.

BIBLIOGRAPHY

Accardi, Maria T. *Feminist Pedagogy for Library Instruction*. Duluth, MN: Library Juice Press, 2013.

Association of College and Research Libraries. *Framework for Information Literacy for Higher Education*. Chicago: American Library Association, 2015. www.ala.org/acrl/standards/ilframework.

Battista, Andrew. "Universities Pay Twice for Information." *The Politics of Information* (blog), January 21, 2014. http://carmichaeldigitalprojects.org/politicsofinfo/?p=199.

Booth, Char. *Reflective Teaching, Effective Learning: Instructional Literacy for Library Educators*. Chicago: American Library Association, 2011.

Cahoy, Ellysa, and Robert Schroeder. "Embedding Affective Learning Outcomes in Library Instruction." *Communications in Information Literacy* 6, no. 1 (2012): 73–90.

Carillo, Ellen. "'Feminist' Teaching/Teaching 'Feminism.'" *Feminist Teacher* 18, no. 1 (2007): 28–40.

Crabtree, Robbin, David Alan Sapp, and Adela C. Licona, eds. *Feminist Pedagogy: Looking Back to Move Forward*. Baltimore, MD: Johns Hopkins University Press, 2009.

Elmborg, James. "Critical Information Literacy: Implications for Instructional Practice." *Journal of Academic Librarianship* 32, no. 2 (2006): 192–99.

Farkas, Meredith. "'I Need Three Peer-Reviewed Articles' or the Freshman Research Paper." *Information Wants to Be Free* (blog), October 27, 2011. http://meredith.wolfwater.com/wordpress/2011/10/27/i-need-three-peer-reviewed-articles-or-the-freshman-research-paper/.

Gentry, Hannah. "Critical Thinking and Education: Questions to Consider." *The Politics of Information* (blog), February 22, 2014. http://carmichaeldigitalprojects.org/politicsofinfo/?p=308.

———. "Peace Out." *The Politics of Information* (blog), April 22, 2014. http://carmichaeldigitalprojects.org/politicsofinfo/?p=308.

———. "Social Media and Volunteerism." *The Politics of Information* (blog), February 4, 2014. http://carmichaeldigitalprojects.org/politicsofinfo/?p=286.

———."Writing for Wikipedia or: How I Learned to Stop Worrying and Love Coding." *The Politics of Information* (blog), April 15, 2014. http://carmichaeldigitalprojects.org/politicsofinfo/?p=492.

Hollister, Christopher V., ed. *Best Practices for Credit-Bearing Information Literacy Courses*. Chicago: Association of College and Research Libraries, 2010.

Kuhlthau, Carol C. "Inside the Search Process: Information Seeking from the User's Perspective." *Journal of the American Society for Information Science* 42, no. 5 (1991): 361–71.

Leonard, Anne, and Maura A. Smale. "The Three-Credit Solution: Social Justice in an Information Literacy Course." In *Information Literacy and Social Justice: Radical Professional Praxis*, edited by Lua Gregory and Shana Higgins, 143–62. Duluth, MN: Library Juice Press, 2013.

Mackey, Thomas P., and Trudi E. Jacobson. *Metaliteracy: Reinventing Information Literacy to Empower Learners*. Chicago: Neal-Schuman, 2014.

———. "Reframing Information Literacy as Metaliteracy." *College and Research Libraries* 72, no. 1 (2011): 62–78. doi:10.5860/crl-76r1.

Metaliteracy.org. "Goals and Learning Outcomes." Updated September 11, 2014. http://metaliteracy.org/learning-objectives.

Morrone, Melissa, ed. *Informed Agitation: Library and Information Skills in Social Justice Movements and Beyond*. Duluth, MN: Library Juice Press, 2014.

Pilkington, Kayla. "Interview with Dr. Matthews and Anonymous Student." *The Politics of Information* (blog), January 21, 2014. http://carmichaeldigitalprojects.org/politicsofinfo/?p=225.

Project SAILS. "Project SAILS Skills Sets." Last modified March 14, 2013. www.projectsails.org/SkillSets.

———. "Sample Questions from Our Information Literacy Assessment." Last modified September 4, 2012. www.projectsails.org/SampleQuestions.

Rheingold, Howard. *Net Smart: How to Thrive Online*. Cambridge, MA: MIT Press, 2012.

Saunders, Katie. "The End: Final Reflection." *The Politics of Information* (blog), April 22, 2014. http://carmichaeldigitalprojects.org/politicsofinfo/?p=549.

———. "How Do I Spread a Message of the Digital Divide?" *The Politics of Information* (blog), April 22, 2014. http://carmichaeldigitalprojects.org/politicsofinfo/?p=561.

———. "Q and A: How Not Having Internet Access Would Affect Our Everyday Lives." *The Politics of Information* (blog), February 19, 2014. http://carmichaeldigitalprojects.org/politicsofinfo/?p=331.

———. "Questions to Consider." *The Politics of Information* (blog), March 19, 2014. http://carmichaeldigitalprojects.org/politicsofinfo/?p=414.

Swokowski, Rachael. "Interview with Feminist Extraordinaire: Tanya Hoang." *The Politics of Information* (blog), February 4, 2014. http://carmichaeldigitalprojects.org/politicsofinfo/?p=270.

————. "Test Scores May Not Have All the Answers: Understanding as a New Educational Approach." *The Politics of Information* (blog), February 11, 2014. http://carmichaeldigitalprojects.org/politicsofinfo/?p=300.

Thomas, Michael, ed. *Deconstructing Digital Natives: Young People, Technology, and the New Literacies*. New York: Routledge, 2011.

Wallis, Lauren, and Andrew Battista. *Authorize This!* (zine). Accessed March 15, 2015. www.joomag.com/en/newsstand/authorize-this/0220614001388692589?ref=ib.

BARBARA J. D'ANGELO
and BARRY M. MAID

3

Metaliteracy Learning of RN to BSN Students

A Fusion of Disciplinary Values and Discourses

FOR ALMOST TWO DECADES, WE HAVE BEEN WORKING IN THE gray area between Library and Information Science (LIS) and Writing Studies (WS). We have looked at the Association of College and Research Libraries' *Information Literacy Competency Standards for Higher Education* (ACRL *Standards*) and the Council of Writing Program Administrators' "Outcomes Statement for First Year Composition (3.0)" (WPA OS),[1] analyzed them, and integrated them to create a unified set of outcomes for the undergraduate degree Technical Communication (TC) Program at Arizona State University (ASU). We then mapped relevant outcomes to individual courses within the TC Program to facilitate course design and assessment.[2] The resulting TC Program outcomes reflect a "meta" approach to information literacy and writing/communication and presuppose the theoretical and practical ties that bind them.

Metacognition plays a role in the pedagogy of our courses and in the assessment of the TC Program using capstone ePortfolios.[3] This approach also reflects our interest in whether our students are able to transfer what they learn related to both information and writing. We are not unique in this concern; however, our combined perspectives to fuse knowledge from LIS and

WS have led us to expand our attention to emerging teaching-for-transfer research,[4] threshold concepts, and metaliteracy.

In this chapter, we report on our development of a discipline-specific writing and research course for ASU's undergraduate nursing program, TWC361: Writing for Healthcare Management. We were able to draw on our experience within the TC Program to fuse disciplinary knowledge from two disciplines for TWC361 by integrating an additional discipline in nursing. Collaboration with our nursing colleagues has enabled us to continually revise the course, resulting in improvement of course design, ongoing refinement of course outcomes, and course assessment. Although not initially designed using metaliteracy learning objectives, the course reflects concepts underpinning metaliteracy: encouragement of critical thinking, collaborative practices, and metacognition, all of which are needed for both the consumption and production of knowledge.

We set out to discover how metaliteracy aligns with disciplinary writing outcomes through a case study of the course. In addition, we examine how well the course currently meets metaliteracy goals and learning objectives by evaluating student work. Prior to describing the course and what we found, we review related literature from the fields of LIS, WS, and nursing to set the context within disciplinary perspectives.

RELATED LITERATURE

Library and Information Science and Writing Studies

LIS and WS have shared a long-standing collaborative partnership in higher education. This partnership is articulated in the literature of both disciplines,[5] through presentations at conferences such as the as the annual conference of the Association of College and Research Libraries (ACRL) and the Georgia Conference on Information Literacy. The ACRL *Standards*, however, have faced criticism as being overly focused on discrete skills. This is not surprising given that both the ACRL *Standards* and WPA OS were created as a way to establish outcomes (or competencies) that are assessable. However, research in both LIS and WS has demonstrated that both information literacy and writing are grounded in process approaches,[6] and that information literacy is a far more complex literacy that is situated and contextual.[7]

Mackey and Jacobson proposed reframing information literacy as metaliteracy in an overarching approach to integrate emerging technologies in today's social media environment and to unify multiple literacy types.[8] As a comprehensive framework, metaliteracy promotes critical thinking and collaboration. In recognition of the differences between traditional print media and today's dynamic social media information platforms, metaliteracy reframes information literacy to recognize that students are both consumers and producers of information. Further, it conceptualizes information literacy away from a model based on discrete skills to one that exists within a framework that can be contextualized. The metaliteracy learning objectives are grounded in four domains—behavioral, cognitive, affective, and meta-cognitive[9]—in a learner-centered model to facilitate a process in which learners are active participants, collaborators, producers, and communicators of information.

As a comprehensive and unifying framework, metaliteracy extends beyond standards and outcomes and has influenced the development of the ACRL's *Framework for Information Literacy for Higher Education*.[10] Although not explicit, we can see the same influences shaping disciplinary documents and work within WS. In 2008 the WPA OS was revised to more explicitly incorporate technology, and it underwent further revision in 2014. Further, in recognition that student learning encompasses more than outcomes, the Council of Writing Program Administrators, in conjunction with the Conference on College Composition and Communications, adopted the *Framework for Success in Postsecondary Writing*,[11] which focuses on eight habits of mind. Rather than outline skills, the habits of mind are a set of attitudes that are intended to help students become better writers and learners. By encouraging students to develop these attitudes, instructors may help students to meet the outcomes defined by the earlier WPA OS. The eight habits of mind explicate similar traits as the metaliteracy domains:

> **Curiosity**—the desire to know more about the world
>
> **Openness**—the willingness to consider new ways of being and thinking in the world
>
> **Engagement**—a sense of investment and involvement in learning
>
> **Creativity**—the ability to use novel approaches for generating, investigating, and representing ideas
>
> **Persistence**—the ability to sustain interest in and attention to short- and long-term projects
>
> **Responsibility**—the ability to take ownership of one's actions and understand the consequences of those actions for oneself and others
>
> **Flexibility**—the ability to adapt to situations, expectations, or demands
>
> **Metacognition**—the ability to reflect on one's own thinking as well as on the individual and cultural processes used to structure knowledge[12]

As we can see, LIS and WS have moved in the same direction to incorporate both outcomes/objectives and dispositions in key documents and foundational principles intended to facilitate teaching, learning, and assessment.

Disciplinary Perspectives: Nursing

The connection between LIS and WS often is articulated or manifested in first-year composition courses, particularly the second-semester composition course focused on research (commonly known as English 102 or Composition II). However, all kinds of communication, including written communication, are important to disciplinary discourse. Nurses, in particular, exist within sophisticated information environments in which work takes place in inter-disciplinary teams including medical personnel, pharmacists, home health care workers, social workers, patients, and more. For undergraduate nursing education, the importance of communication practices can be seen in two of nursing's disciplinary documents related to undergraduate education. Accreditation standards for undergraduate nursing degrees require programs to meet expectations set forth by the American Association of Colleges of Nursing (AACN) in *The Essentials of Baccalaureate Education for Professional Nursing Practice*,[13] which incorporates expectations for both information management and interprofessional communication and collaboration. Interprofessional communication and collaboration competencies are further elaborated by AACN in *Core Competencies for Interprofessional Collaboration*,[14] which identifies and delineates eight communication core competencies related to the organization and presentation of information and the appropriate use of technologies.

Clearly, nurses must communicate effectively with team members; however, nurses also self-identify as patient advocates and educators. In fact, patients themselves are identified as a member of the interprofessional health care team. Information management and the use of various technologies also play significant roles in competencies expected of practicing nurses. As a result, nurses' information and communication landscapes are complex, requiring them to collect and analyze information that is then communicated to various audiences in a variety of different media.

Two disciplinary values further provide connections to WS and LIS: evidence-based practice and reflective practice. Evidence-based practice emphasizes the use of research to inform clinical practice and patient care. Much of the nursing disciplinary literature related to information literacy typically addresses it by focusing on the need for students to learn to use disciplinary databases to find research studies or other clinical information. Others, however, emphasize the need for nurses to be information literate beyond the collection of information and to engage in critical thinking to understand why and when information is needed, be able to analyze information within the context of clinical practice, and develop lifelong learning abilities.[15]

However, nurses' information and communication practices involve more than traditional print sources; they involve drawing upon and sharing information from many different types of sources to construct knowledge for effective practice. These sources may include government or quasi-governmental sites (e.g., Centers for Disease Control and Prevention, National Institutes of Health, World Health Organization), well-known or reputable health/medical organizations (e.g., Mayo Clinic), condition-specific associations (e.g., American Cancer Society), reference apps on smartphones or tablets (e.g., to locate drug information), and intranet-based sources used by their employer (e.g., patient instructional handouts). Bonner and Lloyd have further shown, in a study of renal nurses, that nurses gather information from multiple epistemic, social, and corporeal sources to enable practice and to ensure quality patient care.[16] Nurses, therefore, are situated within socially constructed discourse communities in which information is accessed and shared from multiple types of sources and media to construct meaning. These discourse communities extend beyond nurses themselves to interdisciplinary care teams composed of individuals, including patients, with different expertise and knowledge.

Further, reflective practice is a disciplinary value for nurses that fosters self-awareness for the purpose of cultivating conceptual thinking and decision making and/or changes in practice. It fosters empathy to nurture the human connections and compassion needed for patient care. Reflective practice also is considered a way to develop lifelong learning in a profession in which knowledge evolves rapidly and new information emerges from disparate sources. In short, reflective practice is metacognition.

UNDERGRADUATE NURSING METALITERACY CASE STUDY

The online RN (Registered Nurse) to BSN (Bachelor of Science in Nursing) Program at ASU emphasizes written and oral communication skills, clinical reasoning, and technology skills. Students enrolled in the program have completed their associate's degree and are returning to school to earn their BSN. The student population tends to consist of a mix of students who have just completed their associate's degree and those who have been in the workplace for several years and are returning to school.

Writing for Healthcare Management

TWC361: Writing for Healthcare Management, a junior-level course, is the first course taken by students in the program and is required of all majors; only RN–BSN majors are enrolled. Developed in collaboration between technical communication faculty and nursing faculty, the goals of the course are focused on three areas: to develop students' professional writing abilities, to develop students' information literacy, and to help students use technology effectively. Although the course was developed collaboratively, the course is housed in the TC Program administratively and coordinated by a TC faculty member, who is one of the authors of this chapter. TC instructors teach multiple sections each term. Most of the sections incorporate ASU's course management system (CMS), while others feature the Digication ePortfolio software as part of a pilot program.

To develop the course, we mapped relevant TC Program outcomes to the course and associated outcomes with each assignment so that students can clearly identify how each activity meets overall course goals. Outcomes are used as the basis for grading assignments, with a rubric that lists outcomes and specifies how they apply for that assignment. We continually revise the course to ensure it meets goals for the RN–BSN degree. For example, in spring 2015, we added the AACN interprofessional communication competencies to the list of outcomes and rubrics so that students can clearly see how they relate to existing outcomes and assignments.[17]

The course was therefore developed within the outcomes framework that we use for all courses in the TC Program. We did not use metaliteracy objectives to create or revise the course due to logistical and disciplinary context. Logistically, the course was developed in 2010—before the final version of the article on metaliteracy was first published.[18] Contextually, using TC Program outcomes and interdisciplinary competencies places the course within the overall framework of the broader curriculum for both the TC Program and the RN–BSN program. While this may seem like an issue of semantics, the use of disciplinary language to articulate disciplinary values helps students to learn that language is a part of becoming socialized into the discipline. However, the course does fall under the umbrella of the metaliteracy framework to facilitate student learning. To illustrate, we have aligned metaliteracy learning objectives with TC Program outcomes and interprofessional competencies in table 3.1.

Our alignment of metaliteracy learning objectives not only shows that the course fits within the metaliteracy umbrella but clearly demonstrates that metaliteracy signifies a unifying literacy and, importantly, that it much more clearly unifies domains with learning objectives. The *Framework for Success in Postsecondary Writing* does articulate attitudes representative of the affective domain.[19] Metacognition is also recognized within WS as an integral part of teaching and learning. However, the habits of mind are not explicitly articulated in the WPA OS.[20] As a result, instructors are left to make connections and attempt to incorporate them in pedagogy and in assessment practices. On the other hand, metaliteracy much more clearly identifies domains in a way that facilitates teaching and the development of pedagogical methods.

TABLE 3.1

Comparison of TWC361 Outcomes and Competencies
with Metaliteracy Learning Objectives

TC PROGRAM OUTCOMES (TWC361)	INTERPROFESSIONAL COMPETENCIES (TWC361)[a]	METALITERACY LEARNING OBJECTIVES[b]
Rhetorical Knowledge • Identify, articulate, and focus on a defined purpose • Respond to the need of the appropriate audience • Adopt appropriate voice, tone, and level of formality • Use appropriate technologies to organize, present, and communicate information to address a range of audiences, purposes, and genres	• Choose effective communication tools and techniques, including information systems and communication technologies, to facilitate discussions and interactions • Use respectful language appropriate for a given situation	• Demonstrate the ability to translate information presented in one manner to another in order to best meet the needs of particular audiences; integrate information from multiple sources into coherent new forms (3.5; M) • Produce original content appropriate to specific needs in multiple media formats; transfer knowledge gained to new formats in unpredictable and evolving environments (goal 3.7; B) • Determine scope of the question or task required to meet one's needs (goal 4.1; C) • Reevaluate needs and next steps throughout the process (goal 4.2; C)
Critical Thinking, Reading, and Writing • Use information, writing, and reading for inquiry, learning, thinking, and communicating • Understand that research and writing are a series of tasks including accessing, retrieving, evaluating, and synthesizing appropriate data and information from sources that vary in content, format, structure, and scope	• Express one's knowledge and opinions to team members with confidence, clarity, and respect, working to ensure common understanding of information and decisions • Recognize how one's own uniqueness, including experience level, expertise, culture, power, and hierarchy within the health care team, contributes to effective communication and positive interprofessional working relationships	• Place an information source in its context (goal 1.1, C) • Distinguish between editorial commentary and information presented from a more research-based perspective (goal 1.2; C) • Determine the value of formal and informal information from various networked sources (goal 1.3; C) • Value user-generated content and critically evaluate contributions made by others; see self as a producer as well as consumer of information (goal 3.8; A)

(cont.)

TABLE 3.1

Comparison of TWC361 Outcomes and Competencies
with Metaliteracy Learning Objectives (cont.)

TC PROGRAM OUTCOMES (TWC361)	INTERPROFESSIONAL COMPETENCIES (TWC361)[a]	METALITERACY LEARNING OBJECTIVES[b]
• **Critical Thinking, Reading, and Writing** (cont.)		• Compare the unique attributes of different information formats and have the ability to use effectively and to cite information for the development of original content (goal 3.3; B) • Demonstrate the ability to think critically in context and to transfer critical thinking to new learning (goal 4.5; M) • Demonstrate self-empowerment through interaction and the presentation of ideas; gain the ability to see what is transferable, translatable, and teachable (learners are both students and teachers) (goal 4.10; M) • Use self-reflection to assess one's own learning and knowledge of the learning process (goal 4.4; M)
Processes • Be aware that it takes multiple drafts to create and complete a successful text • Develop flexible strategies for generating, revising, editing, and proofreading • Critique their own and others' works • Develop research and writing strategies appropriate to the context and situation • Understand the collaborative and social aspects of research and writing processes	• Listen actively, and encourage ideas and opinions of other team members • Give timely, sensitive, instructive feedback to others, responding respectfully as a team member to feedback from others	• Take responsibility for participation in collaborative environments (goal 3.2; A) • Participate conscientiously in collaborative environments (goal 3.1; B) • Effectively communicate personal and professional experiences to inform and assist others; and recognize that learners can also be teachers (goal 3.6; B) • Communicate effectively with collaborators in shared spaces and learn from multiple points of view (goal 4.7; M)

TC PROGRAM OUTCOMES (TWC361)	INTERPROFESSIONAL COMPETENCIES (TWC361)[a]	METALITERACY LEARNING OBJECTIVES[b]
Processes (cont.)		• Recognize that learning is a process and that reflecting on errors or mistakes leads to new insights and discoveries (goal 4.8; M)
Knowledge of Conventions • Learn standard tools for accessing and retrieving information • Learn common formats for different genres • Control surface features such as syntax, grammar, punctuation, and spelling • Apply appropriate means of documenting work		• Use technology to build a positive Web presence (goal 2.3; B) • Demonstrate the importance of matching information needs and search strategies to appropriate search tools (goal 4.3; C) • Articulate the necessity of attribution when borrowing the intellectual property of others, regardless of format (goal 2.6; A) • Identify the context for which accurate attribution is needed and consistently apply that attribution (goal 2.7; C)

NOTE: Letter coding for the metaliteracy domains: B = behavioral; C = cognitive; A = affective; M = metacognitive.

[a] Interprofessional competencies are quoted from AACN, *Core Competencies for Interprofessional Communication*.
[b] Learning objectives are quoted from Metaliteracy.org, "Goals and Learning Objectives."

Course Structure and Assignments

The first assignment in TWC361 asks students to compose a Hallmarks of Professionalism e-mail to their instructor in which they use course readings and their own experience to analyze how writing and communication are characteristics of professionalism for nurses. The remainder of the course revolves around a workplace role-playing scenario with a set of sequenced assignments that concludes in a patient education video presentation:

- Brainstorming session to select a specific topic and patient population for the patient education presentation
- Research log to collect sources

- Annotated bibliography to summarize, evaluate, and reflect upon sources
- Proposal to a supervisor for approval of the topic and specific patient audience
- Presentation of the educational message to the specific patient audience

The sequencing of assignments accomplishes two purposes: First, it steps students systematically through the process involved to propose and create the presentation (video). Second, because students are required to collect and use information for two different audiences and purposes related to the same project, they must articulate, understand, and apply information contextually. Because the final products of the scenario are composed in different genres and media (a traditional print memo for the proposal and a video for the presentation), students must grasp the conventions of communicating in each genre as well as develop the cognitive ability to shape the information they have collected and analyzed to meet the challenges of presenting information in different media.

The course ends with one final metacognitive statement in the form of a memo to the course instructor. This final assignment draws upon our philosophical approach to teaching and assessment of learning in which metacognition is used for two purposes: First, metacognitive statements are an integral component of program assessment using ePortfolios. Second, we use metacognitive statements as assignments within courses to help students articulate the why and how of their learning. Our use of a final metacognitive statement in TWC361 follows this approach.

Metacognition, however, is a learned practice. Even with prompts, students are likely to describe what they did instead of reflect on how or why to articulate their learning. We take several steps to help students learn to develop the ability to compose metacognitive statements while they reflect on their work, experience, and progress throughout the course. During the first week of the course, students view a video explaining what reflection is and, equally important, what it is not so that they have an understanding of what is expected in their reflective statements. In addition, during the first week of the course, students read about nursing portfolios as well as the importance of reflective practice to contextualize metacognition within their profession. Within the course structure, students complete a metacognitive piece for each assignment, responding to specific prompts that prod them to articulate how course concepts apply to the specific assignment and how application of concepts differed from one assignment to another. Each of these pieces receives feedback from the instructor so that students learn the "how to" of metacognition.

APPLICATION OF METALITERACY LEARNING OBJECTIVES

Multiple metaliteracy learning objectives are manifested in the course and are aligned with TC Program outcomes and interprofessional competencies as shown in table 3.1. In this section, we describe more specifically how each assignment in the course scenario relates to metaliteracy objectives.[21]

Hallmarks of Professionalism E-mail

In the Hallmarks of Professionalism e-mail assignment, students are asked to discuss the types of writing and communication they do and why. In addition, students are asked to analyze why writing is a "hallmark of professionalism" for nurses and to provide examples from course readings and their experience. This metacognitive assignment sets the tone for the course by asking students to immediately reflect on their attitudes, behavior, and knowledge about writing within their profession. The intent of the assignment draws upon the metacognitive domain of metaliteracy, in particular, metaliteracy goal 4, "demonstrate ability to connect learning and research strategies with lifelong learning processes and personal, academic, and professional goals."[22]

Brainstorming

The role-playing scenario begins with a brainstorming task in which students are asked to suggest potential topics for the patient education presentation and collaborate to refine and focus their selections. We encourage students to begin preliminary research and reading to help narrow their focus on a topic and a specific patient population. Brainstorming takes place using the discussion board (in sections using a CMS) or ePortfolios to facilitate feedback and collaboration as students select and refine their topic. This, in turn, leads students to reevaluate their selection and focus. This assignment facilitates students' ability to determine the scope of their task early in the process and then to continually reevaluate that scope and their research needs throughout the process.

Research Log

Once students have completed brainstorming, they use a research log to identify their search strategies to collect information and data. Part of the goal for this activity is to require students to articulate the following:

- Databases or information sources they selected to search
- Their use of keywords to demonstrate that they have searched for information that meets the purpose of the research
- How they revised searches in an iterative process based on results from initial searches
- Why they have selected sources from their results based on how sources will be used for their upcoming assignments

The assignment not only formalizes their search process but also requires students to think critically to determine the value of the information they have found. As such, they must articulate the purpose for which information will be used and the expectations of the target audience. For example, an empirical research article from a medical journal would represent the type of information that the reader of a proposal might expect and that would be most persuasive. Empirical research might also inform the student as he or she applies information to create an accurate, credible, and current presentation targeted to patients. However, for the purpose of the presentation itself, a patient audience is more likely to expect practical information from such sources as the Centers from Disease Control and Prevention or the Mayo Clinic than empirical research. Students, therefore, meet three metaliteracy objectives: First, they place information sources in context of their assigned tasks to write a proposal and prepare a presentation. Second, students demonstrate the importance of matching the information needs they identified to search strategies by articulating databases searched, keywords used, and revisions to searches. Third, students also distinguish between editorial commentary and information presented from a more research-based perspective by articulating how selected sources will meet the purpose of upcoming assignments and the types of sources that would be expected from their audiences for those assignments.

Annotated Bibliography

In the follow-up annotated bibliography assignment, students summarize, evaluate, and reflect upon the sources they have collected in more depth. To do this assignment well, students must thoroughly read sources so that they are able to concisely paraphrase them, assess their validity and credibility, and then reflect upon how they will use them specifically for the proposal and presentation assignments. Several metaliteracy objectives come into play for this assignment. To complete this assignment effectively, students must translate information presented in one manner to another, integrate information from multiple sources, think critically in context to evaluate sources thoroughly, and accurately attribute information.

Proposal

Students then move on to application of their research in a proposal to a supervisor within the role-playing scenario. They draft their proposal and then work in groups to provide one another with feedback before they revise and submit their final proposal in traditional print memo format. Although the context of the assignment is different, the same three metaliteracy objectives are addressed as in the annotated bibliography assignment. Students must translate information presented in one manner to another in order to best meet the needs of particular audiences—in this case, a hypothetical supervisor. Students must also integrate information from multiple sources into coherent new forms—their proposal—by thinking critically to apply information in an appropriate way for the purpose and audience of the assignment. Finally, students must accurately and consistently attribute sources of information.

Presentation

In the last assignment in the role-playing scenario, students use VoiceThread to compose and create their presentations and then post the URLs to the CMS or their ePortfolios so that other students and the instructor may view and comment on the final product. Students are familiar with doing patient education as nurses. However, the assignment does present challenges: The information they collected is no longer presented as evidence to support a proposed idea; it now has to be adapted and remixed to educate patients who have different levels of knowledge and experience. In addition, students must tackle the conventions of the genre—understanding the need to combine text, visuals, and audio for an effective video presentation. This assignment pushes students to demonstrate that they are able to translate information presented in one manner (the proposal) to another (the presentation) and thereby meet the needs of two different audiences by integrating information from multiple sources into coherent new forms. As a result, students must think critically within the context of their assignments and transfer their learning from one assignment to another.

Final Reflection

The purpose of this final assignment is twofold: First, it requires students to summarize and describe their learning. Second, and most important, it asks students to reflect upon what they have learned and to articulate how that learning will be applicable to their future writing as students and professionals. By articulating future application, it is hoped that students recognize and conceptualize that what they have learned is transferable to other contexts beyond this one course, including the remaining classes in their degree program and in their current and future careers. As such, the assignment draws upon metaliteracy objectives related to metacognition and asks students to demonstrate the ability to think critically in context and to transfer critical thinking to new learning by assessing their own learning. Students often reflect upon self-empowerment related to their learning and articulate what they have learned as transferable and translatable to upcoming courses and to their careers.

ASSESSMENT

Informal Assessment

Based on instructor observation of student engagement in sessions that use the ePortfolio software and sessions that use the CMS, students using ePortfolios are more engaged in both constructing an individualized presence and collaborating with one another. The ePortfolio software used for the course gives students the opportunity to "personalize" the look of their portfolio in a way that is not possible in a CMS. We provide students with a template; however, many take the time to change the style of the portfolio by adjusting colors and adding a different header photo and icon. In addition, self-introductions in the CMS sections tend to be straightforward formal texts; even though the CMS allows for adding photos, students never do. Self-introductions in ePortfolios tend to be very different; students introduce themselves professionally *and* personally, with information and photos of families, pets, or themselves at work. As a result, engagement with one another seems to be higher as students respond to one another's introductions in a much more engaging manner (more often and in more depth). This engagement tends to hold true through the brainstorming assignment. While students are required to post feedback, we do not specify how often or how much. Again anecdotally, in sections using ePortfolios, students seem to engage more by responding to multiple students with feedback, advice, and suggestions based on their experience as nurses and encouragement as they continue with the project. We interpret this engagement within the metaliteracy learning objectives as "use technology to build a positive web presence," "participate conscientiously in collaborative environments," and "take responsibility for participation in collaborative environments" because students do seem to take more initiative and time to personalize their portfolios within the context of the course and to engage with one another.[23]

As noted earlier, metacognition plays a significant role in the course. All students engage in metacognition on some level. Undoubtedly, some compose their reflections in a way to meet course requirements only while others spend considerable time reflecting on their work, what influenced it, and how learning key writing concepts will continue to help them improve academically as they continue with their courses in the RN–BSN program and then as professionals in the workplace. The prompts are designed to push students beyond description to self-assessment and analysis of their work so that they engage in metacognition. Metacognition is valued in all of the disciplines represented in the design of this course, and through their written reflections, students enhance their metacognitive abilities.

Formal Assessment

Each semester we formally assess the course by randomly selecting three reflective statements from the final course assignment in each course. These statements are scored by two faculty members independent of the course (one from Nursing, one from Technical Communication) using a scoring guide based on the four categories of the TC Program outcomes that represent the concepts, knowledge, and abilities for the course.

In fall 2014, two sections used Digication ePortfolios (total of six student statements selected) and five used the CMS only (sixteen student statements selected). Average scores were slightly higher for the categories of Rhetorical Knowledge, Processes, and Knowledge of Conventions for the ePortfolio statements. The average score for ePortfolio statements in the Critical Thinking, Reading, and Writing category, however, was more than 0.5 higher than the average score for CMS statements. Given the higher number of CMS statements scored compared to the number of ePortfolios, it is impossible to know if the higher Critical Thinking score was due to differences in the students or to the platform. This may be the subject of a future study. In particular, one area of interest is whether the use of ePortfolios facilitates metacognition in some way that contributes to critical thinking. For now, the data we obtained is shown in table 3.2.

TABLE 3.2

Average Scores for Reflective Statements

OUTCOMES CATEGORY	AVERAGE ePORTFOLIOS SCORE	AVERAGE CMS SCORE
Rhetorical Knowledge	3.6	3.4
Critical Thinking, Reading, and Writing	3.75	3.22
Processes	3.33	3.28
Knowledge of Conventions	3.25	3.22

NOTE: Rated on a 4-point scale; $N = 6$ for ePortfolios; $N = 16$ for CMS.

Portfolio Coding

We wanted to learn more specifically how metaliteracy learning objectives were manifested in this course. We coded documents from the six ePortfolios from the fall 2014 sections that used Digication. For coding, we selected additional assignments relevant to metaliteracy outcomes. Specifically, we coded the Hallmarks of Professionalism e-mail; the brainstorming session; the reflective statements that are associated with the research log, proposal, and presentation assignment; and the final reflective statement. Documents for the CMS sections were not coded; logistically, other than the reflective statement, the assignments were not available for analysis for the study. This is a limitation of the study; however, we believe coding the documents from the ePortfolios provides us with a good snapshot of metaliteracy learning objectives prevalent in the course. This information is also relevant for us since ePortfolios are likely to be used in all sections in an upcoming course revision.

We used the metaliteracy learning objectives as codes that were assigned to a course assignment once per document. For example, if a student cited multiple sources in an assignment, the code for the related metaliteracy learning objective, for example, 2.7 ("Identify the context for which accurate attribution is needed and consistently apply that attribution"[24]), was assigned just once. In some cases, objectives were manifested in explicit statements by the students that they had done something (in particular, behavioral or cognitive objectives), whereas in other cases objectives were manifested implicitly in statements about what students had learned, how they had learned from mistakes, or how they would use what they had learned in the future (affective and metacognitive objectives).

The results depicted in table 3.3 show the high level of attention paid to searching and analyzing sources in the research log and annotated bibliography assignments. The ability to synthesize and integrate information is a difficult task and one that takes experience and practice. However, students clearly articulate that they have spent time and effort to evaluate sources within the context of their intended use for assignments.

Using APA (American Psychological Association) style is a significant outcome for nursing students and is an emphasis in the RN–BSN program.[25] In TWC361, the only aspect of APA style that is emphasized is citation formatting. It is not surprising, then, that objective 2.7 received the highest number of code instances (see table 3.4). This code was assigned when students cited a source within an assignment. Code 2.6 was assigned if a student specifically articulated a reason for citing a source (the need to attribute or acknowledge others' work). As nurses, students in this course refer frequently to documentation in the context of patient records. This type of documentation was assigned code 2.5 when students specifically referred to the need to document accurately for ethical, legal, or regulatory purposes.

TABLE 3.3

Metaliteracy Objectives Assessment, Goal 1

1. Evaluate content critically, including dynamic, online content that changes and evolves, such as article preprints, blogs, and wikis	
OBJECTIVE	**NUMBER OF INSTANCES**
1.1 Place an information source in its context (B,C)	6
1.2 Distinguish between editorial commentary and information presented from a more research-based perspective (C)	7
1.3 Determine the value of formal and informal information from various networked sources (scholarly, user-generated) (C)	2
1.4 Evaluate user response as an active researcher; understand the differing natures of feedback mechanisms and context in traditional and social media platforms (B, C)	0
1.5 Appreciate the importance of assessing content from different sources, including dynamic content from social media, critically (A)	6

NOTE: The goal and corresponding learning objectives are from Metaliteracy.org, "Goals and Learning Objectives."

TABLE 3.4

Metaliteracy Objectives Assessment, Goal 2

2. Understand personal privacy, information ethics, and intellectual property issues in changing technology environments	
OBJECTIVE	**NUMBER OF INSTANCES**
2.1 Differentiate between the production of original information and remixing or repurposing open resources (C)	0
2.2 Distinguish the kinds of information appropriate to reproduce and share publicly, and private information disseminated in more restricted/discreet environments (C)	0
2.3 Use technology to build a positive web presence (B)	4
2.4 Apply copyright and Creative Commons licensing as appropriate to the creation of original or repurposed information (B)	0
2.5 Recognize the ethical considerations of sharing information (A)	4
2.6 Articulate the necessity of attribution when borrowing the intellectual property of others, regardless of format (A)	2
2.7 Identify the context for which accurate attribution is needed and consistently apply that attribution (C, B)	8

NOTE: The goal and corresponding learning objectives are from Metaliteracy.org, "Goals and Learning Objectives."

TABLE 3.5

Metaliteracy Objectives Assessment, Goal 3

3. Share information and collaborate in a variety of participatory environments	
OBJECTIVE	**NUMBER OF INSTANCES**
3.1 Participate conscientiously in collaborative environments (B)	0
3.2 Take responsibility for participation in collaborative environments (A)	1
3.3 Compare the unique attributes of different information formats (e.g., scholarly article, blog, wiki, online community), and have the ability to use effectively and to cite information for the development of original content (B)	8
3.4 Describe the potential impact of online resources for sharing information (text, images, video, and other media) in collaboration with others (A)	0
3.5 Demonstrate the ability to translate information presented in one manner to another in order to best meet the needs of particular audiences; integrate information from multiple sources into coherent new forms (M, C)	8
3.6 Effectively communicate personal and professional experiences to inform and assist others; and recognize that learners can also be teachers (A, B)	2
3.7 Produce original content appropriate to specific needs in multiple media formats; transfer knowledge gained to new formats in unpredictable and evolving environments (B)	0
3.8 Value user-generated content and critically evaluate contributions made by others; see self as a producer as well as consumer of information (A)	0
3.9 Be open to global perspectives; use communication with others in a global context to encourage deep learning (A)	1

NOTE: The goal and corresponding learning objectives are from Metaliteracy.org, "Goals and Learning Objectives."

In table 3.5, the eight instances of learning objective 3.5 are not surprising. Searching for, collecting, analyzing, and presenting information based on the rhetorical situation is a significant outcome for this course. Because students use researched information to compose two different documents in two different genres (proposal and presentation), it is also not surprising that objective 3.3 was coded in eight instances. Objectives related to participation and collaboration were not assigned; however, this is due more to the nature of the documents coded than to a lack of participation. All students participate and collaborate in their ePortfolios, both to assist one another with brainstorming and to comment and discuss other course concepts. Few, however,

TABLE 3.6

Metaliteracy Objectives Assessment, Goal 4

4. Demonstrate ability to connect learning and research strategies with lifelong learning processes and personal, academic, and professional goals	
OBJECTIVE	NUMBER OF INSTANCES
4.1 Determine scope of the question or task required to meet one's needs (C)	6
4.2 Reevaluate needs and next steps throughout the process (C)	3
4.3 Demonstrate the importance of matching information needs and search strategies to appropriate search tools (C)	4
4.4 Use self-reflection to assess one's own learning and knowledge of the learning process (M)	7
4.5 Demonstrate the ability to think critically in context and to transfer critical thinking to new learning (M)	2
4.6 Value persistence, adaptability, and flexibility (M)	0
4.7 Communicate effectively with collaborators in shared spaces and learn from multiple points of view (M)	3
4.8 Recognize that learning is a process and that reflecting on errors or mistakes leads to new insights and discoveries (M)	4
4.9 Engage in informed, self-directed learning that encourages a broader worldview through the global reach of today's information technology (M)	0
4.10 Demonstrate self-empowerment through interaction and the presentation of ideas; gain the ability to see what is transferable, translatable, and teachable (learners are both students and teachers) (M)	6
4.11 Conclude that metaliteracy is a lifelong value and practice (M)	0

NOTE: The goal and corresponding learning objectives are from Metaliteracy.org, "Goals and Learning Objectives."

mention this collaboration in their reflective statements. It is unclear why this is so; perhaps, as nurses, they consider collaboration second nature and not something that needs to be reflected upon as learned.

The number of cognitive and metacognitive objectives prevalent in coding correlates with ePortfolio scores in which the Critical Thinking, Reading, and Writing and Rhetorical Knowledge categories received the highest average scores (see table 3.6). Students not only reflected upon their own learning but also discussed their perceptions of having grown as writers and an understanding of how they would be able to use what they learned in future courses or their workplace (transfer).

CONTRIBUTION/INNOVATION

Mackey and Jacobson have demonstrated the relationship of various literacies and the unifying nature of metaliteracy.[26] For a course like TWC361, based on the need to address the outcomes or objectives from multiple disciplines, as well as the real-world application of course concepts, this unification is even more important. In our own work, we had previously fused the outcomes of two disciplines and then expanded to incorporate a third discipline in TWC361. The alignment of metaliteracy to those outcomes is providing an additional framework to facilitate further course development.

The design and development of TWC361 continues to evolve since its first iteration in 2011. We have learned from teaching the course (our own metacognitive reflective practice), working with our nursing colleagues, and integrating the scholarship of multiple disciplines (WS, LIS, and nursing). Most notably, metacognition has become an increasingly important concept for us, as it presents significant potential for moving students from a mechanical approach to research and writing to one that is more informed by sophisticated concepts and reflection so that they are able to transfer what they learned to other contexts. We now recognize that we had already integrated many of the metaliteracy goals and objectives into the course design and need to develop others that are relevant. Further, metaliteracy has provided us with a framework for more fully understanding the connection between various domains (which we see related to the habits of mind articulated in the *Framework for Success* document[27]) and outcomes/objectives.

Our contribution, and potential innovation, however, is the "meta" approach to course design and to model a contextual approach to fusing multiple "literacies" and "outcomes or objectives" through valuing shared responsibility and accountability for student achievement and transfer of knowledge. As a framework for fusing multiple literacies under one umbrella, metaliteracy is prevalent in the course in multiple ways. Given the number of writing courses in higher education, both first-year writing and advanced disciplinary writing, the work we present here represents a model for how fusing of literacies can work for writing courses. In addition, our process of aligning metaliteracy to disciplinary outcomes/competencies related to LIS and WS potentially provides a model for doing the same for other disciplines in which disciplinary standards are used.

This contribution also continues the work we did previously to merge the ACRL *Standards* and the WPA OS into one outcomes statement. By more clearly demarcating how metaliteracy objectives align with our current approach, we hope to further show the intersections among disciplines and the shared responsibility for student learning among faculty in multiple disciplines, librarians, and students themselves.

CONCLUSION

For twenty years, we have been working in, thinking about, and writing about the space where LIS and WS coalesce. We have noted parallel and overlapping movements in both disciplines. Now, in our collaboration with nursing, we can see that our previous work of melding concepts from two disciplines is serving us well as we develop and teach a discipline-specific writing course that also stresses information practices. We can also see, by our case study, that the metaliteracy framework enables us to even better understand what our students have learned. The use of metacognition has played a key role in that understanding. Increasingly, we have adapted this course to help students to learn how to reflect upon and articulate what they have learned. We believe that this sort of metacognition facilitates transfer, as students come to recognize and articulate that what they learn is transferrable to other contexts, both academically and professionally. For us, our understanding of the metaliteracy framework extends beyond one course. Our work is evolving toward greater definition and integration of threshold concepts.[28] With the advent of the *Framework for Information Literacy for Higher Education* grounded in threshold concepts and metaliteracy,[29] our work on the TC Program outcomes needs revisiting. The emphasis on threshold concepts and metaliteracy is also pushing our work to explore more fully the use of metacognition and the teaching-for-transfer model of pedagogy recently introduced in WS.

Beyond our own work, our contribution is relevant to others who work in WS and to librarians who collaborate with them to help them understand how writing and information literacy intersect, both in traditional print and evolving digital media. We also recognize that the reflective practice perspective that is so strong in nursing helps our disciplinary colleagues understand our emphasis on metacognition. Lastly, we believe that an understanding of the metaliteracy framework will help us and other educators to develop a range of discipline-specific writing and research courses.

NOTES

1. Association of College and Research Libraries (ACRL), *Information Literacy Competency Standards for Higher Education* (Chicago: American Library Association, 2000), www.ala.org/acrl/standards/informationliteracycom petency; Council of Writing Program Administrators (CWPA), "WPA Outcomes Statement for First-Year Composition (3.0)" (approved July 17, [2000, 2008] 2014), http://wpacouncil.org/positions/outcomes.html.
2. Barbara J. D'Angelo and Barry M. Maid, "Moving Beyond Definitions: Implementing Information Literacy Across the Curriculum," *Journal of Academic Librarianship* 30, no. 3 (2004): 212–17; Barbara D'Angelo and Barry

M. Maid, "Assessing Outcomes in a Technical Communication Capstone," in *Handbook of Research on Assessment Technologies, Methods, and Applications in Higher Education*, ed. Christopher Schreiner (Hershey, PA: IGI Global, 2009), 152–166.

3. D'Angelo and Maid, "Assessing Outcomes."

4. Kathleen B. Yancey, Liane Robertson, and Kara Taczak, *Writing Across Contexts: Transfer, Composition, and Sites of Writing* (Boulder, CO: Utah State Press, 2014).

5. Jean Sheridan, ed. *Writing-Across-the-Curriculum and the Academic Library: A Guide for Librarians, Instructors, and Writing Program Directors* (Westport, CT: Greenwood Press, 1995); Rolf Norgaard, "Writing Information Literacy: Contributions to a Concept," *Reference and User Services Quarterly*, 43, no. 2 (2003): 124–30; Rolf Norgaard, "Writing Information Literacy in the Classroom: Pedagogical Enactments and Implications," *Reference and User Services Quarterly* 43, no. 3 (2004): 220–26; Donna Mazziotti and Teresa Grettano, "'Hanging Together': Collaboration between Information Literacy and Writing Programs Based on the ACRL Standards and WPA Outcomes," in *Proceedings of the ACRL 2011 Conference* (Chicago: American Library Association, 2011), 180–90, www.ala.org/acrl/sites/ala.org.acrl/files/content/conferences/confsandpreconfs/national/2011/papers/hanging_together.pdf; Barry M. Maid and Barbara J. D'Angelo, "The WPA Outcomes, Information Literacy, and Challenges of Outcomes-Based Curricular Design," in *Teaching and Assessing Writing: A Twenty-Fifth Anniversary Celebration*, ed. Norbert Elliott and Leslie Perelman (New York: Hampton Press, 2012), 99–112.

6. Carol Kuhlthau, *Seeking Meaning: A Process Approach to Library and Information Services* (Westport, CT: Libraries Unlimited, 2004); Linda Flower and John R. Hayes, "A Cognitive Process Theory of Writing," *College Composition and Communication* 32, no. 4 (1981): 365–87.

7. Christine Bruce, *The Seven Faces of Information Literacy* (Blackwood, South Australia: Auslib Press, 1997); Mandy Lupton, *The Learning Connection: Information Literacy and the Student Experience* (Blackwood, South Australia: Auslib Press, 2004); Norgaard, "Writing Information Literacy: Contributions"; Annemaree Lloyd, *Information Literacy Landscapes: Information Literacy in Education, Workplace and Everyday Contexts* (Oxford, UK: Chandos Publishing, 2010).

8. Thomas P. Mackey and Trudi E. Jacobson, "Reframing Information Literacy as a Metaliteracy," *College and Research Libraries* 72, no. 1 (2011): 62–78, doi:10.5860/crl-76r1.

9. Thomas P. Mackey and Trudi E. Jacobson, *Metaliteracy: Reinventing Information Literacy to Empower Learners* (Chicago: Neal-Schuman, 2014).

10. Association of College and Research Libraries (ACRL), *Framework for Information Literacy for Higher Education* (Chicago: American Library Association, 2015), www.ala.org/acrl/standards/ilframework.

11. Council of Writing Program Administrators (CWPA), National Council of Teachers of English (NCTE), and National Writing Project (NWP), *Framework for Success in Postsecondary Writing* (January 2011), http://wpacouncil.org/files/framework-for-success-postsecondary-writing.pdf.

12. Ibid., 1.

13. American Association of Colleges of Nursing (AACN), *The Essentials of Baccalaureate Education for Professional Nursing Practice* (Washington, DC: American Association of Colleges of Nursing, 2008).

14. American Association of Colleges of Nursing (AACN), *Core Competencies for Interprofessional Collaboration* (Washington, DC: Interprofessional Education Collaborative, 2011).

15. Julianne Cheek and Irene Doskatsch, "Information Literacy: A Resource for Nurses as Lifelong Learners," *Nurse Education Today* 18, no. 3 (1998): 243–50; Marc Forster, "A Phenomenographic Investigation into Information Literacy in Nursing Practice— Preliminary Findings and Methodological Issues," *Nurse Education Today* 33, no. 10 (2013): 1237–41, doi:10.1016/j.nedt.2012.05.027.

16. Ann Bonner and Annemaree Lloyd, "What Information Counts at the Moment of Practice? Information Practices of Renal Nurses," *Journal of Advanced Nursing* 67, no. 6 (2011): 1213–21.

17. CWPA, NCTE, and NWP, *Framework for Success.*

18. Mackey and Jacobson, "Reframing Information Literacy."

19. CWPA, NCTE, and NWP, *Framework for Success.*

20. CWPA, "WPA Outcomes Statement."

21. Metaliteracy.org, "Goals and Learning Objectives," updated September 11, 2014, http://metaliteracy.org/learning-objectives.

22. Ibid.

23. Ibid.

24. Ibid.

25. American Psychological Association (APA), *Publication Manual of the American Psychological Association*, 6th ed. (Washington, DC: American Psychological Association, 2010).

26. Mackey and Jacobson, *Metaliteracy.*

27. CWPA, NCTE, and NWP, *Framework for Success.*

28. Jan H. F. Meyer and Ray L. Land, "Threshold Concepts and Troublesome Knowledge (2): Epistemological Considerations and a Conceptual Framework for Teaching and Learning," *Higher Education* 49, no. 3 (2005): 373–88.

29. ACRL, *Framework for Information Literacy.*

BIBLIOGRAPHY

American Association of Colleges of Nursing (AACN). *Core Competencies for Interprofessional Collaboration*. Washington DC: Interprofessional Education Collaborative, 2011.

————. *The Essentials of Baccalaureate Education for Professional Nursing Practice.* Washington, DC: American Association of Colleges of Nursing, 2008.

Association of College and Research Libraries (ACRL). *Framework for Information Literacy for Higher Education.* Chicago: American Library Association, 2015. www.ala.org/acrl/standards/ilframework.

————. *Information Literacy Competency Standards for Higher Education.* Chicago: American Library Association, 2000. www.ala.org/acrl/standards/ informationliteracycompetency.

Bonner, Ann, and Annemaree Lloyd. "What Information Counts at the Moment of Practice? Information Practices of Renal Nurses." *Journal of Advanced Nursing* 67, no. 6 (2011): 1213–21.

Bruce, Christine. *The Seven Faces of Information Literacy.* Blackwood, South Australia: Auslib Press, 1997.

Cheek, Julianne, and Irene Doskatsch. "Information Literacy: A Resource for Nurses as Lifelong Learners." *Nurse Education Today* 18, no. 3 (1998): 243–50.

Council of Writing Program Administrators (CWPA). "WPA Outcomes Statement for First-Year Composition (3.0)." Approved July 17, (2000, 2008) 2014. http:// wpacouncil.org/positions/outcomes.html.

Council of Writing Program Administrators (CWPA), National Council of Teachers of English (NCTE), and National Writing Project (NWP). *Framework for Success in Postsecondary Writing* (January 2011). http://wpacouncil.org/files/framework -for-success-postsecondary-writing.pdf.

D'Angelo, Barbara J., and Barry M. Maid. "Assessing Outcomes in a Technical Communication Capstone." In *Handbook of Research on Assessment Technologies, Methods, and Applications in Higher Education*, edited by Christopher Schreiner, 152–66. Hershey, PA: IGI Global, 2009.

————. "Moving Beyond Definitions: Implementing Information Literacy Across the Curriculum." *Journal of Academic Librarianship* 30, no. 3 (2004): 212–17.

Flower, Linda, and John R. Hayes. "A Cognitive Process Theory of Writing." *College Composition and Communication* 32, no. 4 (1981): 365–87.

Forster, Marc. "A Phenomenographic Investigation into Information Literacy in Nursing Practice—Preliminary Findings and Methodological Issues." *Nurse Education Today* 33, no. 10 (2013): 1237–41. doi:10.1016/j.nedt.2012.05.027.

Kuhlthau, Carol. *Seeking Meaning: A Process Approach to Library and Information Services.* Westport, CT: Libraries Unlimited, 2004.

Lloyd, Annemaree. *Information Literacy Landscapes: Information Literacy in Education, Workplace and Everyday Contexts.* Oxford, UK: Chandos Publishing, 2010.

Lupton, Mandy. *The Learning Connection: Information Literacy and the Student Experience.* Blackwood, South Australia: Auslib Press, 2004.

Mackey, Thomas P., and Trudi E. Jacobson. *Metaliteracy: Reinventing Information Literacy to Empower Learners.* Chicago: Neal-Schuman, 2014.

————. "Reframing Information Literacy as a Metaliteracy." *College and Research Libraries* 72, no. 1 (2011): 62–78. doi:10.5860/crl-76r1.

Maid, Barry M., and Barbara J. D'Angelo. "The WPA Outcomes, Information Literacy, and Challenges of Outcomes-Based Curricular Design." In *Teaching and Assessing Writing: A Twenty-Fifth Anniversary Celebration*, edited by Norbert Elliott and Leslie Perelman, 99–112. New York: Hampton Press, 2012.

Mazziotti, Donna, and Teresa Grettano. "'Hanging Together': Collaboration between Information Literacy and Writing Programs Based on the ACRL Standards and WPA Outcomes." In *Proceedings of the ACRL 2011 Conference*, 180–90. Chicago: American Library Association, 2011. www.ala.org/acrl/sites/ala.org.acrl/files/content/conferences/confsandpreconfs/national/2011/papers/hanging_together.pdf.

Metaliteracy.org. "Goals and Learning Objectives." Updated September 11, 2014. http://metaliteracy.org/learning-objectives.

Meyer, Jan H. F., and Ray L. Land. "Threshold Concepts and Troublesome Knowledge (2): Epistemological Considerations and a Conceptual Framework for Teaching and Learning." *Higher Education* 49, no. 3 (2005): 373–88.

Norgaard, Rolf. "Writing Information Literacy: Contributions to a Concept." *Reference and User Services Quarterly* 43, no. 2 (2003): 124–30.

————. "Writing Information Literacy in the Classroom: Pedagogical Enactments and Implications." *Reference and User Services Quarterly* 43, no. 3 (2004): 220–26.

Sheridan, Jean. *Writing-Across-the-Curriculum and the Academic Library: A Guide for Librarians, Instructors, and Writing Program Directors*. Westport, CT: Greenwood Press, 1995.

Yancey, Kathleen B., Liane Robertson, and Kara Taczak. *Writing Across Contexts: Transfer, Composition, and Sites of Writing*. Boulder, CO: Utah State Press, 2014.

AMANDA SCULL

4

Where Collections and Metaliteracy Meet

Incorporating Library-Owned Platforms into
Open and Collaborative Library Instruction

A S BOTH A COLLECTION DEVELOPMENT LIBRARIAN AND AN
instructor, I am keenly aware of how work in one area informs work in
the other. Contact with students through instruction gives me perspective
on the resources they need, and comprehensive knowledge of the library's
resources helps me to direct students to the proper resource at the appropriate time. Mason Library at Keene State College, like many academic libraries,
has moved toward curation and creation of content through an institutional
repository, sponsorship of events that showcase faculty and student work,
research guides, and new initiatives in the archives. Yet the majority of teaching that the librarians do is still focused on large databases and expensive subscription content. Because I suspect that this is the case in many libraries, I
suggest that we consider alternative ways to teach while showcasing and contributing to library-curated content.

This chapter discusses institutional repositories and research guides as
two library initiatives that are ideal for use in instruction provided by librarians, whether this takes the form of one-shot sessions, a librarian embedded
within a course, or a full course taught by a librarian. While there is a great
deal of literature about the implementation and reception of institutional

repositories, it is only recently that the literature reflects the use of the repository to teach and foster student research. The time is therefore right to examine the institutional repository through the lens of metaliteracy, as this comprehensive model provides opportunities to teach students the research process from knowledge acquisition through scholarly dissemination in an online, open access environment. This chapter presents ideas for implementing such instruction through the application of the metaliteracy learning objectives and discusses the means of assessment. By the end of this chapter, readers will come away with new ideas that will allow them to rely less on costly subscription content while promoting the local collections they are curating.

CONTEXT

Academic library collections are in a state of flux. Many libraries are developing electronic collections and purchasing fewer print volumes, preferring to allocate library space to study areas, cafés, and learning commons instead of stacks. Patron-driven and demand-driven acquisitions are replacing the "just in case" model of purchasing with the "just in time" model of purchasing.[1] The rising cost of subscriptions coupled with decreasing budgets has led collection development librarians to rethink the ways in which they license or purchase materials and how those materials are used. There are issues of off-site accessibility, and a surprising number of vendors still do not offer proxy authentication as an access option to academic institutions.

At Keene State College, professors are requiring fewer expensive textbooks and relying on more dynamic online content, such as blogs and open access articles, in the classroom. Books are used less often, as research papers often require the use of peer-reviewed scholarly articles. Consequently, circulation is decreasing as students become more accustomed to electronic resources and spend less time in the stacks selecting resources.[2] From an instructional standpoint, the prevalence of wikis, social media, and blogs in the classroom presents valuable opportunities for participatory learning consistent with the objectives of metaliteracy, which represents an instructional shift away from skills development and toward collaborative production of information through these interactive technologies.[3] However, while information creation is happening on new platforms, the search for information through librarians' instruction is often centered on the database tutorial. Students are still being taught how to locate and evaluate scholarly material in subscription databases, consistent with previous skills-based models of information literacy. It is time for librarians to rethink their lessons to include or even focus on library-curated collections and open access platforms in instruction. There is great potential for encouraging collaboration, contribution to the scholarly process, and engagement with dynamic content through institutional repositories, research guides, and open access journals. Use of these platforms in library instruction can decrease the library's dependence on costly subscription databases while also providing instruction that is relevant to twenty-first-century learners. Students who do not pursue graduate studies might not have access to expensive databases after they graduate, and if they learn information skills in a closed, pretested environment, there is no guarantee that they will be able to apply those skills to open access resources in their careers or future research pursuits. Promotion of research activities through these avenues helps librarians prepare lifelong researchers regardless of where students might go after graduation.

It is important to briefly clarify that the platforms on which libraries create content, from research guide software to website servers, have a cost associated with them. These are not free resources like blogging sites or wikis. However, that cost is often not only significantly less than the cost of a large database subscription but also associated with creating large amounts of *unrestricted*, *owned* content. Springshare's LibGuides platform costs up to $1,099 and the average cost that libraries paid for Bepress's Digital Commons in 2013 was $20,000.[4] Compare those amounts to the $72,536 a Research 2 institution paid in 2009 for access to Taylor and Francis journals or the $89,190 spent by a Master's university for an annual subscription to an Elsevier bundle, and a $20,000 subscription that enables the creation and dissemination of original content appears to be a reasonable investment.[5] Additionally, if the library budget were to be reduced, libraries may lose the leased platforms but still keep the material they created on them.

CONNECTING COLLECTIONS AND INSTRUCTION

Institutional Repositories

In 2012, the Directory of Open-Access Repositories reported 1,857 institutions supporting institutional repositories, platforms on which academia, nonprofits, research centers, and other institutions archive their research output and institutional memory.[6] In 2013, the Directory of Open Access Journals listed nearly 10,000 fully open journals, which publish original peer-reviewed content, in a number of disciplines.[7] The growth of open access publishing in the past ten years represents a shift in scholarly communication from journals that require authors to surrender their copyright and restrict access to research behind an expensive paywall to a model in which researchers can share their work and ideas with a broader audience. As peer-reviewed open-access journals such as *PLoS* and repositories like PubMed demonstrate that open-access content can be both high quality and sustainable, the infrastructure of open access continues to improve and its acceptance and adoption are widespread.[8]

In many colleges and universities institutional repository initiatives are undertaken by the library. Mason Library at Keene State College, for example, is in the process of getting its institutional repository off the ground, focusing on the digitization and inclusion of a number of archival collections as well as the solicitation of student and faculty research. Many institutional repositories are completely open access, while others require an affiliation with the institution to freely access content. Institutional repositories allow for self-archiving within an institution on a platform where faculty and students can present their work accessibly to others in the institution and in the field without the obstacle of a paywall. Some institutions, like Keene State College, even use their institutional repositories as a platform to start their own online open-source journals in which to publish student and faculty research. In these ways institutional repositories provide a ready-made space for students to learn about the scholarly process in its entirety more easily than they would in established peer-reviewed publications. Within the institutional repository they can be both consumers and creators in a local context that is meaningful to them.

Teaching through an Institutional Repository

The learning objectives of metaliteracy include the ability to share, collaborate, and contribute to participatory environments, and there are already a growing number of initiatives that provide excellent models of how to incorporate an institutional repository into this type of instruction. For example, at Keene State College students in the history department combine primary source literacy and digital literacy by transcribing Civil War–era letters that are added to the institutional repository. Each record includes the name of the student responsible for the transcription, thereby recognizing the student's work and providing an opportunity for him or her to include it in a portfolio or later research. At the University of Illinois at Urbana-Champaign, students participating in courses that are part of the Ethnography of the University Initiative conduct research through the institutional repository and then build on existing collections by contributing their own work at the end of the course. Faculty who teach within the program have the benefit of new research foci each semester, and students receive what is likely their first experience with the scholarly communication process. The coursework also includes a poster presentation session so that students learn the entire process, from identifying relevant sources in the institutional repository, through authors' rights and copyright, all the way to presentation and dissemination.[9]

An institutional repository also provides students with a tangible example of the research process within their own academic context, so it is important to show students how they can use the institutional repository to help them develop ideas for research or conduct a portion of their literature review. An effective way to introduce students to open access and the scholarship cycle is to spend time in one-shot instruction sessions demonstrating the use of the institutional repository's interface. This approach expands the conversation about the content available and the materials. As a librarian at the School for International Training (SIT) Graduate Institute, which has a robust institutional repository of students' capstone papers and presentations, I frequently taught students the importance of using the institutional repository to examine the work of their predecessors in order to identify gaps in the research or areas of inquiry that had been exhausted before embarking upon their own research. Analyzing the work of their predecessors encourages students to think about their own research and writing, and the institutional repository is a venue in which they understand their participatory role in the scholarly community. Papers from the institutional repository often appeared as part of their literature reviews alongside articles obtained from established journals. Students using the institutional repository for research will likely have questions about reliability of sources, availability of full text, citing preprints or unpublished papers, or how an article can be in both a journal and the institutional repository. These questions enable conversations about information and scholarly processes.

Students may also want to know whether their own papers and research can be submitted to the institutional repository. Librarians should consider solicitation of student contributions to the institutional repository as an avenue for teaching copyright and intellectual property issues. Many institutional repositories accept student research alongside archival materials and faculty publications as academia begins to recognize the value of encouraging research at the undergraduate level. If the repository does not already have a policy for accepting student research, the literature certainly supports efforts to change that. Many institutions, including the SIT Graduate Institute, have digital collections of student theses and dissertations, while others like Utah State University have expanded their student collections to include research, posters, and creative work in addition to those traditional capstone collections.[10] Some institutional repositories, such as Western Oregon University's, are even defined as student-centric and maintain student research as the bulk of the collection.[11] Showcasing faculty work and archival material is still important to draw users in to the institutional repository, but there should be a sizable space for student contributions as well.

Application of Metaliteracy Learning Objectives

The Association of College and Research Libraries' (ACRL) *Information Literacy Competency Standards for Higher Education*, which most academic librarians have used as a guideline for the past fifteen years, focus heavily on skills development.[12] While skills development is both important and necessary, students must also develop higher-order thinking in order to assess and deploy those skills effectively. Teaching through an institutional repository expands students' metacognitive processes in a way that teaching through subscription databases does not. The processes for searching a database and an institutional repository are very similar, but the range of content that students must evaluate in an institutional repository is often more diverse (including manuscripts, preprints, and presentations, for example) than that of an article database. Advanced searching options that reduce the need for evaluation, such as limitation to peer-reviewed content, will likely not be available in the institutional repository, and students must therefore examine their own abilities to conduct an effective search and evaluate content, make the necessary adjustments to their paradigms of how to do those things, and recognize when their skill set is not adequate and needs further development.

Moreover, students will see the institutional repository as more of a community than a subscription database can be. They are likely to recognize the names of faculty, staff, and students whose scholarly contributions reside in the institutional repository, thereby teaching them by example that user-generated content has value to the institution and to the scholarly community. The obvious participatory nature of an institutional repository, an important facet of the metaliteracy goal to "share information and collaborate in a variety of participatory environments,"[13] is a significant benefit that cannot be matched by most library databases. Students become consumers of community-driven information and producers of information that can be included to advance that community.

The submission of content also presents the opportunity to develop the way in which students think about their research strategies and abilities. Teaching through the institutional repository provides an opportunity to expose students to information ethics and intellectual property in a way that goes beyond rote memorization, such as a presentation about plagiarism. Students will experience firsthand the importance of understanding information ethics and intellectual property because they will be adding their own work to the information environment. Submission of a student's work into an institutional repository is an excellent way to engage that student in the scholarly process from absorbing to creating information, but it will also make him or her think about the implications of having original work available to others on the Web. Questions posed may include these: How comfortable are the students with their work being used by others? What if they were to be plagiarized? Worse, what if they were to be accused of plagiarism? These types of questions represent a higher order of thinking than the understanding of when and how to cite. Students must consider the ethical implications of sharing information and critically evaluate their own contributions and how they might be used, thereby engaging with the second goal of the metaliteracy learning objectives, "understand personal privacy, information ethics, and intellectual property issues in changing technology environments."[14]

Assessment

The emphasis on metacognition in this type of instruction poses an inherent problem when approaching assessment, namely, that skill development is easily assessed whereas thinking processes are not. The best way to assess this type of instruction may differ for each instructor, but it is important to recognize that pre- and posttests, a feedback rating form, or other quantitative measurement are not likely to yield useful results. Instructors may consider asking students to write brief self-reflections about the instruction and their research process. Students might also include a meta-writing component with a draft of their paper, wherein they write notes throughout the paper about how they found the information they used, their evaluative process, and their decisions about how to synthesize the information. Instructors could also hold small group discussions or focus groups to talk with students about what did and did not work for them. The final product will of course be graded, but the useful assessment of the metaliteracy practices in this case will come from encouraging open, reflective dialogue.

As an aside, many institutional repository platforms provide statistics on how often a particular item is viewed or downloaded, and instructors should view these statistics on their students' work regularly, if possible. While the statistics cannot provide any type of useful assessment for the students who submitted the work in prior semesters, they can demonstrate to new students embarking upon this type of research that the work they do is important and will be utilized.

RESEARCH GUIDES AS METALITERACY PLATFORMS

Institutional repositories provide a space in which students can engage with the research process and share their own scholarship, which is a participatory environment in its own right, but extensive digital collaboration requires a different medium. A growing understanding of the need to engage students in collaborative learning has led many library instructors to embrace the use of blogs, wikis, and social media in the classroom. However, much of the literature on digital projects presents the use of platforms that are not connected to the library or institution, such as Wikispaces or WordPress.[15] While it is true that such projects can help students learn how to evaluate and work with digital content that constantly evolves (the basis of the first goal of the metaliteracy learning objectives, "evaluate content critically, including dynamic, online content that changes and evolves"[16]) they can also pose problems. Writing papers, creating posters, or designing presentations means students leave a course with tangible products that they can include in a portfolio or build upon in future research. If they create wikis or blogs instead, the transient nature of the Web means that those materials they have worked to create could become inaccessible if content is removed or links are changed. Additionally, wikis and blogs are platforms that anyone on the Web can utilize for any means, so there is nothing about those sites that connects students' work with their academic institution or shows that content was created as part of scholarly pursuits. Projects used in instruction that are contained within a course management system, like Wikispaces, pose similar access issues, as they are closed when the course ends and cannot be shared within the scholarly community.

Many academic libraries are already using one system that can address these issues by providing a space for students to create and engage with information that will be branded within the institution and remain accessible to them. Springshare's LibGuides platform is a space to create research guides with a number of elements: different tabs across the top of the page for multiple subtopics, boxes for text or search widgets, and Web linking and embedding capabilities. While not all libraries subscribe to the platform, it is widely used: in early 2013, more than 2,000 libraries were using Springshare's LibGuides and there were 125,000 guides in existence.[17] Most of these research guides are created by librarians, but there is enormous potential for having students contribute to the guide collection through research and creation. The development of LibGuides immerses students in the technology-rich collaborative ethos of metaliteracy while also benefiting the library via the creation of new resources.

Student Creation of LibGuides

Implementing a LibGuide creation project requires a semester-long commitment, giving librarians who do not teach full courses the opportunity to collaborate with faculty and thereby maintain an ongoing presence in a course throughout the semester. The actual work that students will do on their LibGuides occurs autonomously and outside of class, but the librarian will need to provide guidance and instruction through multiple class sessions or tutorials in the course management system. Additionally, the LibGuide creation should be conducted as a group project to reduce individual workload, to ensure higher quality of content for the finished product, and to encourage the collaboration that is a cornerstone of metaliteracy.

The project begins with what looks like a "traditional" information literacy instruction session in which a librarian teaches students how to identify and evaluate sources. It is important, however, that in-depth coverage is given to Web and open access resources. Because LibGuides are themselves open access, people outside of the institution will be able to view the guide, but an abundance of subscription content from databases and journals means that most of the content will be hidden behind a proxy wall. It is helpful to frame this discussion with students as one of appropriateness of content for the medium, conjoining metaliteracy practice with the ACRL's "Information Creation as a Process," part of its *Framework for Information Literacy for Higher Education*.[18] Students should understand that not every medium is appropriate for every type of content, and that the type of container has implications for how information will be used. LibGuides are an open access resource available to general Web traffic but are also a library resource, so there is a balance to be struck between scholarly content and open access resources. It is therefore advisable to not only encourage but also require a variety of resource types for inclusion in students' LibGuides, including scholarly articles, blogs, multimedia, websites, photos, social media, and other appropriate content.

A second session provides students with instruction on how to use the platform, which is simple and does not require any coding or other technical experience, and some best practices for Web design, such as layout and color schemes. If a librarian chooses to provide this information through the course management system, he or she might do so by creating a tutorial video or interactive module to walk students through the process. Students can then embark upon the project on their own; they can get together as a group to work on the guide, they can assign tabs or sections and work on their own sections individually, they can use it as a group communication space much like a Google Doc, and they can move things around and edit them freely. The pages remain private until the librarian approves them to be changed to public status.

One major benefit to students of this type of project is that LibGuides provide the option for students to include their own research activities, and librarians interested in piloting a LibGuides project may choose to start with upper-level or research courses for this reason. Students may be encouraged to create an extra tab or section in their LibGuide to showcase their own research findings. In this way, they pull together all of the information they have collected and then move the research forward through their contributions. Others in the field and within the institution will be able to access that work and build upon it. An excellent example of this occurs at the SIT Graduate Institute, where graduate students in a research course create LibGuides and include the results of their research (often surveys and interviews). The first few tabs on the LibGuides provide a wealth of background information obtained through their research, and the final tab contains graphs, tables, charts, and descriptions of the students' research findings.[19] Creation of the research tab helps students learn how to present research findings in a more visual way than they do when they write a paper, and many of them use the page as a reference point for continuing their research in their practical placements or as a piece of their professional portfolios.

Application of Metaliteracy Learning Objectives

Librarians strive through instruction of any type to teach students the importance of evaluating information, but a LibGuide project puts that instruction into a new perspective. The conversation about scholarly versus nonscholarly sources as a means of evaluation is outdated, and this project provides the environment in which librarians can bring it up-to-date. According to the objectives of the first metaliteracy goal, students must "appreciate the importance of assessing content from different sources" and "determine the value of formal and informal information from various networked sources."[20] This means demonstrating to students that every type of information has an appropriate setting, and if it is not scholarly we do not automatically eliminate it from the conversation. By requiring students to explore a variety of source types to include in their LibGuides, librarians help students become digital researchers who are prepared for whatever environment they find themselves in—even if it is not an academic database.

In their original article introducing the concepts of metaliteracy, Mackey and Jacobson presented a number of abilities that today's digital researchers must have and that can be developed through the creation of open educational resources like LibGuides. For example, they indicate that researchers "must contextualize . . . information within a decentered environment that connects the professional and novice and makes accessible both formal and informal sources of information."[21] This perfectly describes the environment of the LibGuides, which are open source and therefore available on the Web to any researcher regardless of skill level and which allow for the synthesis of several different types of information sources. Students will need to know how to navigate such environments, and allowing them to create one is an excellent way to immerse them in that type of digital learning. Mackey and Jacobson also acknowledge that today's information seekers "may use factors such as . . . succinctness of the material, visual presentation and usability, and other elements that we now consider to locate information," which requires students to consider additional elements of design and presentation.[22] Asking students to think about the ways in which they themselves identify relevant information and how they use it develops a metacognitive process that they will both employ and further explore through the creation of a LibGuide that other researchers will evaluate in the same manner.

Finally, the third goal of the metaliteracy learning objectives, "share information and collaborate in a variety of participatory environments," is directly addressed by this project.[23] By expanding the LibGuide platform's potential beyond a static page and into a collaborative, dynamic space, instructors can take the traditional model of group work and shift it into an environment where students can collaborate on the shared guide online. Students in a group will all locate and evaluate information independently, but they then must discuss, evaluate, and synthesize the information collaboratively as well as design the page itself. When employed in a blended or an online program, the LibGuide may even become a platform for group discussion. This overlaps somewhat with the second learning goal addressing information and ethics and should lead students to ask the same types of questions relating to plagiarism and intellectual property as those discussed in the section about institutional repositories. There is, however, the added component of shared contributions. Students will share credit for their work with others throughout their academic and professional careers but might not consider the difference that makes to their understanding of ethics and intellectual property. Are individual contributions being made ethically? If one member of the group plagiarizes, what will the consequences be for the group as a whole? How will future researchers attribute the work of the group?

Assessment

As discussed in the section about institutional repositories, assessment can be a difficult venture in metaliteracy instruction given its qualitative nature. However, assessment of a LibGuide project is somewhat easier because instructors will have a finished product that they can grade and use to assess the efficacy of the project. When conducting an assessment of a LibGuide, a rubric can be used to assess the quality and relevance of content, proper attribution, and design elements (see figure 4.1 for an example). This is also a method of quality control—students can be informed that they must score at a certain level on the rubric in order for their guide or tutorial to be made public and thus represent the library. Assessment of this project is connected to the metaliteracy learning objectives by the expectation that the LibGuide created is reflective of the students' thinking processes during creation. An instructor is not just looking for demonstration of skills like proper citation or the application of keywords for searching but, rather, evaluating the thought process that went into the design and presentation of the information, the depth of understanding of the research process represented by the variety of sources presented, and the success of collaborative efforts illustrated by the cohesiveness of the finished product.

A reflective writing piece can also give the instructor some insight into the ways students approached the project and whether or not they grasped the intended concepts. The first time this project was conducted at the SIT Graduate Institute, students were given a survey to complete. The survey was intended to assess the project itself and provide feedback for making changes to it, but student responses to open-ended questions were very thoughtful about how they divided up work, what types of sources they found challenging or easy to evaluate and use, and how they decided the best ways to tie in their

	EXCELLENT (3)	**ACCEPTABLE (2)**	**POOR (1)**
Content and Research	Content demonstrates critical thinking about relevant and appropriate resources as evidenced by inclusion of information from a variety of formats (both formal and informal) that are suitable to the topic. The topic is fully represented by thorough research, and information from a variety of sources is synthesized and presented coherently.	Content includes information in at least three types of appropriate formats and includes both formal and informal sources. There may be some gaps in the presentation of the topic or missing content that required further research. Information may not be synthesized attentively, and it may be obvious which information was contributed by which student.	Content does not demonstrate critical analysis of information needs. Content includes only one or two formats and does not provide a complete picture of the topic. There is little to no synthesis of information from different sources.
Organization	Organization of the LibGuide demonstrates attention to presentation and consideration of a user's movement through the page. Content is grouped within relevant tabs and has a logical flow.	Organization of the LibGuide has a navigable flow, but use of relevant tabs and boxes is minimal. Content is understandable but not logically organized.	Organization of the LibGuide does not have a logical flow, and usability is low. There is little to no use of relevant tabs and boxes, and content is not grouped within any themes or chronologically.
Aesthetics	LibGuide demonstrates students' consideration of design and invites use. Appropriate images are included, and there is a balance between text and nontext content. Color scheme is present but does not distract from content.	LibGuide demonstrates some consideration of design, but design elements may be distracting or unbalanced. LibGuide may rely too heavily on text or visual material at the expense of content navigability.	LibGuide demonstrates no consideration of design elements. LibGuide may lack any color scheme or images and rely entirely on text.
Student Research	Students demonstrate critical analysis of the research process by incorporating background research sections with their own research section in a way that is logical and contributes to the user's understanding. Background information is relevant to the topic of the students' research and identifies the gap that students' research fills.	Students demonstrate research skills through presentation of their own research, but background information may lack synthesis with research contribution. It may be unclear how the background information relates to the current research or what knowledge gap is being addressed.	Students do not present their own research. Student may not provide adequate background information on the topic. Background information may be unrelated to research presented.

SOURCE: Adapted from the rubric in Amanda Scull, "Fostering Student Engagement and Collaboration with the Library: Student Creation of LibGuides as a Research Assignment," *The Reference Librarian* 55, no. 4 (2014): 318–27.

FIGURE 4.1
LibGuide Assessment Rubric

own research. Students seemed to view the survey as more metacognitive reflection than technical feedback, which provided an unexpected but useful means of assessment.

DISCUSSION

The fourth and final goal of the metaliteracy learning objectives states that students should "demonstrate ability to connect learning and research strategies with lifelong learning processes and personal, academic, and professional goals."[24] Providing instruction through an institutional repository or a Lib-Guide, resources that are branded and part of the institution, allows students to include their work in professional portfolios or continue to build on the research they conducted. Rather than just teaching skills, instructors who embark upon these metaliteracy initiatives may contribute to the formation of a student's future academic or professional path. Librarians are moving toward a model of instruction that does not pigeonhole information sources into easy, discrete categories like authoritative or nonauthoritative, scholarly or popular, and reliable or unreliable but instead develops students' thinking about information sources in a more flexible and contextually based way.

In order to serve this shift and ensure the relevance of the library in the Google age, we must redefine the library collection. The *Oxford English Dictionary* defines a collection as "a number of objects collected or gathered together."[25] There was a time when this simple definition suited library collections, most of which were comprised of the number of volumes on the shelves. Later that definition was expanded to include digital objects as well, and the "collection" encompassed the electronic books, journals, and databases that came to define the twenty-first-century academic library. Today open educational resources, like institutional repositories and research guides, are once more leading us to redefine the library collection. Amid budget crises and high prices, the collection has become an amalgam of books, subscriptions, and carefully curated open educational resources for which librarians advocate and solicit content. By redefining the collection under these terms, librarians can innovate and adapt their instruction in ways that engage students with collaboration, varied content, and the literacies demanded of today's scholars and workforce. Instruction and collections can intersect in a more engaging way than was ever possible under the traditional definition.

Moreover, this redefinition ensures the relevance of the library collection in an academic environment that now spans multiple formats. Students in blended or online programs need and deserve the attention of librarians as much as on-campus students, but they are not interested in the books on the shelves that might be hundreds of miles away. Having the ability to shift instruction into that environment is a major benefit of librarians embracing the possibilities of their own platforms and other open educational resources. Instead of missing the opportunity to provide information literacy instruction to the growing number of students taking courses online, librarians will be set up to be embedded in courses with projects and lessons that have already been adapted to the Web.

CONCLUSION

Institutional repositories and LibGuides are certainly not the only ways in which librarians can utilize content held institutionally to facilitate metaliteracy. Students can create video tutorials for resources or particular skills based on metaliteracy instruction that will serve future students. Institutional archivists can foster primary source literacy through work in the archive. Students can participate in institutional or departmental conferences, preparing presentations or posters with the assistance of librarians. The platform may vary but the objective remains: to foster metaliteracy with more of the content that libraries create instead of focusing so heavily on purchased content or generic Web platforms, benefiting both the library and the students it serves. This shift will not be easy, and it will require librarians to dedicate time and resources to evaluate their current models of instruction and how they might be adapted. However, it is initiatives like these that will guarantee that librarians maintain an important role in blended and online courses as well as on campus, in addition to ensuring the continued relevance of library collections and instruction.

Last year during a virtual conference presentation, I asked my audience if we were tired of the phrase "Library 2.0" yet, because in academia, adapting our work to digital and open source environments is no longer the revolutionary vision of the future library. It is what we do and who we are every day. The metaliteracy learning objectives provide the support and justification for our instruction to change accordingly and to support our campus communities, both online and in person, as they engage responsibly with the scholarly community in a digital environment.

NOTES

1. Marcia L. Thomas, "Disruption and Disintermediation: A Review of the Collection Development and Management Literature, 2009–10," *Library Resources and Technical Services* 56, no. 3 (2012): 183–98.
2. This observation is the result of a review of circulation statistics and a syllabus analysis that were recently completed as part of a collection assessment.
3. Thomas P. Mackey and Trudi E. Jacobson, "Reframing Information Literacy as a Metaliteracy," *College and Research Libraries* 72, no. 1 (2011): 70, doi:10.5860/crl-76r1.

4. LibGuides pricing information was obtained from the Springshare website, www.springshare.com/libguides. Bepress pricing information is not available on its website; this figure was obtained from a 2014 interview with the company's CEO: Richard Poynder, "Interview with Jean-Gabriel Bankier, President and CEO of Bepress," *Open and Shut?* (blog), April 5, 2014, http://poynder.blogspot.com/2014/04/interview-with-jean-gabriel-bankier.html.

5. Theodore Bergstrom, Paul Courant, R. Preston McAfee, and Michael Williams, "Evaluating Big Deal Journal Bundles," *Proceedings of the National Academy of Sciences of the United States of America* 111, no. 26 (2014): 9426.

6. Stephen Pinfield, Jennifer Salter, Peter A. Bath, Bill Hubbard, Peter Millington, Jane H. S. Anders, and Azhar Hussain, "Open-Access Repositories Worldwide, 2005–2012: Past Growth, Current Characteristics and Future Possibilities," *Journal of the American Society for Information Science and Technology*, article preprint (2013): 16.

7. Heather Joseph, "The Open Access Movement Grows Up: Taking Stock of a Revolution," *PLoS Biology* 11, no. 10 (2013): e1001686, doi:10.1371/journal.pbio.1001686.

8. Joseph, "Open Access Movement Grows Up."

9. Merinda Kaye Hensley, "The Poster Session as a Vehicle for Teaching the Scholarly Communication Process," in *Common Ground at the Nexus of Information Literacy and Scholarly Communication*, ed. Stephanie Davis-Kahl and Merinda Kaye Hensley (Chicago: Association of College and Research Libraries, 2013), 123–41.

10. Danielle Barandiaran, Betty Rozum, and Becky Thoms, "Focusing on Student Research in the Institutional Repository," *College and Research Libraries News* 75, no. 10 (2014): 546–49.

11. Erin Passehl-Stoddart and Robert Monge, "From Freshman to Graduate: Making the Case for Student-Centric Institutional Repositories," *Journal of Librarianship and Scholarly Communication* 2, no. 3 (2014): eP1130, doi:10.7710/2162-33091130.

12. Association of College and Research Libraries, *Information Literacy Competency Standards for Higher Education* (Chicago: American Library Association, 2000), www.ala.org/acrl/standards/informationliteracycompetency.

13. Metaliteracy.org, "Goals and Learning Objectives" (updated September 11, 2014), http://metaliteracy.org/learning-objectives.

14. Ibid.

15. Frank Boateng and Yan Quang Liu, "Web 2.0 Applications' Usage and Trends in Top US Academic Libraries," *Library Hi Tech* 32, no. 1 (2014): 120–38.

16. Metaliteracy.org, "Goals and Learning Objectives."

17. Jennifer Emanuel, "A Short History of Library Guides and Their Usefulness to Librarians and Patrons," in *Using LibGuides to Enhance Library Services*, ed. Aaron W. Dobbs, Ryan L. Sittler, and Douglas Cook (Chicago: American Library Association, 2013), 12.

18. Association of College and Research Libraries, *Framework for Information Literacy for Higher Education* (Chicago: American Library Association, 2015), www.ala.org/acrl/standards/ilframework.
19. Amanda Scull, "Fostering Student Engagement and Collaboration with the Library: Student Creation of LibGuides as a Research Assignment," *The Reference Librarian* 55, no. 4 (2014): 318–27.
20. Metaliteracy.org, "Goals and Learning Objectives."
21. Mackey and Jacobson, "Reframing Information Literacy," 73.
22. Ibid.
23. Thomas P. Mackey and Trudi E. Jacobson, *Metaliteracy: Reinventing Information Literacy to Empower Learners* (Chicago: American Library Association, 2014), 88–90.
24. Ibid., 90–91.
25. *Oxford English Dictionary*, s.v. "collection, n." (accessed March 2015), www.oed.com.

BIBLIOGRAPHY

Barandiaran, Danielle, Betty Rozum, and Becky Thoms. "Focusing on Student Research in the Institutional Repository." *College and Research Libraries News* 75, no. 10 (2014): 546–49.

Bergstrom, Theodore, Paul Courant, R. Preston McAfee, and Michael Williams. "Evaluating Big Deal Journal Bundles." *Proceedings of the National Academy of Sciences of the United States of America* 111, no. 26 (2014): 9425–30.

Boateng, Frank, and Yan Quang Liu. "Web 2.0 Applications' Usage and Trends in Top US Academic Libraries." *Library Hi Tech* 32, no. 1 (2014): 120–38.

Emanuel, Jennifer. "A Short History of Library Guides and Their Usefulness to Librarians and Patrons." In *Using LibGuides to Enhance Library Services*, edited by Aaron W. Dobbs, Ryan L. Sittler, and Douglas Cook, 3–22. Chicago: American Library Association, 2013.

Hensley, Merinda Kaye. "The Poster Session as a Vehicle for Teaching the Scholarly Communication Process." In *Common Ground at the Nexus of Information Literacy and Scholarly Communication*, edited by Stephanie Davis-Kahl and Merinda Kaye Hensley, 123–41. Chicago: Association of College and Research Libraries, 2013.

Joseph, Heather. "The Open Access Movement Grows Up: Taking Stock of a Revolution." *PLoS Biology* 11, no. 10 (2013): e1001686. doi:10.1371/journal.pbio.1001686.

Mackey, Thomas P., and Trudi E. Jacobson. *Metaliteracy: Reinventing Information Literacy to Empower Learners*. Chicago: American Library Association, 2014.

———. "Reframing Information Literacy as a Metaliteracy." *College and Research Libraries* 72, no. 1 (2011): 62–78. doi:10.5860/crl-76r1.

Metaliteracy.org. "Goals and Learning Objectives." Updated September 11, 2014. http://metaliteracy.org/learning-objectives/.

Passehl-Stoddart, Erin, and Robert Monge. "From Freshman to Graduate: Making the Case for Student-Centric Institutional Repositories." *Journal of Librarianship and Scholarly Communication* 2, no. 3 (2014): eP1130. doi:10.7710/2162-33091130.

Pinfield, Stephen, Jennifer Salter, Peter A. Bath, Bill Hubbard, Peter Millington, Jane H. S. Anders, and Azhar Hussain. "Open-Access Repositories Worldwide, 2005–2012: Past Growth, Current Characteristics and Future Possibilities." *Journal of the American Society for Information Science and Technology*, article preprint (2013).

Scull, Amanda. "Fostering Student Engagement and Collaboration with the Library: Student Creation of LibGuides as a Research Assignment." *The Reference Librarian* 55, no. 4 (2014): 318–27.

Thomas, Marcia L. "Disruption and Disintermediation: A Review of the Collection Development and Management Literature, 2009–10." *Library Resources and Technical Services* 56, no. 3 (2012): 183–98.

SANDRA K. CIMBRICZ
and LOGAN RATH

5

Empowering Learners to Become Metaliterate in a Digital and Multimodal Age

THIS CHAPTER EXPLORES WHAT A LIBRARIAN AND PROFESSOR learned about teaching the many literacies important to learning and living in a digital and multimodal age. Our collaboration centers on a newly created, hybrid graduate course focused on the teaching and learning of critical multiliteracies in grades 5–12. The collaborative dimension of our work proved powerful throughout the course, especially after the course ended. Once we examined our efforts to promote metacognitive reflection, empowerment, collaborative sharing, and creation and use of information in its many forms and places, we realized that this course was essentially metaliteracy in practice.[1]

This discovery broke new ground for our teaching and inspired us to reexamine several course artifacts. For instance, we looked at student feedback and commentary, both written and spoken, as well as student products and teaching notes collected during and at the end of the course. Our collaborative reflection on this experience raised two specific questions:

- What did we learn about helping teachers become not just critically multiliterate but metaliterate?

- What value does metaliteracy hold for our instructional practice, as teacher educators, and for those interested in teaching for learning the many different, but related literacies vital to living in a digital and multimodal age?

Revisiting course artifacts in light of these two questions gave us cause to think about text more broadly and as information in all possible forms and environments, especially those enabled by technology. This analysis also led us to see metaliteracy as an effective way to frame and approach this course as well as teaching for literacy and learning writ large. As a result, we contend that metaliteracy provides the ends and means for realizing what is vital to teaching and learning literacy in the twenty-first century. Specifically, metaliteracy allowed us to

- make sense of the growing list of literacies largely enabled by technology;
- identify areas of strength and weakness in our own instructional practices; and
- Adapt a meaningful model to improve the teaching and learning of literacy in the twenty-first century.

WHY CRITICAL MULTILITERACIES?

The decision to offer the course EDI 728: Critical Multiliteracies, 5–12, reflects efforts to expand our college's Master's in Childhood Literacy (Birth–6) program to include adolescence literacy (grades 7–12). This expansion allowed students enrolled in this program, all of whom hold initial teacher certification, to grow professionally by preparing them to become literacy specialists within B–12 schools.[2]

The idea of *multiliteracies* attends to the diversity of language and culture and the multiple dimensions of visual, aural, and media in multimodal texts, largely enabled by technology.[3] With this expanded definition, literacy becomes less of a singular "thing" and more of a set of shifting or adaptive practices for communication among individuals and groups within social and cultural settings, or *multiliteracies*.[4] Moreover, the socially situated practices of meaning-making using "text" more broadly defined move to the fore.[5] That is, text included, but was not limited to, what is written or "print based." When coupled with the intent of helping others explore multimodal literacies as a set of social practices through which they can critique and take action in the world, the concept of *critical multiliteracies* is somewhat accurate for this context.[6] That said, a clear understanding of what critical multiliteracies "is" remains elusive still, especially when we consider the many literacies central to twenty-first-century life.

Our deliberation on course artifacts led us to conclude that Mackey and Jacobson's metaliteracy model effectively unifies and expands the characteristics and purposes of the many related literacies important to living in a digital and multimodal age, including, but not limited to, critical multiliteracies. This framework also provides a clear and comprehensive understanding of what knowledgeable, critical, empowered, and metacognitive users and creators of text (more broadly conceived as information) think about and do so that these teachers, as learners, could in turn help their students do the same.

INDIVIDUAL AND SOCIAL TRANSFORMATION FOR A GREATER GOOD

This course centered on notions of learner empowerment and the idea that education is a vehicle for individual and social transformation. Accordingly, the overarching goal of this course was to assist B–12 teachers pursuing a Master of Science in Education in Literacy to help adolescents acquire, develop, and expand upon the many literacies they need to

- succeed in school;
- find meaningful work;
- pursue their own goals and interests throughout their lives; and
- appreciate, participate, and contribute to society as informed and productive citizens.

Another core commitment was the belief that educational decisions are more equitable and just when teachers thoughtfully consider those whose interests, experiences, and welfare are affected by the decisions they make. These goals significantly shaped the overall course design, specific assignments, and expectations for student learning. These same aims also led us to ground our deliberation of course artifacts in participatory action research.[7] By doing so, we were able to engage in metaliteracy as a model for learning about our own literacy as well as that of our students.

In the next section, we describe the course goals pertinent to this study's methodology and overall design.

METHODOLOGY

Study Design

Participatory action research (PAR) differs from *practical* action research in that it has a distinct social justice theoretical orientation.[8] Goals associated with PAR are emancipatory and transformative in nature and focus on "life-enhancing changes" for the participants and the researcher.[9] According to Kemmis and McTaggert and as summarized in Plano Clark and Creswell,[10] PAR, as a distinct form of inquiry, is

- a social process in which researchers deliberately explore the relationship between the individual and other people;
- participatory;
- practical and collaborative;
- "emancipatory in that it helps unshackle people from the constraints of irrational and unjust structures that limit self-development and self-determination";[11]
- aimed at helping "people recover and release themselves from the constraints embedded in social media (e.g., their language, their modes of work, their social relationships of power)";[12] and
- reflexive (e.g., recursive or dialectical) and focused on bringing about change in practices.

Practical research and participatory action research have their differences but also share a number of characteristics. Both, for example,

- have a practical focus;
- ask teachers-as-researchers to be self-reflective and "turn the lens on their own educational classroom, school or practices";[13]
- require collaboration with others so that a larger good can be served;
- approach research "as a dynamic process" that involves "spiral[ing] back and forth between reflection about a problem, data collection and action";[14]
- ask the action researcher to formulate "an action plan in response to the problem";[15] and
- necessitate sharing what is gained with others who can use this research to promote transformative change of their own.

These goals well align with course aims related to developing "particular knowledge, capabilities, and dispositions that grow and spur change that makes the world better for the teachers, themselves, and the literacy instruction they design for adolescents with whom they are working and/or will work."[16] These course outcomes were not created with metaliteracy in mind. Nevertheless, they embody the learner- and learning-focused principles of metaliteracy as both a mind-set and as a set of social practices through which to use information to think critically and take purposeful action in the world. Table 5.1 illuminates the alignment between the core course and metaliteracy learning objectives that our deliberation would eventually reveal.

E-mail reminders were sent to individuals whose projects provided noteworthy variation and an opportunity for us to dig deeper. In so doing, we were

TABLE 5.1

Mapping of Core Metaliteracy Learning Objectives with EDI 728 Learning Objectives

EDI 728 LEARNING OBJECTIVES[a]	CORE METALITERACY LEARNING OBJECTIVES[b]	AS MADE EVIDENT VIA . . .
Construct theorized understandings of critical literacy and multiliteracies	Produce original content in multiple media formats	Course readings; weekly writings; digital Note Take, Make, and Share project; One-on-One Summative Assessment
Use multiliteracies and multimodalities to build understanding, engage and critique, and take social action	Create a context for user-generated information; share information in participatory environments	Weekly writings; digital Note Take, Make, and Share project; One-on-One Summative Assessment
Develop skill in using multiple technological tools for representing thinking and for teaching and learning	Understand format type and delivery mode; create a context for user-generated information	Digital Note Take, Make, and Share project; One-on-One Summative Assessment
Examine and use multiple literacies and multimodalities to create meaningful learning experiences and assessments respectful of a critical multiliteracies framework and aligned with the learning standards of English Language Arts and the content areas	Create a context for user-generated information; evaluate dynamic content critically; evaluate user feedback as active researcher	Course readings; weekly writings; digital Note Take, Make, and Share project; One-on-One Summative Assessment
Identify strategies for effectively engaging students in critical multiliteracies through reading, writing, speaking, and viewing multimodal texts in content areas across the curriculum	Create a context for user-generated information; understand personal privacy, information ethics, and intellectual property issues; share information in participatory environments	One-on-One Summative Assessment
Explore digital writing workshop as a framework for multimodal composing	Understand format type and delivery mode; create a context for user-generated information; share information in participatory environments	Weekly writings; digital Note Take, Make, and Share project; One-on-One Summative Assessment

[a]Cimbricz, "EDI 728 Syllabus."
[b]Mackey and Jacobson, "Reframing Information Literacy."

able to attain a purposeful representative sample ($n = 11$; nine females and two males) of the overall class composition ($N = 24$). Pertinent details about the artifacts we examined are provided in the section to follow.

Data Collection and Analysis

Multiple and varied course artifacts, specifically, course instructor notes, student feedback and commentary, both written and spoken, and student products, specifically the digital Note Take, Make, and Share project and the One-on-One Summative Assessment, were collected at the beginning, during, and at the end of the course. Data were triangulated ex post facto[17] and in relation to our two research questions. To reiterate, we wondered what these course artifacts revealed about

- how to help others become not just multiliterate but metaliterate; and
- the value metaliteracy holds for our instructional practice, as teacher educators, and for those who are interested in teaching for learning the many literacies important to living in a digital and multi-modal age.

Sandra's notes and analytic memo writing before, during, and after the course would "lay the groundwork for these questions."[18] Similar to journal entries or blogs, analytic memos are "sites of conversation with ourselves about our data"[19] and learning spaces where Sandra recorded and reflected upon what she was observing and thinking during the span from initial planning through postcourse assessment. This writing allowed Sandra to make sense of what students were learning *through* and *as a result of* this course so that she, in turn, could make changes for her students' and her own literacy and instructional practices potentially more transformative and life enhancing. Unbeknownst to Sandra, researcher reflexivity around analytic memo writing and the idea of "thinking critically about what you are doing and why, confronting and often challenging your own assumptions, and recognizing the extent to which your thoughts, actions, and decisions shape how you research and what you see"[20] are parallel tenets of reflexivity and empowerment foundational to the "meta" in metaliteracy.[21]

Sandra's analytic memo writing based on student feedback revealed a number of patterns. First, fourteen (or 61 percent) of the students wanted to better understand what a number of literacies, including but not limited to critical multiliteracies, meant and looked like in action (i.e., definitions, specifics, examples). Second, many of these students also explicitly or implicitly stated that they wanted to understand the relationships between and among these many literacies. The remaining 39 percent, on the other hand, wanted to learn how to incorporate these literacies into their instructional practice. In addition, most students were interested in the potential for motivation, engagement, and learning.

This first cycle of analysis led Sandra to take three pivotal actions. First, she continued investing time writing analytic memos based on student feedback and her notes as the course instructor. Second, she decided to use Selber's categories of functional, critical, and rhetorical literacy to help students better understand and relate the many literacies they identified. [22] Selber's work initially made the most sense in relation to critical multiliteracies. Third, she asked Logan, the college's librarian and instructional technology specialist, to actively support her students and her as they sought to become more literate collectively and individually.

Student Feedback and Instructor Field Notes

Student feedback collected throughout and at the end of class and instructor field notes captured student reflection upon the process of creating course assignments. In addition, instructor field notes importantly captured student reflection upon the process related to each assignment. These notes provided access to student thinking "in" and "on" action. Here, the analytic distinction between *behavior* and *action* is noteworthy. According to Erickson, behavior refers to only the physical act, whereas action refers to both the physical act (or behavior) plus the meaning humans attach to it. [23] We included these data sources because we were interested in what students created as critical and empowered consumers of new media and multiple literacies, and in the meaning or significance they attached to the designing, making, and doing of this work. As Rowsell suggests, "learning in a digital and multimodal age is no longer simply about being critical consumers of technologies and new media, rather it is about designers, makers, and doers." [24] Concomitantly, "metaliteracy is an integrated framework that is metacognitive and promotes empowerment through the collaborative production and sharing of information." [25] Metaliteracy, we would realize, values creation as much as consumption, [26] thus making it a more apt framework for any course where students are required to produce and reflect upon the many literacies important to learning in the twenty-first century.

We also analyzed two assignments, the digital Note Take, Make, and Share (NTMS) and the One-on-One Summative Assessment, for several reasons. First, these assignments comprised 40 percent of the course grade. Second, considerable activity—inside and outside of class—focused on scaffolding successful completion of these assignments. Third, students identified these two assignments in their end-of-course evaluations as the most significant or valuable to their learning. Most important, these two assignments emphasized key aspects of metaliteracy, specifically, metacognitive reflection related to goal setting, empowerment, and the sharing, participation, creation, and use of knowledge and information in networked spaces, both collaboratively and independently. [27]

These two assignments provided students with multiple and varied opportunities to explore "new and multiple media, literacies, practices and processes." [28] Both assignments also asked students to self-assess and "monitor and regulate their learning processes to accomplish the learning goals they set."[29] Student discussion of and reflection on the process and product associated with these two assignments held considerable value. Student feedback—collected along the way—further served to monitor and drive course content and activities on an as-needed basis. A great deal of time and effort were invested throughout the course to

- create an environment (online and face-to-face) where all felt safe to take the kind of risks critical to worthy intellectual, emotional, and social growth;
- design purposeful learning experiences that honored where they were, the "funds of knowledge" they currently possessed, what they learned or gained, and that meaningfully expanded their world related to course goals as well as their own goals; and
- provide the experiences, support, and feedback that would spur critical thinking, meaningful learning, and life-enhancing changes.

The effective integration of behavioral, cognitive, affective, and metacognitive domains, we would discover, is also critical to creating the conditions, contexts, and environment ripe for developing metaliterate learners.[30] In the next section, we describe these two course assessments and their relationship to metaliteracy in greater detail.

ASSESSMENT

Digital Note Take, Make, and Share

For the NTMS, students demonstrated their ability to contribute as well as take, make, and share digital notes mindful of "author's craft, genre study, and digital writing" (and what some might call critical digital literacy or rhetorical literacy[31]) based on the recommendations found in the course text, *Crafting Digital Writing: Composing Texts across Media and Genres.*[32] Digital writing, as Hicks defines it, is "writing that is produced using various electronic media and shared on-line."[33] To determine what students already knew and wanted to learn more about (and before they had read any of the course texts), students responded via Google Docs to the same two question stems that corresponded to the content focus of chapters 3, 4, 5, 6, and 7 of Hicks's book (i.e., web texts, presentations, audio texts, video texts, and social media, respectively). To ascertain prior knowledge and interest around "Crafting Web Texts" (Hicks's chapter 3), for instance, students were asked the following questions:

1A. What do you currently know about crafting *web texts*?
1B. What more do you want to learn about crafting *web texts*?[34]

Interestingly, although we did not ask students to read or respond to what other students wrote, student entries (like the following one) soon showed that they were reading and responding to others' comments on their own:

> I never heard the term web text before. Like many others [in class]
> I only know what I have read in my classmates' responses. Basically,
> I believe that it is any form of online media that enables people to
> connect with one another and communicate. I hope [to] gain a better
> understanding of the term throughout the course and learn how to use
> it in my classroom. (6.2.14)

Once students had responded to all of the questions, they were asked which of the five areas (web texts, presentations, audio texts, video texts, and social media) they knew the least about. They were then charged with becoming resident experts of digital writing for the area in which they needed to improve the most.

Students read all of the chapters in Hicks's book, paying special attention to the chapter they were assigned, and his Wikispace[35] (which includes links to numerous resources for each chapter). After exploring these resources, they were encouraged to find others of value.

They also responded to a second set of follow-up questions via Google Docs. The same set of question stems was tweaked to reflect the content focus of each chapter. For Hicks's "Crafting Web Texts" (chapter 3), students were asked the following:

2A. What information—about crafting *web texts*—did you find most useful and why?

2B. What was (were) your favorite idea(s) about learning to craft *web texts* and why?[36]

Blank pages quickly became sixteen pages as student responses to the four questions filled the Google Docs files for each of the chapters. While we expected students to share information freely in this open learning environment, we were delighted to see them organically engage in ways that demonstrated that they were learning *with* and *from* one another. Students quickly began experimenting with font styles and inserting links to videos or websites that related to the conversation at hand. One student shared that she wanted to learn how to create a multimodal web text based on a poem she had seen online:

> I personally would like to learn more about new technologies available to implement in a [digital poem] https://www.youtube.com/watch?v=17i3LrSDsFA. I feel out of the loop (and a little old school) with the new era of technology and want to learn more about them! I think this will help with an engaging presentation, as well as utilize many resources that I know are out there. (6.2.14)

For the next phase of the NTMS project, students were asked to think about the distinctions between taking or recording notes and making notes of one's own. After working with partners, in small groups, and then debriefing as a whole, the class agreed upon the criteria by which all NTMS products would be assessed. Provided in the following list are the jointly created criteria used to adjudge the quality of digital notes that teams collaboratively wrote for their respective chapters. Comments that Sandra added are in parentheses.

Quality NTMS product criteria:

1. *Should clearly and concisely identify key points for each chapter* (Each assigned chapter has the word "crafting" in the title. That's important! Rather than creating a presentation that tells us about the genre or topic [say video text], share KEY POINTS that Hicks identifies as important to "crafting" a particular kind of text. Be sure to explicitly connect to Hicks's recommendations. If you quote any of his ideas, be sure to clearly and appropriately cite using APA.)

2. *Are well-organized and easy to follow and understand*

3. *Are interesting (e.g., appealing) and engaging (e.g., interactive)* (Remember: How do you bring words and ideas to life using the tools and information available to you? Create with intention and consider what Hicks identifies in his MAPS heuristic [i.e., mode, media, audience, purpose, situation].[37])

4. *Have long-term value for your and your classmates' purposes* (i.e., These notes could be used a year from now and you would have the information you need to understand and use them.)

Resident experts of the same chapter became members of the learning design team charged with collaboratively taking, making, and sharing digital notes for their respective chapters. To ramp up the assignment's potential value to the entire class and to demonstrate effective pedagogy, groups needed to thoughtfully draw upon all of their classmates' responses provided around the four chapter questions (i.e., what they already knew, were interested in, reported most useful and interesting). Teams of five created digital notes made available on Google Docs for all to access, review, and keep. In addition, digital learning design teams also presented their NTMS products to the class during face-to-face meetings. Before sharing their face-to-face presentations, however, each member of the design team first identified at least one area around which he or she wanted specific feedback from the class.

As teams shared their digital NTMS, they were asked the following questions:

- What did you do?
- What was your process?
- What choices did you make and why?
- What did you learn?
- What challenges and successes did you have?
- How can you apply this to teaching adolescents?

Classmates provided constructive feedback specific to each of the digital writer's stated goals after the design teams concluded their presentations.

Prompts such as these were provided to guide the feedback process: *One thing I appreciated around what you did in relation to Goal X . . .* ; *In terms of Goal X, you might want to think about . . .* ; *One thing that might get in the way of your desire to achieve X is . . . .* Once teams had received feedback from their classmates, they also received e-mail feedback from Sandra. Here is an example of what the feedback looked like:

Dear Students A, B, C, and D,

Your chapter submission thoughtfully and explicitly speaks to major themes and ideas found in this chapter. Originality, insight, and depth-of-thought are demonstrated throughout. Key ideas are clear, detailed, and accurate.

Overall, you effectively integrate traditional text, social media, and digital text into notes in ways that meet the criteria the class identified. You clearly distinguish when you're taking notes and when you're making notes. WOWZA. Props to you when you explicitly cite Hicks and page numbers: YES! You do much to add your own "digital" or "idea" sparkle. The way in which you embedded additional sources and web links was clear, crisp, and noteworthy. By the way: Now that you've learned about the "They Say/I Say" sentence starters,[38] consider using them when you do embed quotes into your notes. That you have an amazing essential question around "what media do you follow" and that you now have 25 followers on Twitter (including Hicks) blows my mind. WOOT! WOOT!

You purposefully use white space and text features/structures that make the text or information stand out clearly. You use text structures and features that make your digital notes invitational and interactive. The last two major sections powerfully reflect all that you have learned about creating digital text. At times, the visual presentation in the Prezi tended to undermine the incredibly thoughtful provision of information within. Please consider revisiting each slide with what Hicks identifies as important to crafting slide shows.

The combination of all of the resources into one set of notes proved helpful. Still, consider including some of the conversational glue you provided in class on June 24th. Doing so would help readers more smoothly transition from one section to the next and promote a better sense of why you present the information in this "order" and how the information relates.

You all demonstrated an ability to craft digital note taking, making, and sharing that showed a remarkable awareness of and respect for an audience with many preferences. As a result, your notes demonstrate your growth AND furthered all of our learning.

Your next steps? Consider what is essential to this process and product in relation to what Crockett et al.[39] identify around SOLUTION fluency (p. 27), INFORMATION fluency (p. 38), CREATIVITY fluency (p. 50), MEDIA fluency (p. 64), and COLLABORATION fluency (p. 74). There is so much more to this process and product than meets the eye.

Write on,
Sandra

NTMS: Metaliteracy in Practice

Upon reflection, the NTMS assignment champions a number of metaliteracy goals. Metaliteracy goal 1, or the typical library instruction goal of "evaluat[ing] content critically,"[40] was foundational to not only this course but also this assignment. More interestingly though, this assignment speaks to metaliteracy goal 3: "Share information and collaborate in a variety of participatory assignments."[41] The digital NTMS required students to "produce information in open and online communities" as well as synthesize and adapt "information so that it effectively moves from one format . . . to another."[42] This overarching goal, which "includes several new objectives that represent all four domains,"[43] makes this particular project an especially powerful example of metaliteracy in practice.

Creating and sharing this assignment operated in an open, social, environment—Google Docs. This type of collaborative space brings in metaliteracy goal 2 and "understand[ing] personal privacy, information ethics, and intellectual property issues in changing technology environments."[44] Google Docs allowed for a level of transparency in learning not normally available inside the learning management system. Students were able to see the learning in process, which opened the "door to sharing the process of learning, not only the final product."[45] Moreover, the interactions that occurred online and in class extended beyond the "traditional learning space" and allowed "for dialogue among peers and between the teacher and learner in new ways."[46] In our experience, this level of transparency encouraged participants, who were not merely engaged but empowered as collaborative and metaliterate learners. For example, Google Docs became a common learning space where students could meet at any time to freely exchange ideas and information independently and collaboratively. As the class progressed, ownership for this online environment shifted. Instead of this being Sandra's or any individual's learner space, it became "our" space for learning and interacting collectively.

One-on-One Summative Assessment

The second assignment that students identified as especially powerful was the One-on-One Summative Assessment. For this assignment, every student met with Sandra for twenty to thirty minutes to share what he or she had learned in relation to the course objectives.[47] During this meeting and what is best described as an oral defense, students identified

- three of the most significant things they had learned around critical multiliteracies and why these three "things" were most significant to them as learners and/or teachers of literacy and

- three actions they planned to take based on what they wanted to strengthen and why.

To prepare their defense for the One-on-One, students used the same set of questions to self-assess and gauge their learning throughout the course. These questions, we discovered, are especially well aligned with the kinds of meta-cognitive reflection critical to developing metaliterate learners:

- What am I learning/have I learned about what is important to educating critically, multiliterate students, in grades 5–12?
- What meaning or significance does all of what I am learning hold for me, for my instructional practice, and the teacher I want to or can be(come)?

In preparing for this meeting, students created digital writing based on an idea or topic of their choosing to communicate and demonstrate the extent to which they were critically multiliterate. They also knew that they would need to make explicit their decision-making process and intentionality surrounding the digital writing they chose to create. Ultimately, this meeting was the reflective opportunity (face-to-face or cyber) where they needed to make clear what literacies they had learned, what literacies they have yet to learn, and the value this learning holds for them as critical consumers and producers of text, all of which are key to the metaliteracy framework.

One-on-One Summative Assessment: Metaliteracy in Practice

The reflective, metacognitive aspect of the One-on-One assignment aligned with metaliteracy goal 4 and the "ability to connect learning and research strategies with lifelong learning processes and personal, academic, and professional goals."[48] In asking students to "use self-reflection to assess . . . [their] learning and knowledge of the learning process" and "demonstrate the ability to think critically in context and to transfer critical thinking to new learning,"[49] the idea of thinking critically about one's thinking for the goal of future learning or transfer became a focal point of the assignment and course. According to Mackey and Jacobson, "metacognition allows for ongoing critical thinking that builds on previous experience so that learners adapt to new information situations."[50] In retrospect, metaliteracy helped us better define and support what metacognition and reflexivity look like in practice. The reflective pieces of the One-on-One assignment asked students to think critically about what they had learned, give voice to what they found meaningful, and consider how their worldview had changed around text, multimodal text, literacy, and literacy education.

■ ■ ■ ■ ■

As a result of this experience, we plan to incorporate the aspect of the metaliteracy framework that promotes metacognition to improve the One-on-One Summative Assessment and the digital Note Take, Make, and Share project in future iterations of this course.

The digital NTMS project and the One-on-One assignment assessments reflect a commitment to providing students with an opportunity to discover and experiment with new and multiple literacies and media through the creation of digital texts of their own choosing and design. Exploring student thinking—via written and spoken commentary and feedback—throughout these assignments, either individually or collaboratively achieved, was also valued. The course instructor's notes and analytic memo writing also provided reflective pedagogical insights about the students' learning as well as Sandra's own throughout the course.

In the collaborative decision to root our deliberation on course artifacts in participatory action research,[51] we analyzed this data "as a dynamic process . . . spiral[ing] back and forth between reflection about a problem, data collection and action."[52] This approach also engaged us in the study of metaliteracy and informed our practice, since we learned about our own literacy as well as that of our students.

WHAT WE LEARNED

Examination of all of this data and reflective practice ultimately led us to see metaliteracy as an effective way to frame and approach the teaching and learning of critical multiliteracies, as well as teaching for literacy and learning writ large. In this section, we share what we learned about the value metaliteracy holds for

- helping teachers become not just critically multiliterate, but metaliterate; and
- teacher educators of literacy and those interested in teaching for learning the many different, but related literacies vital to living in a digital and multimodal age.

In the end, the construct of metaliteracy allowed us to

- make sense of the growing list of literacies largely enabled by technology;
- identify areas of strength and weakness in our own instructional practices; and
- ascertain a meaningful course of action to improve the teaching and learning of literacy in the twenty-first century.

One theme that emerged from Sandra's analytic memo writing throughout the course was the need to make sense of the many literacies valued in today's world. As mentioned previously, we, as well as the students enrolled in this course, struggled to make sense of the growing list of multiple literacies, including, but not limited to, critical multiliteracies (e.g., critical literacy, new literacies, multiliteracies, digital literacies, multimodal literacies, information literacy, twenty-first-century literacies and/or fluencies). Ultimately, critical multiliteracies is just one of the many literacy models worth considering when designing for today's complex learning environment. Because we valued other literacies and a comprehensive approach to literacy education, Sandra, Logan, and the students ultimately questioned why critical multiliteracies was the defined set of literate practices the course creators initially privileged. For us, this set of hashtags captured our collective insights very well: #MANYLITER-ACIES #MULTI-LITERACIES #CRITICALMULTI-LITERACIES: HUH?

Based on our observations, students benefited from exploring multiliteracies as a set of social practices through which they could critique and take action in the world. The digital NTMS and One-on-One products revealed, for example, that students did indeed become more informed, critical, and practiced users and creators of digital writing. As one student explained in her One-on-One, knowledge was power, but gaining it did not make the process of learning any less overwhelming:

> I struggled with how to present this information. I looked all over Hicks and other resources. One of the most helpful, and overwhelming, was the 50+ web ways to tell a story. I was excited and ready to use Vuvox Collage [that Hicks recommends] but it turned out to be defunct. Then I looked at some other programs but they were complicated, unwieldy, or cost money. Then I tried a Glogster, I signed up and started making one but it looked busy and I found it too limiting. In the end I decided to use a PowerPoint because that is a medium I can easily use in class.

Selber's categories of functional, critical, and rhetorical literacy did help students better understand the relationships among some of the many literacies students deemed valuable.[53] Still, they found these categories fell short when they attempted to describe what they learned as both teachers and learners. In contrast, the metaliteracy framework foregrounds the metacognitive dimension of learning and thus provides a context for our students and for us to experience and reflect on specific learning in this course.

Likewise, Mackey and Jacobson's construct of metaliteracy unites and broadens the teaching and learning of the many different, yet related literacies important to twenty-first-century life in a clear and inclusive way.[54] From a critical multiliteracies perspective, bridging the literacies that adolescents use outside of school with the literacies they use in school is central. These outside-of-school literacy practices and interests are worthy of attention—so much so that EDI 728 was created to broaden literacy to include multiple and varied literacies central to more richly supporting adolescents' ongoing literacy development, learning, and future success in college, in the workplace, and in life. Metaliteracy is "a way to raise critical concerns about literacy . . . in a social media age."[55] As a result, we contend that the metaliteracy framework provides an effective way to frame and approach metacognitive learning and interrelated literacies.

At the same time, changes in technology (e.g., the Internet, multimodal technology, and digital media) and contemporary writing research challenged us to rethink what counts as text. In the world of schools, literacy is typically defined as the ability to make and convey meaning using language (which includes other sign systems, such as color, sound illustration, movement, etc.) and print-based text in ways that particular individuals, communities, and society value and privilege.[56] In a digital and multimodal world, consideration of multimodality, design, and production became paramount.[57] The Association of College and Research Libraries' (ACRL) *Framework for Information Literacy for Higher Education*, informed by metaliteracy, inspired us to see any piece of writing or communication "offer" as information rather than text.[58] Redefining text as information, in all of its various forms, was one of the most beneficial links between critical multiliteracies and metaliteracy that allowed us, as course instructor and librarian, to use a shared mind-set and vocabulary.

Metaliteracy also provided us with a model to develop, think critically about, and empower our own literate selves and instructional practices, as well as the students enrolled in this course. From our analysis of course artifacts, for example, we gained the sense that we had assumed much about the extent to which our students were literate. We presumed, for example, that because they lived in a world that required competencies relating to computing and the use of multimodal environments, the students would know how to use new tools and would be able to easily create new information in a variety of contexts and formats. This was not the case. Save for the digital NTMS, the One-on-One products gravitated toward individual preferences, strengths, and paths of efficiency in a five-week course. Experimentation and risk were evident in students' summative assessments, but both the course instructor and the students wanted increased specificity about what being critically multiliterate looked like and meant for teachers as learners. The metaliteracy framework provides that.

Being metacognitive about one's own literacies was essential to student success in this class. As the students developed an awareness of their own metaliteracy and reflected on "how and why they learn, what they do and do not know, their preconceptions, and how to continue to learn,"[59] they created action steps around areas in need of development and strengthening. When students reflected on what they knew, did not know, and wanted to know more about, they discovered that despite wanting to help adolescents become knowledgeable, critical, empowered, and metacognitive users and creators of language, text, and technology, *they* needed to be knowledgeable, critical, empowered, and metacognitive users and creators of language, text, and technology first. Their status as graduate students did not guarantee that they, themselves, had met or could meet all of these expectations. This discovery prompted Sandra to ask Logan, a contributor to the goals of metaliteracy,[60] to provide direct instruction in support of increasing students' literacies as well as the course instructor's. His understanding of and support for metaliteracy would prove invaluable, and this opportunity to be a part of metaliteracy in practice influenced his own thinking about the original goals and objectives.

As transformative teacher educators, we wanted all of our students to walk away from the course feeling empowered by having learned something that improved their understanding and/or instructional practices around emerging literacies. Indeed, as Wiggins and McTighe remind us, "The point of learning anything is to make it our own, and to have it culminate in some new power and perspective."[61] Their quote echoes nicely with Mackey and Jacobson's assertion that "metaliteracy empowers learners to be active and collaborative participants while encouraging metacognitive reflection."[62] For some of the teachers enrolled in this class, being more critically multiliterate meant that they had learned something that inspired them to think or act differently. Others suggested that they had gained greater appreciation for something they already knew, believed, or could do. Even more suggested that they were empowered when they discovered or learned something new and now had another tool, skill, or possibility available to them as a result. It is this empowerment created by metacognitive reflection that gave us yet another reason to see metaliteracy as a more powerful way to frame the learning objectives of this course than we had previously envisioned.

All told, there was considerable worth in discovering the complex nature of critical multiliteracies, as it led us to understand and appreciate metaliteracy as an applied construct and allowed us to become more aware of our own metaliteracy. Looking to the future iterations of this course, and its counterpart, Critical Multiliteracies, Birth–6, we plan on amending the course objectives to include the participatory, empowering, and metacognitive facets of metaliteracy gained from this study. Furthermore, we plan on introducing metaliteracy as a foundational concept important to all of the coursework within our college's literacy programs.

CONCLUSION

Our examination of what B–12 teachers reported and demonstrated learning in this course suggests that metaliteracy is an effective overarching concept for literacy teacher educators to consider for several reasons. First, metaliteracy integrates digital technologies, multimodality, and print-based literacies. Second, it foregrounds the metacognitive aspect vital to advancing literate practices and habits of mind that better prepare learners for today's world and a future yet to be. Third, metaliteracy provides teachers a comprehensive and comprehensible way to thoughtfully develop their own (and their students') literacies critical to teaching and learning in a digital and multimodal age. For us, the goals and learning objectives of metaliteracy explored in this study—specifically, critical evaluation, learner empowerment through the creation and transformation of meaning, and metacognitive reflection—provide worthy aims that powerfully engage learners of all ages.

NOTES

1. Thomas P. Mackey and Trudi E. Jacobson, *Metaliteracy: Reinventing Information Literacy to Empower Learners* (Chicago: Neal-Schuman, 2014).
2. College Senate, The College at Brockport, "Literacy Education B–12 Proposal" (n.d. #72_10–11GC, The College at Brockport, 2011), 1.
3. Susan Sandretto and Jane Tilson, "Reconceptualising Literacy: Critical Multiliteracies for 'New Times'" (Teaching and Learning Research Intitative, 2013), 3.
4. Kathy Ann Mills, "A Review of the 'Digital Turn' in the New Literacy Studies," *Review of Educational Research* 80, no. 2 (2010): 247.
5. Elizabeth Birr Moje, "Standpoints: A Call for New Research on New and Multi-literacies," *Research in the Teaching of English* 43, no. 4 (2009): 348–62.
6. Michèle Anstey and Geoff Bull, *Teaching and Learning Multiliteracies: Changing Times, Changing Literacies* (Newark, DE: International Reading Association), 37–38.
7. Vicki L. Plano Clark and John W. Creswell, *Understanding Research: A Consumer's Guide* (Upper Saddle River, NJ: Merrill/Pearson Educational, 2010).
8. Ibid.
9. John W. Creswell, *Educational Research: Planning, Conducting, and Evaluating Quantitative and Qualitative Research* (Boston: Pearson, 2012).
10. Stephen Kemmis and Robin McTaggart, "Participatory Action Research: Communicative Action and the Public Sphere," in *The SAGE Handbook of Qualitative Research*, ed. Daniel Perrin and Eva-Maria Jakobs (Berlin: De Gruyter, 2014), 251–53; Plano Clark and Creswell, *Understanding Research*, 374.
11. Plano Clark and Creswell, *Understanding Research*, 374.
12. Ibid.
13. Creswell, *Educational Research*, 586.
14. Ibid., 587.
15. Ibid.

16. Sandra K. Cimbricz, "EDI 728 Syllabus, Summer 2014" (Department of Education and Human Development, The College at Brockport, 2014), 2.

17. Paul W. Vogt, *Dictionary of Statistics and Methodology: A Nontechnical Guide for the Social Sciences* (Thousand Oaks, CA: SAGE Publications, 2005), http://srmo.sagepub.com/view/dictionary-of-statistics-methodology/n706.xml.

18. Johnny Saldaña, *The Coding Manual for Qualitative Researchers* (Thousand Oaks, CA: SAGE Publications, 2013), 41.

19. Adele Clarke, *Situational Analysis: Grounded Theory after the Postmodern Era* (Thousand Oaks, CA: SAGE Publications, 2005), 202.

20. Jennifer Mason, *Qualitative Researching* (Thousand Oaks, CA: SAGE Publications, 2002), 5.

21. Mackey and Jacobson, *Metaliteracy*, 6.

22. Stuart A. Selber, *Multiliteracies for a Digital Age* (Carbondale, IL: Southern Illinois University Press, 2004), 25.

23. Frederick Erickson, "Qualitative Methods in Research on Teaching," in *Handbook of Research on Teaching*, ed. M. C. Wittrock and American Educational Research Association, 3rd ed. (New York; London: Macmillan; Collier Macmillan, 1986), 119–61.

24. Jennifer Rowsell, *Working with Multimodality: Rethinking Literacy in a Digital Age* (New York: Routledge, 2013), 163.

25. Mackey and Jacobson, *Metaliteracy*, 84.

26. Ibid., 88–89.

27. Ibid.

28. Moje, "Standpoints," 348.

29. Priscilla L. Griffith and Jiening Ruan, "What Is Metacognition and What Should Be Its Role?" in *Metacognition in Literacy Learning: Theory, Assessment, Instructions, and Professional Development*, ed. Susan E. Israel, Cathy Collins Block, Kathryn L. Bauserman, and Kathryn Kinnucan-Welsch (Mahwah, NJ: Erlbaum Associates, 2005), 16.

30. Mackey and Jacobson, *Metaliteracy*.

31. Troy Hicks and Daniel Perrin, "Beyond Single Modes and Media: Writing as an Ongoing Multimodal Text Production," in *Handbook of Writing and Text Production*, ed. Daniel Perrin and Eva-Maria Jakobs (Berlin: De Gruyter, 2014), 251–3; Stephen B. Kucer, *Dimensions of Literacy: A Conceptual Base for Teaching Reading and Writing in School Settings*, 4th ed. (New York: Routledge, 2014); Selber, *Multiliteracies for a Digital Age*.

32. Troy Hicks, *Crafting Digital Writing: Composing Texts across Media and Genres* (Portsmouth, NH: Heinemann, 2013).

33. Ibid., 4.

34. Ibid., 28–60.

35. Troy Hicks, "The Digital Writing Workshop—Crafting_Digital_Writing" (companion page to Hicks, *Crafting Digital Writing*, accessed April 18, 2015), http://public.eblib.com/choice/publicfullrecord.aspx?p=1347020.

36. Hicks, *Crafting Digital Writing*, 28–60.

37. Ibid., 21.

38. Gerald Graff and Cathy Birkenstein, *"They Say/I Say": The Moves That Matter in Academic Writing* (New York: W. W. Norton, 2014), xvii.

39. Lee Crockett, Ian Jukes, and Andrew Churches, *Literacy Is Not Enough: 21st-Century Fluencies for the Digital Age* ([Kelowna, BC]; [Thousands Oaks, CA]: 21st Century Fluency Project; Corwin, 2011), 27, 38, 50, 64.

40. Thomas P. Mackey and Trudi E. Jacobson, "Reframing Information Literacy as a Metaliteracy," *College and Research Libraries* 72, no. 1 (2011): 87, doi:10.5860/crl-76r1.

41. Mackey and Jacobson, *Metaliteracy*, 88.

42. Ibid., 89.

43. Ibid., 88.

44. Ibid.

45. George Siemens, "Teaching as Transparent Learning," *Connectivism*, April 28 (2009), www.connectivism.ca/?p=122.

46. Thomas P. Mackey, "Transparency as a Catalyst for Interaction and Participation in Open Learning Environments," *First Monday* 16, no. 10 (2011), 8, www.firstmonday.org/ojs/index.php/fm/article/view/3333.

47. Cimbricz, "EDI 728 Syllabus."

48. Mackey and Jacobson, *Metaliteracy*, 90.

49. Metaliteracy.org, "Goals and Learning Objectives" (updated September 11, 2014), http://metaliteracy.org/learning-objectives.

50. Mackey and Jacobson, *Metaliteracy*, 90.

51. Plano Clark and Creswell, *Understanding Research*.

52. Creswell, *Educational Research*, 587.

53. Selber, *Multiliteracies for a Digital Age*, 25.

54. Mackey and Jacobson, "Reframing Information Literacy," 70; Mackey and Jacobson, *Metaliteracy*, 22–27.

55. Mackey and Jacobson, *Metaliteracy*, 6.

56. Kucer, *Dimensions of Literacy*.

57. Rowsell, *Working with Multimodality*.

58. Association of College and Research Libraries, *Framework for Information Literacy for Higher Education* (Chicago: American Library Association, 2015), www.ala.org/acrl/standards/ilframework; Mackey and Jacobson, "Reframing Information Literacy."

59. Metaliteracy.org, "Goals and Learning Objectives."

60. Ibid.

61. Grant P. Wiggins and Jay McTighe, *Schooling by Design: Mission, Action, and Achievement* (Alexandria, VA: Association for Supervision and Curriculum Development, 2007), 13.

62. Mackey and Jacobson, *Metaliteracy*, 28.

BIBLIOGRAPHY

Anstey, Michèle, and Geoff Bull. *Teaching and Learning Multiliteracies: Changing Times, Changing Literacies*. Newark, DE: International Reading Association, 2006.

Association of College and Research Libraries (ACRL). *Framework for Information Literacy for Higher Education*. Chicago: American Library Association, 2015. www.ala.org/acrl/standards/ilframework.

Cimbricz, Sandra K. "EDI 728 Syllabus, Summer 2014." Department of Education and Human Development, The College at Brockport, 2014.

Clarke, Adele. *Situational Analysis: Grounded Theory after the Postmodern Turn*. Thousand Oaks, CA: SAGE Publications, 2005.

College Senate, The College at Brockport. "Literacy Education B–12 Proposal." n.d. #72_10–11GC. The College at Brockport, 2011. www.brockport.edu/collegesenate/resolutions/2010-2011%20Resolutions/2010-2011-38res.pdf.

Creswell, John W. *Educational Research: Planning, Conducting, and Evaluating Quantitative and Qualitative Research*. Boston: Pearson, 2012.

Crockett, Lee, Ian Jukes, and Andrew Churches. *Literacy Is Not Enough: 21st-Century Fluencies for the Digital Age*. [Kelowna, BC]; [Thousand Oaks, CA]: 21st Century Fluency Project; Corwin, 2011.

Erickson, Frederick. "Qualitative Methods in Research on Teaching." In *Handbook of Research on Teaching*, edited by M. C. Wittrock and American Educational Research Association, 3rd ed., 119–61. New York; London: Macmillan; Collier Macmillan, 1986.

Graff, Gerald, and Cathy Birkenstein. *"They Say/I Say": The Moves That Matter in Academic Writing*. New York: W. W. Norton, 2014.

Griffith, Priscilla L., and Jiening Ruan. "What Is Metacognition and What Should Be Its Role?" In *Metacognition in Literacy Learning: Theory, Assessment, Instruction, and Professional Development*, edited by Susan E. Israel, Cathy Collins Block, Kathryn L. Bauserman, and Kathryn Kinnucan-Welsch, 3–18. Mahwah, NJ: L. Erlbaum Associates, 2005.

Hicks, Troy. *Crafting Digital Writing: Composing Texts across Media and Genres*. Portsmouth, NH: Heinemann, 2013.

———. "The Digital Writing Workshop—Crafting_Digital_Writing." Companion page to *Crafting Digital Writing: Composing Texts across Media and Genres*, by Troy Hicks (Portsmouth, NH: Heinemann, 2013). Accessed April 18, 2015. http://digitalwritingworkshop.wikispaces.com/Crafting_Digital_Writing.

Hicks, Troy, and Daniel Perrin. "Beyond Single Modes and Media: Writing as an Ongoing Multimodal Text Production." In *Handbook of Writing and Text Production*, edited by Daniel Perrin and Eva-Maria Jakobs, 251–53. Berlin: De Gruyter, 2014. http://public.eblib.com/choice/publicfullrecord.aspx?p=1347020.

Kemmis, Stephen, and Robin McTaggart. "Participatory Action Research: Communicative Action and the Public Sphere." In *The SAGE Handbook of Qualitative Research*, edited by Norman K. Denzin and Yvonna S. Lincoln, 3rd ed., 559–604. Thousand Oaks, CA: SAGE Publications, 2005.

Kucer, Stephen B. *Dimensions of Literacy: A Conceptual Base for Teaching Reading and Writing in School Settings.* 4th ed. New York: Routledge, 2014.

Mackey, Thomas P. "Transparency as a Catalyst for Interaction and Participation in Open Learning Environments." *First Monday* 16, no. 10 (2011). www.firstmonday.org/ojs/index.php/fm/article/view/3333.

Mackey, Thomas P., and Trudi E. Jacobson. *Metaliteracy: Reinventing Information Literacy to Empower Learners.* Chicago: Neal-Schuman, 2014.

———. "Reframing Information Literacy as a Metaliteracy." *College and Research Libraries* 72, no. 1 (2011): 62–78. doi:10.5860/crl-76r1.

Mason, Jennifer. *Qualitative Researching.* Thousand Oaks, CA: SAGE Publications, 2002.

Metaliteracy.org. "Goals and Learning Objectives." Updated September, 11, 2014. http://metaliteracy.org/learning-objectives/.

Mills, Kathy Ann. "A Review of the 'Digital Turn' in the New Literacy Studies." *Review of Educational Research* 80, no. 2 (2010): 246–71.

Moje, Elizabeth Birr. "Standpoints: A Call for New Research on New and Multi-literacies." *Research in the Teaching of English* 43, no. 4 (2009): 348–62.

Plano Clark, Vicki L., and John W. Creswell. *Understanding Research: A Consumer's Guide.* Upper Saddle River, NJ: Merrill/Pearson Educational, 2010.

Rowsell, Jennifer. *Working with Multimodality: Rethinking Literacy in a Digital Age.* New York: Routledge, 2013.

Saldaña, Johnny. *The Coding Manual for Qualitative Researchers.* Thousand Oaks, CA: SAGE Publications, 2013.

Sandretto, Susan, and Jane Tilson. "Reconceptualising Literacy: Critical Multi-literacies for 'New Times.'" Teaching and Learning Research Initiative, 2013. http://54.79.73.135/sites/default/files/projects/Sandretto_Summary_final_1.pdf.

Selber, Stuart A. *Multiliteracies for a Digital Age.* Carbondale, IL: Southern Illinois University Press, 2004.

Siemens, George. "Teaching as Transparent Learning." *Connectivism*, April 28 (2009). www.connectivism.ca/?p=122.

Vogt, W. Paul. *Dictionary of Statistics and Methodology: A Nontechnical Guide for the Social Sciences.* Thousand Oaks, CA: SAGE Publications, 2005. http://srmo.sagepub.com/view/dictionary-of-statistics-methodology/n706.xml.

Wiggins, Grant P., and Jay McTighe. *Schooling by Design: Mission, Action, and Achievement.* Alexandria, VA: Association for Supervision and Curriculum Development, 2007.

MICHELE R. SANTAMARIA
and KATHRYN M. MONCRIEF

6

Metacognition Meets Research-Based Learning in the Undergraduate Renaissance Drama Classroom

"I FELT LIKE I LEARNED MORE ABOUT COLLABORATING AND working in a group than I did about research. The group process felt the most important." This quote, drawn from a student's survey response, emphasizes collaboration in the research-based learning experience in an undergraduate Renaissance Drama classroom at Washington College during the fall of 2014. Upon completion of the project, our teaching team of Kathryn, the professor, and Michele, the librarian, reflected further about collaboration itself, with implications both for metaliteracy and for joint research in the humanities. From a disciplinary perspective, it is important to note that in the humanities, in contrast to other disciplines, particularly science, technology, engineering, and math (STEM) education, the notion of solo research and publication continues to dominate. In the undergraduate humanities classroom, this paradigm is frequently replicated with students researching and writing as individuals, rather than working in groups, collaborating with one another, or with the professor.

On the other hand, with this project, the teaching team of librarian and professor invited students to collaborate with one another and with us, with the goal of making a contribution to a digital, open access project known as

FIGURE 6.1
Project Levels of Collaboration

the Map of Early Modern London (MoEML). This open access project represents an international collaboration, as noted in the project's student survey, which asked students to rate their feelings about this statement: "At the end of the MoEML module, I value collaborative work more highly (both with my classmates and with an international project)." The survey was created by MoEML in order to assess the efficacy of their pedagogical partnerships and to assist in making the process smoother for professors and students. In dialogue with the survey results, we offer a diagram to help convey the nested levels of collaboration involved in this project, in contrast with the first circle representing the model of the "Solo Humanities Scholar" (see figure 6.1).

In this chapter, we analyze how metaliteracy was intrinsic to the experience of undergraduate Renaissance Drama students embarking upon collaborative research, nested within various cooperative ventures. This collaborative research was incorporated into an open access digital humanities project known as the Map of Early Modern London (MoEML). While not actively promoted as an open educational resource, or OER, the project shares many features with OERs and inspired student contributions that now serve as a collective case study for tracking the development of metaliterate learners. As such, the case study provides a useful model for professors and librarians interested in seeing how students will apply metaliteracy to a range of high-stakes research tasks. To assign students this type of project is to assume that students can come to see themselves as "information producers" and not just "information consumers." As noted by Mackey and Jacobson in their 2014 work on the subject, *Metaliteracy: Reinventing Information Literacy to Empower Learners*, this is a distinction that is vital for reinventing information literacy as metaliteracy.[1] By assigning students a research narrative that was process oriented, as well as a final end product that might be incorporated into the MoEML, we were able to track students' development as metaliterate learners.

Several components of the students' coursework and the nature of the MoEML pedagogical partnership align with aspects of metaliteracy, from its dynamically digital nature to the class's semester-long emphasis on student collaboration. Additionally, in emphasizing undergraduate students' capability as knowledge producers, the assignment worked to empower the students as researchers and writers. The MoEML provides students with an excellent opportunity to engage with critical information literacy. It offers learners an open access alternative to the "knowable reality" of information mediated by undemocratic library practices, as elaborated upon by James Elborg in his exploration of critical information literacy.[2] By drawing key aspects of their research from subscription-based library resources, students would be bringing elements of information guarded behind a paywall into an open access context, an issue that the director of the MoEML, Dr. Janelle Jenstad, addressed during her in-person class visit. This was also an issue that Michele commented upon by emphasizing her support of the endeavor, despite possibly being viewed in a "gatekeeping" kind of capacity as someone who works for an organization paying for information that is not freely available. In keeping with Elborg's formulation of critical information literacy and metaliteracy as a whole, the production of new information during this project did indeed occur within a community of peers, as students were put into teams and wrote group rather than individual essays.

Moreover, students were researching and writing collaboratively, working toward an end product that is also a scholarly collaborative effort. Aside from submitting this project, the students submitted "commonplace books" that tracked their research process more informally. Students also submitted more polished research narratives. The research narratives, the main focus of our analysis, reflect not only upon students' individual metacognition but also upon metacognition as part of a collaborative venture. As such, the narratives also touch upon the other metaliteracy learning domains and offer a compelling snapshot of students' development as metaliterate learners.

In Mackey and Jacobson's revised formulation of metaliteracy learning objectives, they organize metaliteracy learning objectives into four learning domains: behavioral, cognitive, affective, and metacognitive.[3] Being able to track the development of metacognition is essential to teaching it; therefore, the applicability of this case study transcends its particulars. Since the affective domain also played a pivotal role in students' experiences, this is also examined in our analysis. For the most part, positive student emotions created a feeling of empowerment that they were able to meet the project's learning objectives successfully. The collaborative nature of the task cut across the four learning domains, with students becoming metaliterate learners through the process of coming to terms with one another's learning competencies. An understanding of the metaliterate learner provides a comprehensive sense of how the coursework gave students an opportunity to integrate the behavioral, cognitive, and affective domains of learning with metacognition. This holistic perspective is particularly useful given how powerfully the affective dimension played a role in team bonding and effective collaboration.

INSTITUTIONAL AND ASSIGNMENT CONTEXT

Washington College is a small, selective, private liberal arts college, with an enrollment of 1,480 students, located on the eastern shore of Maryland. The school presents itself as a "Writing College." As part of its focus on writing, every first-year student is required to take ENG 101, Literature and Composition. All English 101 instructors emphasize the process of writing, which takes time and requires revision and deliberate work toward a final, polished project. The course stresses thoughtful and responsive reading, critical and imaginative thinking, and effective and well-crafted expository writing. The ability to think critically and write clearly and persuasively is integral throughout the college's curriculum. All students are also required to take two additional courses, offered across the curriculum, designated as "writing intensive." Finally, the college has a robust Creative Writing minor. Creative writing classes, from Introduction to Creative Writing through the upper-level workshops (including Fiction, Poetry, Nonfiction, and others), use not only writing and revision but also ongoing feedback on the process of revision. In short, Washington College students are exposed to significant instruction on the writing process.

In comparison, while information literacy is written into the first-year seminar's curriculum, its integration throughout students' four years at the college is not as consistent as the incorporation of writing. All students at the college are required to complete a senior capstone project, either a thesis or comprehensive exams; many of the capstones focus on research. For those pursuing a research-based capstone, some majors include a junior and/or senior seminar that incorporates research sessions. However, information literacy is not mandated by any curricular requirements. Even some upper-level seminars with a research component do not require information literacy sessions. From this perspective, incorporating a librarian into the project arose from Kathryn's personal and pedagogical belief that collaboration with a librarian would be beneficial to the students given the research challenges that they would be undertaking with this project.

Kathryn's course, ENG/DRA 312: Renaissance Drama, examines early modern English drama, exclusive of Shakespeare, from the 1580s through the 1630s in its unique cultural and historical context. It considers drama as a central cultural performance—both reflecting and creating the dynamic culture of late sixteenth- and early seventeenth-century England—and explores plays by prominent dramatists of the period, including Thomas Kyd, Christopher Marlowe, Ben Jonson, Thomas Middleton, John Webster, and others, in order to understand how the dramas of the age comment on and react to, imagine and subvert, their culture. In the fall of 2014, twenty junior- and senior-level students enrolled in the course. Seventeen of those students were either English or Drama majors; the majority were also Creative Writing minors.

Over the course of the semester, the class participated in a pedagogical partnership with the Map of Early Modern London (MoEML; mapoflondon .uvic.ca). Based on the Agas map (a bird's-eye woodcut from about 1561), the project maps and provides encyclopedia entries for neighborhoods, streets, sites, buildings (including theatres), and the boundaries of London from 1560 to 1640 (see figure 6.2).

The Map of Early Modern London is an impressive open access digital initiative with several social media components, including a blog. Given the growing importance of digital literacy and the rise of digital humanities, the project was an ideal opportunity for the students to develop these skills. The students in the class, in collaboration with one another and with Kathryn, the professor—and working closely with the research librarian, Michele—researched and wrote an article on the Rose Theatre (see figure 6.3). Built in 1587, it is the first theatre on the southern bank of the Thames river in London and one of the most important theatrical sites of the era—Shakespeare's *Titus Andronicus* and *Henry IV, Part 1* premiered there. It is also important archaeologically, as the site was found in 1989 and excavation is still going on there.

As contributors, students reviewed and redacted the secondary research, located the playhouse within London's neighborhoods, summarized the impact of the playhouse on the surrounding sites and streets, and pointed MoEML users to other resources, both print and digital. Students were divided into five groups and worked collaboratively to research the following aspects of the theatre:

1. Location, site, and neighborhood
2. Building architecture/visual images

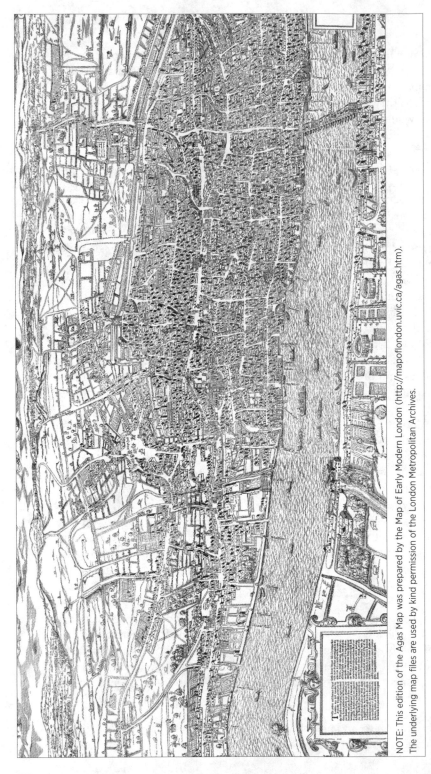

NOTE: This edition of the Agas Map was prepared by the Map of Early Modern London (http://mapoflondon.uvic.ca/agas.htm). The underlying map files are used by kind permission of the London Metropolitan Archives.

FIGURE 6.2

Agas Map

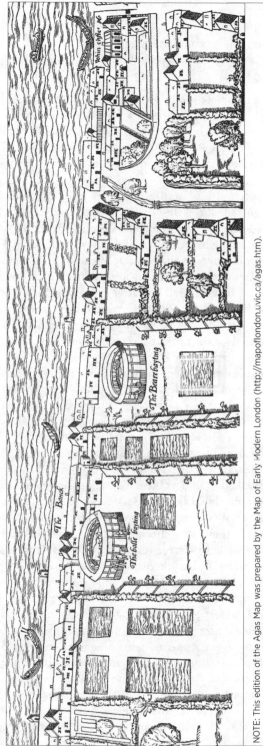

NOTE: This edition of the Agas Map was prepared by the Map of Early Modern London (http://mapoflondon.uvic.ca/agas.htm). The underlying map files are used by kind permission of the London Metropolitan Archives.

FIGURE 6.3

Rose Theatre

3. Owners, players, playing companies, audiences
4. Literary significance, plays, playwrights
5. Archaeology

Each group produced a complete group-written essay, a works cited list, and an annotated bibliography and also made a formal research presentation to the class. The more polished reflection narrative is the main focus of our chapter. The final article on the Rose Theatre, edited by Kathryn, will be peer reviewed and, if deemed of high enough quality, will then be published on MoEML's website.

We began the project with a lecture and class visit from the MoEML Director, Dr. Janelle Jenstad, of the University of Victoria in Canada, and followed this later in the semester with a Skype session with Dr. Jenstad that allowed students to ask follow-up questions once they were engaged in their research. Also in the initial stages of the project, Michele gave a research presentation on the information resources in the library, met with individual students, and wrote a sample of a research narrative as a model for the students. She attended class on the day the students presented their projects and was available for questions. Further, she familiarized herself with the metadata tagging method being used for the project and wrote a simple summary so the students understood their task.

This research-based learning assignment is ideal as a case study for the metacognitive dimension of metaliteracy for a number of reasons. First, by asking students to undertake collaborative project- and research-based learning with real-life impact, the assignment takes student metacognition and metaliteracy as a given: students had to "think about their thinking" or engage in constant metacognitive behavior in order to monitor their own progress throughout the semester and successfully complete the assignment. Second, students were asked to undertake a research assignment that would contribute to an important digital humanities open access project. This real-life impact was pivotal to how students responded both cognitively and affectively to the project. While there were check-in points with the teaching team and the teaching team modeled effective research processes, students mainly consulted among themselves and tracked their own progress in their commonplace books. Given how important student empowerment is to the metaliteracy model, the level of student independence in this project is key to this research-based learning project as a metaliteracy case study. As elaborated upon in *Metaliteracy: Reinventing Information Literacy to Empower Learning*, empowerment truly came from students being able to take on entirely new and participatory roles as metaliterate learners.[4] We saw this at play during various stages of this project. Throughout the semester, students viewed themselves as collaborators, and by the end of the term when their projects came together, they also came to see themselves as authors of information. Ultimately, this project asked them to be translators of information, moving information from a print and online subscription database context into the realm of open access.[5]

Finally, as the semester progressed, the teaching team also grappled in a metacognitive way with their own pedagogical choices, another important element to be considered when it comes to articulating how information literacy can be reenvisioned in order to be implemented as metaliteracy. At the beginning of the semester, we began with a more traditional one-shot session, which did feature an important moment in metaliteracy when a student was asked to function as the teacher. As the term progressed, Michele became more embedded at the students' point of need, fielding questions generated by their work rather than presenting an overview of relevant resources.

LITERATURE REVIEW

One component in the most recent metaliteracy model developed by Jacobson and Mackey is that traditional information literacy competencies—to determine, access, understand, and evaluate information—are enhanced by the infusion of metacognition. As seen throughout *Metaliteracy: Reinventing Information Literacy to Empower Learners*, metacognition is intrinsic to the other dimensions of metaliteracy. Metacognition also plays an important role as one of the four domains to be mastered by a metaliterate learner. For the purposes of this analysis, we look primarily at the metacognitive dimension of metaliteracy.

In its own right and in a broader sense, metacognition includes any knowledge or cognitive process that acts as a referent, monitor, or control to cognition.[6] Thus, as Flavell recognized in his groundbreaking research, metacognition allows us to be able to think about our own thinking.[7] The importance of metacognition to metaliteracy cannot be understated in its impact: it "allows us to move beyond rudimentary skills development and prepares students to dig deeper and assess their own learning."[8]

Most research on metacognition draws a distinction between metacognitive knowledge (or metacognitive awareness) and metacognitive regulation.[9] Metacognitive knowledge or metacognitive awareness refers to learners' thinking about their own thinking; it is this type of metacognition that is most commonly understood as "metacognition." According to Gregory Schraw, metacognitive knowledge can be further broken down into three types: declarative knowledge, procedural knowledge, and conditional knowledge.[10]

As characterized by Negretti in her article analyzing metacognition in student academic writing, declarative knowledge addresses *what* student strategies are, whereas procedural knowledge addresses *how* they will apply these strategies, and conditional knowledge addresses *why* those strategies would work for the particular task at hand.[11] These distinctions will be critical to our case study analysis of the research narratives that were submitted by students in their final research portfolio.

The second broad subcategory of metacognition has to do with metacognitive regulation. This refers to any set of activities that assist students in better regulating their learning. Many research studies indicate that a stronger repertoire of metacognitive regulation improves student performance in a number of ways. Students' regulation of their own cognition allows them to visibly improve their own learning by planning, monitoring, and evaluating.[12] Monitoring ability, or the ability to engage in periodic self-testing, develops fairly slowly and can be quite poor even in adults.[13]

Along with the students' role in the acquisition of greater metacognitive awareness, it is critical to note the role of teachers' metacognitive awareness about their own pedagogical practices. According to the BACEIS model developed by Hartman and Sternberg in 1993, teachers not only have a role in terms of assisting students with the development of metacognitive skills, but they also need to apply metacognition to their instruction, curriculum, and assessment.[14] The BACEIS model covers behavior, affect, cognition, environment, interacting, and systems. Along with its emphasis on teachers' metacognition, the model assists in our case study analysis with its emphasis on affect. As Hartman points out, many metacognitive approaches can be narrow in their approach, "often ignoring the affective domain."[15] On the other hand, the affective domain is critical to Mackey and Jacobson's vision of developing the metaliterate learner.[16] Though our case study analysis will, at times, analyze the metacognitive and affective dimensions separately, we agree with the assessment that the domains are fluid and interrelated and will also strive to demonstrate these interconnections.

Since we were able to see that students progressed through stages or phases in their search process, the work of Carol Kuhlthau is also relevant to our analysis. In terms of students' affective response, the role of uncertainty is most predominant in the research narratives.[17] The constructivist idea of seeking meaning as a type of quest also figured in some students' experience of the project.[18] On the teaching side of the collaboration, Kuhlthau's ideas about the roles of "mediators" in the research process seem particularly relevant to the teaching team's metacognitive reflection about how we would revise our own approach. More will be said on this issue in our conclusion.

Given that the case study is humanities based and situates itself in analysis of students' self-evaluative writing, Raffaella Negretti's 2012 article on metacognition in student academic writing is of particular relevance. In her article, Negretti focuses upon how students' journaling functions as a way of examining how beginning writers use metacognitive awareness to "monitor, self-regulate, and evaluate their writing."[19] Negretti analyzes students' task perception over time by examining their journals, whereas our case study analysis examines students' research narratives drawn from their commonplace book assignments. For Negretti, the key connections are between task perception, metacognitive awareness, and self-regulation. Negretti's article looks at four writing assignments, including one that is research based. While the methodology of this article will be taken as the jumping off point for our case study analysis, it is important to note that Negretti is analyzing novice student writing, whereas this case study focuses upon the work of more advanced writers who have internalized key concepts having to do with revision and peer review.

While Negretti's article provides a relevant, humanities-based framework for breaking down and analyzing individual students' metacognitive steps when it comes to the writing process, metaliteracy provides the collaborative template for tracking how students came to a better understanding of their metacognitive abilities through their interactions with one another. An understanding of the metaliterate learner gives us a holistic sense of how the coursework provided students with an opportunity to integrate the behavioral, cognitive, and affective domains of learning with metacognition. This holistic perspective is of particular use in our analysis given how powerfully the affective dimension played a role in team bonding and effective collaboration.

CASE STUDY AND ANALYSIS

General Methodology and Structure of Coding

Given that Raffaella Negretti's methodology from her 2012 article on novice composition student writers who kept journals best matched both the humanities-based context and the research narratives that were analyzed, it made the most sense to combine this method with an overall sense of how the students were becoming metaliterate learners through the process of collaborative research and writing. While Kathryn assessed students based on disciplinary standards and flagged particularly self-reflective narratives, Michele used the metaliteracy-oriented tracking codes to primarily evaluate the metacognitive dimension of metaliteracy. After Kathryn assessed the research narratives according to her disciplinary learning objectives, the research narratives submitted by students were coded by Michele based on the following categories:

TP for "task perception": Student perception of discrete research tasks was tracked as explained by the assignment handout. Student perception of tasks was looked at in terms of whether or not students were able to transcend the assignment's explanation of the task and think more metacognitively about what they were being asked to do.

SR for "self-regulation": With this code, students were tracked in terms of how they monitored their own progress and made strategic interventions. Included within this coding was also some metacognitive awareness/knowledge, including students' sense of what they were doing with their research strategies, how they were doing research, and why they were choosing to do what they did.

A for "affect": With this code, we looked at how emotion played a role in students' research process and ability to be metacognitive. We looked for moments when students explicitly articulated feeling empowered by certain individual research achievements or by their collaborative work with the other members of their group. We also noted when negatively stressful emotions were foregrounded in their narratives.

Through this coding process, several key themes emerged that help to illuminate the learners' and the teachers' experience of metaliteracy in this research-based learning project. One clear theme was that a greater sense of team cohesion and effective collaboration yielded better research results and a sense of empowerment; the most successful teams succeeded as they developed, collaboratively, into metaliterate learners.

Tracking Task Perception, Metacognitive Knowledge, Self-Regulation, and Affect

Most students were able to articulate what they were doing and how they were doing it once their task perceptions were clarified; that is to say, many narratives began with a sense of feeling lost, albeit, in many cases, excited about the work at hand. Interestingly enough, one student described his group's work as "setting forth," as though embarking on a kind of quest. In this sense, there was a strong resonance with Kuhlthau's groundbreaking work applying the constructivist paradigm to the search process.[20] Most of the students involved in the project needed to sit down with their classmates and begin grappling with concrete research tasks in order to get a better sense of what they were trying to accomplish and how they were trying to do it. In fact, given the themes that emerged through our analysis, it makes sense to talk about the teams in terms of a collaborative/metaliterate continuum, with different teams showing different levels of cohesion. Thus, the chart shown in figure 6.4 establishes teams based on a number order while also presenting them in terms of their levels of cohesion, collaboration, and metaliterate integration across the four learning domains.

While the process of working together helped students to integrate the metaliteracy learning domains, very few students were able to articulate *why* they were doing what they were doing, or the conditional knowledge that is a subcategory of metacognitive awareness. By and large, the students' answers to why they were doing what they were doing were based upon Kathryn's criteria for the assignment. At times, a few students began to realize that some of their tasks were somewhat arbitrary and that there might be overlap

TEAM NUMBER	COHESION	COLLABORATION	METALITERATE INTEGRATION
1	High	High	High
2	Low	Low	Low; two individuals excelled following their own paths
3	Medium	High	Medium
4	Medium	Medium	Medium
5	Low	Low	Low

FIGURE 6.4

Team Identification and Characteristics

between the groups, but rather than think about what that might mean about the enterprise, most worried about keeping on task.

Hence, when one student was able to articulate what, how, and why, as well as contextualize these within the parameters of the contribution to an encyclopedic open access project, his research portfolio really stood out as the most metacognitively aware. In fact, this student was the only one to articulate specifically how particular information might not be suited to the encyclopedia format; a few students were able to make the distinction between information that might be fascinating but not relevant. Thus, we both agreed that this particular student's research process narrative is the most worthy of being submitted as a possible blog entry on MoEML's official website. This student's ability to track his thought process and to self-regulate was unparalleled in comparison to that of the other submitted research portfolios.

It is interesting to note that this student was part of Team 2, a team that was not otherwise distinguished by metaliterate awareness through collaboration and cohesion. In fact, Team 2 had two members who excelled individually on a metacognitive level but who did not excel through collaboration as part of a group. The other member of Team 2 who individually excelled at metacognition generated her own research questions, independent of the assignment sheet. Task perception for many students was clarified only after team meetings, during which most went for a straightforward division of labor, mapping individual assignments to individual list numbers on Kathryn's assignment sheet. Very few groups or individuals strayed from a division of labor based on the handout that they received.

This member of Team 2's generation of her own research questions demonstrated a more sophisticated sense of task perception than was the case for the other students in the class. It is interesting to note that while this particular student ended feeling quite positively about one of her research triumphs, even texting a friend to let her know about it in the moment and highlighting it during her presentation, much of her research narrative was permeated by a sense of negative affect. The student referenced frustration frequently and even described having a tearful panic attack in the submitted research narrative. While the student was able to produce high-quality work, she did not appear to feel an overall sense of empowerment, at least not at the time when she was writing about the experience. More time away from the project may make a critical difference.

Perhaps one reason for the student's negative level of stress might have to do with a much lower sense of group cohesion; while other individual narratives strongly emphasized a sense of "we're in it together" or pleasure in the collaborative process, despite the division-of-labor approach, this particular student did not seem to feel supported by her team members. There was very little mention of interaction with other group members except for checking in about deadlines. The other individual in this team who excelled individually on a metacognitive level never mentioned his other team members in his narrative. The other two individuals in Team 2 were not negative about the project, but neither of them reported that a strong team bond had contributed to their progress.

In contrast, Team 1 worked very well together; strong metacognitive awareness developed through collaboration played a role in a number of ways. To begin with, through the process of working together, each member of Team 1 came to self-identify a particular strength that he or she could bring to the table, independent of the research tasks. As argued by Webb, Schirato, and Danaher, each student had individual literacies, but the students developed metaliteracy only "to the extent that they are able to understand each other's areas of knowledge."[21] Moreover, aside from identifying a good synthesizer and an effective note taker, the team also kept track of positive synergies between different roles. This was the only team that was organized enough to realize that there needed to be tagging done to the final article, and thus the only team that contacted Michele about this process. This contact with Michele about the metadata displayed a very high level of independence and a seriousness of purpose that aligned with these students' feeling empowered as learners. While the team had a leader of sorts, every member of this team seemed to feel empowered enough to believe that his or her individual metacognitive strengths were strong contributors to their overall success; both the process and the product had been truly collaborative for this team, and what they learned from one another would have a long-term or lifelong learning impact.[22]

Like Team 2, Team 4 distinguished itself through half of its members displaying a very strong sense of metacognitive awareness. Similar to Team 2, Team 4 also displayed a weaker sense of team cohesion. In terms of their most impressive intellectual contribution to the research, one team member generated a kind of "authority control" by creating a standardized information-gathering template for all team members to use. While the other groups dealt with the tagging required by the MoEML, this one individual had enough metacognitive awareness to understand why such an approach to information might be beneficial even within the scope of his group.

While the class had its own evaluation survey, the MoEML also has formulated a survey to help evaluate the effectiveness of its pedagogical partnerships. Tagging or coding was referenced much more in the survey done for the MoEML than it was in the research narratives, and the students seemed more interested in it as a process within that context. This might have something to do with task perception. While the students were always aware that their projects might be incorporated into the MoEML, they might have seen their research narrative as more of a class assignment and somehow separate from their digital contribution. Filling out a survey for the digital project could have had them thinking beyond the scope of how they were being assessed for their English class.

Another member of Team 4 distinguished herself metacognitively in a unique way since she approached both the writing and the research as metacognitive processes. Moreover, like the person in Team 2, she did not limit her task perception to what was written down on the class handout. Once the other members of Team 4 supplied her with their information, which was presented in a standardized format thanks to the template, this person created another standardized chart to synthesize all the different pieces of information. With each revision of the chart, she added new content and treated both the research and the writing as iterative processes. As is discussed in the conclusion, one way of reinventing information literacy may be to treat it more the way that we approach the teaching of writing, especially on a campus such as Washington College, with such a robust focus on composition and revision.

That students' approach to writing was far more sophisticated than their approach to research was particularly clear when it came to their approach to generating search strings. Several research narratives referenced trying "every permutation possible" of a search while not indicating having changed a search field, used Boolean operators, or tried advanced search. One student was searching for primary sources by using "primary source" as one of her search terms. It is important to note that none of these students contacted Michele about reformulating a search; the same student who claimed to have tried "every permutation" contacted Michele about an article behind a paywall but never questioned the set of assumptions that kept her from effectively revising her search strategies. The student did not have enough metacognitive awareness to question how she was building her search or why she might want to rethink the search string. While the students were able to produce high-quality work, these metacognitive gaps in terms of search behavior have strong implications for the metacognitive component of metaliteracy and for revising library instructional practices. As discussed in Mackey and Jacobson, students may misconstrue a search strategy as successful when in fact it only "skims the surface without digging deeper."[23]

Finally, another less positive metacognitive trend has to do with the nearly immediate classification of sources as "useful" or "useless" with little evaluation. Michele has seen this even with the most-advanced-level students; once students have grasped that there are peer-reviewed or scholarly sources, many are reluctant to use anything else. Students display an inability to adapt criteria that they have been given to evaluate a source, viewing them in a kind of popular versus scholarly dichotomy. Many students expressed reluctance to use online sources for this project; what they meant was "freely available through the Internet." Almost every research narrative in the case study classified sources at some point as either useful or useless. Given the predominance of this mind-set, one student in Team 1 stood out in her metacognitive self-awareness when she identified herself as an effective "filterer" of information with the ability to "sift" the relevant from the irrelevant. This student also stood out in terms of pointing out how her natural ability to do this improved over the course of the semester. That the student belonged to the team with the highest degree of cohesion and collaboration attests to her development as a metaliterate learner.

The teaching team's metacognitive awareness of pedagogy and collaboration developed through the first iteration of this project. In retrospect, Michele would have suggested meeting with teams once they had started their research process in lieu of, or as a supplement to, meeting with the class as a whole. Since each group's sense of task perception was strongly group driven, it might have incentivized their level of engagement with the instruction if it were tailored to their specific tasks. Since this was research-based learning, it would have made more sense to tailor instruction around specific problems being faced by the group rather than around a general introduction to pertinent resources. Perhaps the most effective element of the whole-class research session that resembled more of a one-shot session was Michele's asking a student to teach RefWorks to his classmates since he had come in with another class the previous week. By incorporating this into the class session, the student functioned as a teacher, one of the key participatory roles for metaliterate learners.

Moreover, a few more metacognitive "check-ins" would have assisted us in keeping track of what was going on in students' minds over time. On the other hand, letting the students go off on their own did have the benefit of conveying to the students that they were truly in charge of their own learning, and this seems to have promoted a greater sense of pride in their teamwork. Returning to Kuhlthau's work on mediators in the research process, it seems that structuring the check-ins as researchers checking in with other researchers would work much better than a check-in reminiscent of "looking over students' shoulders."[24] It was clear on the presentation day that students felt ownership over their work; intrusive check-ins may have conveyed that we did not trust them enough to be independent thinkers and researchers.

ASSESSMENT

Through assessment measures, the teaching team wanted to gauge how successful students had been at research but, more important, how reflective they could be about what they had gained from this experience. Aside from the coding of student narratives, we were also able to see the results of a survey administered by the MoEML on the last day of class. The survey was created by the MoEML to assess the efficacy of their pedagogical partnerships and to assist in making the process smoother for professors and students. Several survey items are tailor-made for a focus on metaliteracy. Four statements that were tested through use of a Likert scale aligned with key learning objectives for the metaliterate learner. The chart in figure 6.5 lists those statements as well as average and median scores for student agreement with those statements, with 1 = not achieved, 2 = somewhat achieved, 3 = achieved, 4 = largely achieved, and 5 = fully achieved.

In fact, question seven in the MoEML survey asks students to evaluate, upon completion of the project, whether or not they "can be not just a knowledge consumer but also a knowledge producer," a question that gets at the core of metaliteracy's goals for learners. In the case of our group of students, the average response was a very solid 3.84, with a median response of 4; this means that students felt that they had more than achieved this goal or, in the case of a 4 score, had "largely achieved" this goal. Nonetheless, the standard deviation for this statement was quite high compared with the statements related to

STATEMENT: At the end of the MoEML module, I . . .	MEAN	MEDIAN	STANDARD DEVIATION
. . . feel I can be not just a knowledge consumer but also a knowledge producer	3.84	4	1.07
. . . value collaborative work more highly (both with my classmates and with an international project)	3.44	4	1.34
. . . think undergraduates and/or graduates are capable of engaging in meaningful research	4.32	5	0.82
. . . am proud of the fact I contributed to a widely used online scholarly resource	4.42	5	0.84
SCALE: 1 = not achieved, 2 = somewhat achieved, 3 = achieved, 4 = largely achieved, and 5 = fully achieved.			

FIGURE 6.5

Survey Statement Analysis

pride in their work and advocating for this type of research as coursework. The standard deviation was greatest when it came to the statement about valuing collaborative work. This fact points to an interesting pattern that does bear itself out in the research narratives: two of the teams definitely flourished as metaliterate learners through collaboration, while the other teams did not see the same gains as teams.

The sense of pride that the students felt in the project was palpable during their presentations and clearly evident in the survey results. As indicated by the lower standard deviations of the last two statements, students felt strongly that they were capable of this kind of meaningful research and were proud of their contribution to this open access project.

CONCLUSION

This case study demonstrates that learners benefit tremendously from collaborative, research-based learning that depends on them working across several domains of metaliteracy. In this analysis, we have focused primarily on the metacognitive and the affective dimensions of metaliteracy. Except for one student who expressed dissatisfaction with the experience, the other nineteen students expressed vocal enthusiasm for the project. A few students articulated their renewed enthusiasm for scholarship and collaboration; some reported having forged a special bond with their team members. Nearly all expressed a strong pride in their work, including those who had some complaints. Students displayed a strong sense of responsibility; nearly all responded to Kathryn's request for revisions to their essays after the conclusion of the semester. The final work product was almost universally outstanding. Four of the five groups produced research and writing that (with some organization and editing by Kathryn) is ready to be incorporated into the final article to be submitted for peer review.

The case study also demonstrates that this experience can be enhanced by collaboration between professors and librarians. The same semester that Kathryn and Michele worked together, there was one other librarian-professor teaching team. Perhaps the expectation is that once students are juniors and seniors they have mastered the kinds of research skills that they will need to undertake this type of project. However, we argue that research is about much more than navigating database interfaces and is, in fact, a metaliteracy with complex cognitive, metacognitive, affective, and behavioral domains, and that collaborations such as this one provide a compelling and potentially more effective model.

By tracking students' task perception and self-regulation, educators can get a better sense of how students are thinking about their thinking and self-regulating their learning through a variety of interventions. Our coding schema could easily be adapted for a number of other research projects if self-reflective narratives are also required; a midpoint or quarterly "meta-cognitive check-in" would assist the teaching team in addressing issues in the moment. This type of insight into student learning from the student lens can assist librarians and professors in terms of revising their own pedagogical practices to address student learning gaps more effectively rather than guessing about those gaps in understanding. In a sense, this is much like requiring students to submit a rough draft of a paper since what is happening in both instances is that someone besides the students is being given access to an unfolding of their thoughts. The less polished the draft or research narrative, the more likely it is that the professor or librarian can track what the student is doing on a metacognitive level and engage in a more complex conversation about the research and/or writing process than would ordinarily be possible. As delineated by Donna Mazziotti (now Donna Witek) and Teresa Grettano, another librarian and English professor team, much can be done in terms of approaching research and writing on a united pedagogical front.[25]

Aside from the pedagogical potential of conceptualizing research and writing as analogous processes, this experience also demonstrates the value of a multilevel collaboration model for humanities research. In a nested model, the humanities researcher moves away from research as a solitary pursuit into a collaboration model that works so well precisely because it opens up teaching and learning into a dynamic information context, one that brings learners closer to one another, to their teachers, and to a much wider community of scholarship.

NOTES

1. Thomas P. Mackey and Trudi E. Jacobson, *Metaliteracy: Reinventing Information Literacy to Empower Learners* (Chicago: Neal-Schuman, 2014), 22–23.
2. James Elborg, "Critical Information Literacy: Implications for Instructional Practice," *Journal of Academic Librarianship* 32, no. 2 (2006): 198.
3. Mackey and Jacobson, *Metaliteracy*, 91.
4. Ibid., 91.
5. Ibid., 89.
6. Robert A. Wilson and Frank C. Keil, *The MIT Encyclopedia of the Cognitive Sciences* (Cambridge, MA: MIT Press, 1999), 355.
7. John Flavell, "Metacognition and Cognitive Monitoring: A New Area of Cognitive-Developmental Inquiry," *American Psychologist* 34, no. 10 (1979): 908.
8. Mackey and Jacobson, *Metaliteracy*, 13.
9. Raffaella Negretti, "Metacognition in Student Academic Writing: A Longitudinal Study of Metacognitive Awareness and Its Relation to Task Perception, Self-Regulation, and Evaluation of Performance," *Written Communication* 29, no. 2 (2012): 143.

10. Gregory Schraw, "Promoting General Metacognitive Awareness," in *Metacognition in Learning and Instruction: Theory, Research and Practice*, ed. Hope J. Hartman (Boston: Kluwer Academic Publishers, 2002), 4.
11. Negretti, "Metacognition in Student Academic Writing," 155.
12. Schraw, "Promoting General Cognitive Awareness," 5.
13. Michael Pressley and Elizabeth S. Ghatala. "Self-Regulated Learning: Monitoring Learning from Text," *Educational Psychologist* 25, no. 1 (1990): 19–33. doi:10.1207/s15326985ep2501_3.
14. Hope J. Hartman, *Metacognition in Learning and Instruction: Theory, Research and Practice* (Boston: Kluwer Academic Publishers, 2002).
15. Hartman, *Metacognition in Learning and Instruction*, xii.
16. Mackey and Jacobson, *Metaliteracy*, 86.
17. Carol Collier Kuhlthau, *Seeking Meaning: A Process Approach to Library and Information Services* (Norwood, NJ: Ablex, 1993), xxiii.
18. Ibid., 36.
19. Negretti, "Metacognition in Student Academic Writing," 147.
20. Kuhlthau, *Seeking Meaning*, 44.
21. Jen Webb, Tony Schirato, and Geoff Danaher, *Understanding Bourdieu* (London: SAGE Publications, 2002), 143.
22. Mackey and Jacobson, *Metaliteracy*, 90.
23. Ibid., 11.
24. Kuhlthau, *Seeking Meaning*.
25. Donna Mazziotti and Teresa Grettano, "'Hanging Together': Collaboration between Information Literacy and Writing Programs Based on the ACRL Standards and the WPA Outcomes," in *Proceedings of the ACRL 2011 Conference* (Chicago: American Library Association, 2011), 180–90, www.ala.org/acrl/sites/ala.org.acrl/files/content/conferences/confsandpreconfs/national/2011/papers/hanging_together.pdf.

BIBLIOGRAPHY

Elborg, James. "Critical Information Literacy: Implications for Instructional Practice." *Journal of Academic Librarianship* 32, no. 2 (2006): 192–99.

Flavell, John H. "Metacognition and Cognitive Monitoring: A New Area of Cognitive-Developmental Inquiry." *American Psychologist* 34, no. 10 (1979): 906–11.

Hartman, Hope J. *Metacognition in Learning and Instruction: Theory, Research and Practice*. Boston: Kluwer Academic Publishers, 2002.

Kuhlthau, Carol Collier. *Seeking Meaning: A Process Approach to Library and Information Services*. Norwood, NJ: Ablex, 1993.

Mackey, Thomas P., and Trudi E. Jacobson. *Metaliteracy: Reinventing Information Literacy to Empower Learners*. Chicago: Neal-Schuman, 2014.

Mazziotti, Donna, and Teresa Grettano. "'Hanging Together': Collaboration between Information Literacy and Writing Programs Based on the ACRL Standards and the WPA Outcomes." In *Proceedings of the ACRL 2011 Conference*, 180–90. Chicago: American Library Association, 2011. www.ala.org/acrl/sites/ala .org.acrl/files/content/conferences/confsandpreconfs/national/2011/papers/ hanging_together.pdf.

Negretti, Raffaella. "Metacognition in Student Academic Writing: A Longitudinal Study of Metacognitive Awareness and Its Relation to Task Perception, Self-Regulation, and Evaluation of Performance." *Written Communication* 29, no. 2 (2012): 142–79.

Pressley, Michael, and Elizabeth S. Ghatala. "Self-Regulated Learning: Monitoring Learning from Text." *Educational Psychologist* 25, no. 1 (1990): 19–33. doi:10.1207/s1532698ep2501_3.

Webb, Jen, Tony Schirato, and Geoff Danaher. *Understanding Bourdieu*. London: SAGE Publications, 2002.

KRISTINE N. STEWART
and DAVID M. BROUSSARD

7

Promoting Empowerment through Metaliteracy

A Case Study of Undergraduate Learning Outcomes

THIS CHAPTER PRESENTS A CASE STUDY THAT ILLUSTRATES how empowered, metaliterate learners were developed through a reinvention of undergraduate learning outcomes. We focus specifically on the competencies in a semester-long (sixteen-week), face-to-face, one-credit, undergraduate course at the University of Missouri. Although the curriculum of the course, Information Use and Student Success (IUSS), was based on the Association of College and Research Libraries' (ACRL) *Information Literacy Competency Standards for Higher Education* from 2000,[1] it has evolved from one that teaches information literacy skills to one that develops metaliteracy competencies. This chapter demonstrates why dramatic changes in today's dynamic information environment required this critical shift to metaliteracy.

Information literacy competency as described by ACRL in 2000 was appropriate for that time; however, the information settings in which students now operate are vastly different. Today's world is socially connected, technology enhanced, and networked through multiple devices and linked communities. Although the standards that guided the creation of IUSS's curriculum and pedagogical goals remained unaltered, the actual content of the course did change. These revisions were made to reflect the transformation we have seen in the information environment and the competencies required for learners to flourish in the current information age. Our new look at the learning outcomes and how to teach information literacy was influenced by "the making, mixing, and sharing of knowledge through multimodal and constantly shifting technologies."[2] This case study shows how this new perspective had a positive impact on the revision process and, ultimately, on the learners in this course.

Metaliteracy provides a framework that expands upon earlier conceptions by Zurkowski and ACRL of what it means to be information literate.[3] The metaliteracy framework developed by Mackey and Jacobson addresses how students both use and produce information.[4] Metaliteracy recognizes that learners are no longer passive information recipients; they now communicate, create, and distribute information in a highly social and participatory information environment. Metaliteracy promotes not only the evaluation and consumption of information but also the production and sharing of information through social media and emerging technologies.[5]

The case study presented here explores how undergraduate students apply metaliteracy abilities to areas of their lives outside of the classroom. The aim is to understand how lifelong learning is manifested through the development of critical thinking in multiple information environments. Using student reflection papers ($N = 127$) as a source of data from IUSS, the real-life applications and contributions of metaliteracy competency are illustrated. The chapter also provides an overview of approaches to metaliteracy instruction and assessment that goes beyond the teaching of skills and tools.

RELATED LITERATURE

The relevant literature that informs this research falls into three main categories: (1) changes in the information environment and the competencies required to flourish in this environment; (2) approaches to the assessment of information literacy skills and metaliteracy abilities; (3) the shift from ACRL's *Information Literacy Competency Standards for Higher Education* to its *Framework for Information Literacy for Higher Education*.[6]

Changes in the Information Environment and Related Competencies

The world has changed drastically since the conception of information literacy by Paul Zurkowski in 1974. The "tools and techniques"[7] referenced by Zurkowski in his seminal report on information literacy are no longer sufficient to survive and thrive in the current information age. To be *truly* information literate, one must have metaliteracy competencies.

We live in a radically different information age—we literally live *in* the information landscape. Our personal and professional lives are based and managed online through social media, online communities, and open learning commons. As Mackey and Jacobson write, "We are constantly on the go as transient digital citizens, and technology is used to get us there and to create and share information in multiple forms (text, image, video, voice, map) from any location along the way."[8] It wasn't until 2005 that a modernized, Global Positioning System (GPS) satellite was launched for use by civilians on mobile phones.[9] Only a decade later, GPS is now embedded in our lives for the purposes of basic navigation and through our use of social media.

The technologies we use on a daily basis are highly social and collaborative. It is for this reason that information literacy has become much more than a set of skills; it is a metacognitive approach to understanding information.[10] To that end, critical reflexivity is a key component of the metaliteracy framework as it empowers students to adapt and change alongside the current information landscape. As a reinvention of information literacy, metaliteracy "prepares our learners to engage in the information environment as active, self-reflective, and critical contributors."[11]

Metaliteracy expands on previous notions of information literacy through a connection to other theories of literacy, but with an added dimension. Metaliteracy provides an "overarching model for connecting related literacies with an emphasis on emerging technologies."[12] This model put forth by Mackey and Jacobson reframes information literacy by integrating a greater understanding of multiple intelligences, multiliteracies, multimodal literacy, and transliteracy.[13] However, metaliteracy differs from these prior theories of literacy because metaliteracy focuses much more on the convergence of related information literacies and the expanded abilities needed to excel across various media formats.[14]

Approaches to Assessment

For over a decade, information literacy instruction, evaluation, and research in the United States have been guided by ACRL's *Information Literacy Competency Standards*.[15] A large portion of the research on information literacy relies on quantitative skill measurements and test scores in evaluation.[16] While these studies lay the groundwork on *what* students learn, they are limited in their explanations of *how* students learn and their actual experiences with information. In order to provide a deeper understanding of what is learned and the ways in which knowledge is applied, quantitative measures must be supplemented with qualitative investigation. This is of particular importance in the current post–information age as information formats are now vastly different. In contrast to physical resources, accessible only in person, we now have "interactive user-generated information written in, referenced to, and shared through a sprawling social network."[17]

The heavy use of quantitative methods of assessment, as noted earlier, is not surprising given the current environment of higher education in which institutions, academic departments, and libraries are increasingly asked to prove their worth.[18] A stark increase in the assessment of student learning for the purposes of institutional effectiveness in American universities occurred after the release of the report *A Test of Leadership: Charting the Future of U.S. Higher Education* by the Commission on the Future of Higher Education.[19] The report emphasized the "importance of objective and direct measurement of student learning outcomes."[20] While the implications of institutional assessment in higher education are less consequential than in K–12, it's important to bear in mind that Millennials grew up under the No Child Left Behind (NCLB) Act and thus have undergone assessments throughout their educational careers. A study of American college students' attitudes toward institutional accountability assessments by Zilberberg and colleagues revealed students regard these assessments with skepticism.[21] Zilberberg's findings also showed that these assessments increase adverse attitudes of students toward assessment, resulting in "undesirable test-taking behavior, thereby compromising validity of inferences made from test scores."[22]

In addition to questions of validity of inferences from quantitative assessment, there is a second area of concern: research and assessment on information literacy competency is, by and large, from the perspectives of librarians and instructors. This is problematic because while this research is informed by instructors' experiences, it lacks the perspectives of the actual learners involved. In an analysis of Bruce's *Seven Faces of Information Literacy*,[23] Andretta discusses the relational frame of information by which learning may be explored, not from the perspective of an information-literate professional (such as a librarian or an academic), but from that of the learner.[24] This holistic approach to information literacy assessment is demonstrated, not through the more traditional quantitative skills assessment, but through an exploration of the qualitative changes in *how* individuals perceive and interact with information and the world around them. This approach facilitates a shift from the perception of the instructor to the views and experiences of learners and allows for more complex understandings of information interaction, competency, and characteristics.[25]

ACRL's *Framework for Information Literacy for Higher Education* emphasizes metaliteracy competencies, which include the ability to adapt to the rapidly changing information environment, high levels of critical thinking, and "analysis about how we develop our self-conception of information literacy as metacognitive learners."[26] ACRL's *Information Literacy Competency Standards for Higher Education* provided a framework "for assessing the information literate individual"[27] through five standards and twenty-two performance indicators. While skills may be measured according to indicators and outcomes, how does one evaluate metaliteracy competencies such as self-reflection? Furthermore, what are the real-life applications of metaliteracy competency?

Transitioning from the Standards to the Framework

ACRL's *Information Literacy Competency Standards for Higher Education* has received criticism in past years for being outdated[28] and too rigid,[29] lacking the full array of information competencies,[30] and "insufficient for the proposed model of information literacy."[31] Although the original *Information Literacy Competency Standards for Higher Education* has met with criticism, so has ACRL's *Framework for Information Literacy for Higher Education*. Less than a month prior to the formal adoption of ACRL's *Framework*, a group of librarians from New Jersey voiced their concerns regarding the *Framework* in an open letter.[32] Primary concerns expressed in this open letter include the implementation of the *Framework*, assessing outcomes of such a "theoretical document,"[33] and the belief that the *Standards* are not outdated.[34]

True to its name, the *Framework* provides a basic structure of "conceptual understandings that organize many other concepts and ideas about information, research, and scholarship in a coherent whole."[35] While it is understandable that the lack of prescribed structure to instruction and assessment in the *Framework* may be intimidating, it also provides librarians and information professionals with the opportunity for further development as professionals. Just as metaliteracy competency requires critical self-reflection of students, it can also assist librarians and instructors in doing the same.

Char Booth's book *Reflective Teaching, Effective Learning: Instructional Literacy for Library Educators* emphasizes the importance of practicing constructive self-awareness in teaching and reflective practices.[36] Think of it as practicing what you preach. Metaliterate individuals have the "capability to adapt to changing technologies and learning environments. . . . This requires a high level of critical thinking and analysis of how we develop our self-conception of information literacy as metacognitive learners in open and social media environments."[37] With the principles of metaliteracy in mind, the *Framework* opens the way and encourages librarians and instructors to redesign courses, collaborate on research, involve students in research and assessment, and engage in a broader dialogue on student learning.[38] ACRL's *Information Literacy Competency Standards for Higher Education* were intended to be as applicable as possible, but in reality, application requires critical reflection as the context of instruction varies by institution. Colleges and universities differ greatly, as does the format of instruction, be it online, in a credit-bearing class, or in a one-shot session in a library.[39]

As an "overarching and unifying framework"[40] built on the core competencies of information literacy, metaliteracy emphasizes the increased roles and responsibilities that students have in not only the consumption but also the creation of new knowledge.[41] Many have had adverse reactions to the *Framework*; however, this is a good thing. Past conceptions of what it means to be "information literate" need to be revitalized and the profession needs to evolve. The academic library does not exist independent of its institutional context. As Beilin and Foasberg conclude in their response to the open letter on the *Framework*:

> Like the rest of academia [we] should put into action the results of research not only produced by ourselves, but throughout academia and beyond (and yes, that includes theory!). . . . were we to avoid theory, we would lose one of our great opportunities of such a revision—the chance to carefully examine what we do and the philosophy that under-lies it.[42]

CONTEXT

This study was conducted at the University of Missouri (MU), which is located in the midwestern United States in central Missouri. MU was the first public university founded west of the Mississippi River (in 1839) and is the largest public research university in the state of Missouri.[43] MU offers over 300 degree programs spread throughout nineteen colleges and schools.[44] Traditional students (aged eighteen to twenty-two) make up 70 percent of MU's enrollment of over 35,000 students.[45] Seventy percent of MU students come from within the state, with minority populations accounting for 16 percent of enrolled students.[46]

Course Context

IUSS is a semester-long (sixteen-week), face-to-face, one-credit, undergraduate course. As a credit-bearing course, IUSS is taught outside of the academic library in a school within the College of Education. In the past, the course was a requirement for all undergraduate students at the university. Presently, it is now listed among many other one-credit courses from which undergraduates may choose to fulfill a student success requirement. Students enrolled in the course are primarily traditional students at the freshman and sophomore levels.

The pedagogical goals of IUSS are to

- teach students research skills using library and online resources;
- teach students search strategies and evaluation techniques to improve academic performance; and
- prepare students for college-level research demands that require students have the ability to frame meaningful questions, understand the structure and content of information resources,

evaluate available information and information sources, and use information resources as genuine learning tools.

As previously stated, IUSS was a course based on ACRL's *Standards*. Although the *Standards* that guided the creation of the IUSS curriculum remained unchanged, along with the pedagogical goals of the course, the actual content of the course and approaches to learning in the course did change.

Information is viewed as a commodity in the ACRL *Standards*, but IUSS aims to promote the development of learners who are more than just information consumers. As addressed in the ACRL *Framework*, information has many different "dimensions of value"; in addition to information's value as a commodity, it is also a means of education, influence, and mode to understand the world.[47] Learners in the twenty-first century are immersed in an entirely new information landscape; they need to be active, self-reflective, and critical contributors in our information society.[48] The metacognitive component of metaliteracy encourages students to concentrate and reflect on their experiences engaging in various information environments where they produce, share, and consume information.[49] As social media have an important role in the lives of students enrolled in IUSS, as Millennials, their highly digital lives and the metacognitive component of metaliteracy were important considerations when making updates to the curriculum.[50]

Changes to IUSS included (1) a new approach to understanding information with an emphasis on the difference between information and knowledge; (2) integration of multimedia exercises and group activities; (3) an investigation of social media sources; (4) the introduction to the management of information found online, both information encountered passively (through social media) as well as serendipitously while searching online.

Curriculum of IUSS

The curriculum of the course is structured around the creation of an annotated bibliography in an assignment we refer to as the Paper Trail. This assignment was created in July 2011 based on an exercise in *Teaching Information Literacy: 50 Standards-Based Exercises for College Students*[51] and adapted in order to facilitate the course's objectives. The assignment was first implemented in the fall semester of 2011 and has been revised three times since then in order to clarify the expectations of the assignment and to reflect the evolving content of the course.

Throughout the semester, students create a written record of the resources they find to answer a research question of their own creation. Students are not expected to write an actual research paper. The Paper Trail is an ongoing project in the class, and students are introduced to or assigned specific portions of the project throughout the semester. The required sections of the Paper Trail assignment are illustrated in table 7.1.

TABLE 7.1

Contents of Paper Trail Assignment

SECTION	ITEM	DETAILS
1	Research statement	Single page with one or two paragraphs describing your topic, how/why you chose it, and the context within which you framed your research
2	Research question	State your research question below your research statement
3	Concept map	Final copy of your concept map (digital copy or a scanned, hand-written copy)
4	Annotated bibliography of relevant and useful sources	Compile all the sources you decide to use in your annotated bibliography; sources should be listed alphabetically by author
5	Research summary	A thoughtful essay on your semester's work

TABLE 7.2

Timetable of the Introduction and Deadlines for Sections of the Paper Trail

	SESSION (WEEK) OF CLASS	
Paper Trail Sections	**Introduced**	**Due**
General overview of Paper Trail project	Session 1	Finals week
Research topics of interest	Session 2	Session 3
Gather possible sources	Session 2	Ongoing
Selection and formulation of research question	Session 3	Session 5
Rough draft	Session 10	Session 13

Dates for the introduction of topics and deadlines for specific portions of the assignment are stated in class and listed in the course schedule as shown in table 7.2. The course schedule is posted in Blackboard and available to students for the entirety of the semester. The semester-long assignment is introduced during the first class session of the semester so that students begin thinking of their research topic immediately. During the second session a description, rubric, and example of the assignment are handed out (an electronic version is also made available to students via Blackboard).

A component of the Paper Trail is the research summary (as noted in table 7.1). The research summary is meant to be a thoughtful reflection on the work completed throughout the students' work on the Paper Trail assignment and has two parts. The first is a reflection on the students' research statement and question; the second is a reflection on the knowledge and information habits they have developed over the semester. It is the second part of the research summary that is used for analysis in this case study.

Earlier renditions of the course, much like ACRL's *Standards*, focused on acquiring skills. IUSS aims to go beyond these traditional conceptions of information literacy to reflect the changes (and challenges) of the post–information -age society. In order to accomplish this, it is crucial that students learn to apply knowledge and conceptions of information and their own learning outside of academia as lifelong learners.

Flavell acknowledged the impact of metacognition on lifelong learning and argued "metacognitive abilities can be developed through teaching strategies."[52] Metacognition requires a high level of critical thinking and moves beyond the development of mere skills. As a metacognitive concept, metaliteracy instruction empowers students to use, change, create, and contribute information sources, critically and in a variety of formats.[53] It is for this reason that metacognition was selected as the conceptual model used to make the transition in IUSS from a skills-based information literacy course to one that encouraged the development of metaliteracy abilities.

As Mackey and Jacobson discuss, literacy has a complex relationship with technology.[54] To foster the development of metaliteracy abilities in IUSS students, new competencies and expanded learning objectives were integrated into the course curriculum. These competencies and learning objectives considered mass media and social media trends that "combine verbal, visual, textual, and aural information."[55] As an example, one course session is focused on news media and is well aligned with the first goal of metaliteracy, "Evaluate content critically, including dynamic, online content that changes and evolves, such as article preprints, blogs, and wikis."[56] Learning objectives in this session include identifying bias, misrepresentation (e.g., overestimating crime rates via sensationalism), and understanding how news media operate within a profit-driven industry. As opposed to teaching basic evaluation skills to students, this session requires students to develop their own abilities and then reflect on their experiences.

This course session incorporates a multimedia format that requires students to evaluate videos as well as examine news articles on the same event in online and traditional formats. Students are provided equal amounts of time with each form of information and then are asked to reflect on the following: facts included, message communicated, the creator, target audience, the purpose of creation, and tone. While this may sound like a very skills-based approach, it wasn't at all. Students were asked to reflect on differences in the formats and types of media and examine how the presence (or lack thereof) of images and audio impact how they receive and evaluate content. Additionally, as a class, students discussed which form of media impacted them the most and why. This allowed the students, themselves, to examine their own information abilities, such as how they may establish authority unknowingly based on the format of information and how they obtained it (e.g., their Internet homepage, through a friend on Facebook, etc.).

METALITERACY CASE STUDY

We chose to use qualitative research methods in this study because we wanted to know *how* students apply the knowledge learned in class outside the confines of the course as opposed to assessing *what* they learned. These types of findings are not ones that can be examined or measured by quantity, frequency, or intensity.[57] More specifically, we wanted to know what non-skills-based outcomes (e.g., lifelong learning) result from metaliteracy competency.

Based on our research objectives, we conducted a qualitative content analysis of the research summaries from the Paper Trail assignments of students. Content analysis is a methodology used to study the content of communication and is frequently used in the analysis of text-based documents.[58] Analysis of student research summaries focused on the subjective meanings that students attributed to their information experiences throughout the semester, both inside and outside of class. This is particularly important in an investigation of metaliteracy abilities because of the emphasis on critical reflection. The metacognitive experience of metaliteracy encourages learners to make decisions based on prior experiences, feelings, and beliefs regarding information and knowledge.[59]

Student summaries used for analysis in this study were collected for one academic school year. This resulted in an initial sample of 152 student papers. Since only a portion of the research summary was used in the analysis, this portion of each paper was extracted and copied into a fresh document in order to keep data from each paper separate and to track the number of student papers available for inclusion in the sample. No identifying information (e.g., name, course section, instructor) was included in this study.

We conducted two rounds of analysis on student papers. We performed relevance (or purposive) sampling during the first round of analysis in order to determine which papers should be included in the study's sample of papers for final analysis. While all student papers included a reflective summary, some of the students failed to answer questions posed to them in the assignment. Consequently, after this first round of analysis our sample was lowered from 152 student papers to 127. While this sampling technique lowered the number of units included in our sample, those student papers selected for inclusion in this analysis all contained relevant information.[60]

Together we read and analyzed the first twenty research summaries. We each took notes during this process and together created an initial list and description of themes to be used as a codebook and measurement instrument (see table 7.3). Although this codebook contains themes that at face value are

TABLE 7.3

Codebook

CODE	ABBREVIATION
Technology–Other	TO
Technology–Library	TD
Technology–Internet Sources and Tools	TI
Citation	Cit
Confidence	Con
Critical Thinking	CT
Evaluation	E
Information Management	IM
Library Skills	LS
Research	R
Search Strategies	SS
Share Information with Others	S
N/A	N/A

associated with information literacy, many of these themes contained deeper levels of meaning than those attributed to the more skills-based approach of information literacy. As an example, in addition to mentioning changes in the ways the student searches for and evaluates information, one student notes, "I am still not an excellent researcher, but my ability to conduct research has improved greatly." Statements such as these demonstrate the use of critical reflection on the process of learning, which in turn provides students with new insight into their own knowledge and abilities. Other themes in the codebook connected to metaliteracy include other forms of technology and Internet sources, citation (many students demonstrated the ability to cite sources but also acknowledged the importance of recognizing ideas and sources), increased confidence, deeper forms of evaluation, information management, research, and sharing information.

As we coded the first twenty research summaries together, we discussed any disagreements we had in coding until an agreement was reached. This was done in order to establish intercoder reliability, thus ensuring reproducibility during the coding of the remaining student papers as well as reliability of this study.[61] Each researcher then worked independently to analyze the remaining 107 student papers. When one of us encountered a statement that could not be easily classified or did not appear to fit any of the themes identified in the codebook, the paper was saved until the end so that we could work together to reach a consensus on its classification.

FINDINGS

Our objectives revolved around gaining an increased understanding of how lifelong learning is manifested through the development of critical thinking skills in the post–information age. In terms of skills-based findings, we were not surprised to learn that many of the students cited increased or new knowledge and skills associated with traditional information literacy, such as the ability to use and locate library resources (e.g., library databases and the library catalog), cite sources correctly, evaluate information, conduct research, and utilize search strategies (see table 7.4 for tallies of individual instances and table 7.3 for the codebook).

TABLE 7.4

Skills-Based Outcomes

TD	CIT	E	IM	LS	R	SS
70	5	83	5	26	8	44

For example, one student references a new approach to research in general:

> I now know where the library is, where to find books, and even where to ask for help. There are writing tutors and people everywhere to help. . . . There are so many databases to find great articles. Before this class, I used Google for everything. I would never branch out from the first page of results.

Along the same lines, another student references an increased knowledge of and ability to access relevant information:

> I would use mainly books and online websites. I overlooked valuable resources such as academic journals, databases, and articles. By learning how these resources help me to get more useful information will also help in expanding my research efforts. I've also learned ways to organize information better and how to expand on topics that I thought I couldn't explain any further.

Students also reference improved search strategies and a basic understanding of evaluation methods:

> I now know how to use the library website and how to navigate databases. . . . I also pay more attention to how I evaluate my sources as well. I never really thought about the credibility of my sources that much. This class has taught me that credibility is actually extremely important.

> I now look for authors and where and when they found their material. I
> have become a lot more conscience [*sic*] of my research.

In addition to the skills-based outcomes associated with information literacy instruction, students also cite instances indicative of metaliteracy instruction. Although the number of instances reported by students is less (see table 7.5), the results are encouraging. Students note a familiarity with new technologies, Internet sources and tools, increased confidence in finding and using information, and sharing information and information competencies with others.

To organize these findings, we refer to four of the goals of Mackey and Jacobson's metaliteracy framework.[62]

TABLE 7.5
Non-Skills-Based Outcomes

TO	TI	CON	CT	S
18	11	24	11	4

GOAL 1
Evaluate content critically, including dynamic online content that changes and evolves, such as article preprints, blogs, and wikis.

In the past, resources were most frequently published in print, making scholarly or popular resources easier to categorize; however, with the rise of digitization, this process is not as simple as it once was. Information is now primarily less structured and easier to access online through social outlets such as blogs, wikis, and social media.[63] Mackey and Jacobson emphasize that metaliterate learners must have an understanding of the format and context of these sources; the element of evaluation plays an important role in this goal.[64]

Several students in IUSS demonstrated their competency in this first goal through reflections regarding their own use of the social media and mass media. One student refers to the use of Twitter, for example: "I learned to be more skeptical of information from every source. Social media like Twitter can be misleading. I've learned to not trust everything you see on a social media website or account." Another student mentions the evaluation of images in the reflection: "It is hard to determine what is real or what is factual on the internet in social media but in this class I did learn how to verify if pictures on twitter are actually real or not."

Additionally, students display a deeper understanding of the format and context of resources; "From one class I learned how visualizing a video and just simply reading an article has a huge effect on my opinion of the situation. I learned that pictures can be more descriptive than words." Another student discusses the importance of understanding the context of information and scope of one's research:

> Multiple news sources are owned by different corporations and you must constantly check the information you find against other information from a different source. This is important because there may be bias towards a subject . . . from one source that could give you something you are not interested in.

GOAL 2
Understand personal privacy, information ethics, and intellectual property issues in changing technology environments.

While the original ACRL *Standards* addressed issues of intellectual property, the state of intellectual property has changed vastly since the *Standards* were written. As Jacobson and Mackey note, "personal privacy has taken on a new meaning in collaborative social settings when users are willing to share so much information online."[65] While Millennials are heavy social media users, Jacobson and O'Keefe[66] and Mackey and Jacobson[67] note that this generation of students is unaware of many related issues concerning their privacy and digital footprint.

One student, concerned with personal online privacy, offers a solution: "I learned about my search history on the Internet and will now use in-private browsing for this." An additional eight students express concern over the implications of browsing history on filter bubbles. Menchaca posits that the implications of the relationship between social media and learning include critical thinking.[68] The implications of which Menchaca spoke were present in student reflections from IUSS. One student states, "I learned that the Internet is tailoring their search results to our own interests." Another student states, "I feel concerned about the information I receive and wonder what information I want is being held back because of the filter bubble."

GOAL 3
Share information and collaborate in a variety of participatory environments.

This third goal is concerned with the collaborative and sharing aspects of metaliteracy, with an emphasis on "producing information in open and online communities."[69] Social media were mentioned in several student reflections, which could be indicative of participation in open and online spaces; however, only one of these statements alludes to the student's actual concerns regarding participation and sharing online: "I feel like I learned to be more cautious now online when I use Facebook."

Metaliterate individuals participate in sharing information both ethically and responsibly. As Mackey and Jacobson note, ideally, this includes both contributing to social spaces as well as reflecting on their own thinking and participation as a collaborative participant.[70] Additional findings in this study include statements by students regarding sharing and collaboration in the participatory environment of their other classes. Student reflections exude confidence and self-empowerment in the abilities they amassed throughout the semester, so much so that students are comfortable sharing their new skills and resources with others:

> On my English paper we had to do an annotated bibliography and I used the CRAAP [currency, relevance, authority, accuracy, purpose] method we learned to figure out if the source was a good source or not. I also suggested to a girl in my English class to use the CRAAP method as well and it really helped her a lot.

Another student states, "I have already once passed on a better way to search to a friend of mine. I showed her that she could find articles using Academic Search Complete; she appreciated it." Knowledge gained through active information seeking, evaluation, and use through in-class collaboration prepared IUSS students to make the transition from learner to teacher when outside of the classroom.

GOAL 4
Demonstrate ability to connect learning and research strategies with lifelong learning processes and personal, academic, and professional goals.

This fourth goal is concerned with the metacognitive dimension of metaliteracy and is a critical component of Mackey and Jacobson's metaliteracy framework. Metacognition is, in essence, thinking about one's own thinking.[71] A metacognitive approach to learning encourages critical thinking based on previous experiences. It assists students in reflecting on and adapting their abilities to changes in the information landscape as well as changes in their own lives through critical thinking and problem solving.[72]

Nearly every student reflection indicates that students believe their abilities to find and use information had improved since the start of class. Some students, however, take their reflections a step further and demonstrate a higher level of critical thinking, for example:

> Some of the things I learned will carry over and be useful for the rest of
> my life. Knowing how to use citations is extremely important for when
> I write research papers or am doing graduate schoolwork in the future.

Although the initial statement by the student is a generic explanation for
what the student has learned in class, the student is able to match these new
abilities with a future aspiration, graduate school. This student also expresses
an awareness of the lifelong value of such abilities, another outcome associated with this fourth goal.

DISCUSSION

The metaliteracy model by Mackey and Jacobson expands upon ACRL's core
components of information literacy through four additional characteristics
of the information environment: collaboration, participation, production (of
information), and sharing (of information).[73] Student papers in this study
reveal that in addition to more traditional outcomes of information literacy
instruction (e.g., use of library resources and evaluation techniques), students
in IUSS also report learning outcomes in line with the four overarching goals
of metaliteracy instruction. Students report using new Internet tools and
resources, express concerns regarding their own information behaviors online
(e.g., social media presence and digital footprints), note increased confidence
in their skills and abilities, and engage in sharing their new knowledge and
skills from class with others. As a model that promotes higher levels of critical thinking and collaboration, metaliteracy instruction eases the transition
between traditional literacy instruction and the online environment in which
students now primarily operate.[74]

Confidence gained from information literacy instruction is often associated with self-perceived competency on behalf of the students in their ability
to perform tasks associated with information literacy. However, as Molteni
and Chan note, students' self-confidence ratings are not reliable indicators of
competence;[75] this is what differentiates the findings of this case study from
others. Student reflections not only indicate self-confidence; they also *demonstrate* ability. By incorporating different types of media into existing curriculum, students become not only skilled researchers but also teachers. IUSS
students demonstrate self-empowerment through interaction and sharing of
knowledge in collaborative environments (both online and in person).

Limitations in this study revolve around the unit of analysis (student
papers) and time constraints. While students will, in theory, write a thoughtful and genuine reflection on their information skills, the unit of analysis in
this study is a graded class assignment and as such may influence what students write. Additionally, this study only covers the use of information skills
and metaliteracy competencies outside of the classroom as the result of current course curriculum.

Future iterations of the course based on the findings of this initial study may be used to learn how different approaches to teaching metaliteracy principles affect how students develop, conceptualize, and apply metaliteracy competencies more specifically in their lives. The most visible gap found in student learning outcomes was in the fourth goal of the metaliteracy model, in which students connect learning with lifelong processes and other long-term goals. After addressing this gap in the curriculum, revisiting student learning outcomes once more may provide insight into different approaches used to develop metaliteracy competencies.

Despite the limitations of this study, student reflection papers reveal that in addition to learning skills associated with more traditional conceptions of information literacy, students are also applying skills and knowledge from class to additional Internet and social media resources. Students communicate an increase in their self-confidence and are empowered to share their knowledge and abilities with others, acting both as learners and teachers.

CONCLUSION

This study presented the learning outcomes of students enrolled in a class, which in addition to the teaching of more traditional conceptions of information literacy also included sessions on the production, sharing, and evaluation of information created in digital environments. Through student reflection papers, this study illustrates how metaliteracy instruction fosters student learning and development outside of the classroom. Furthermore, it provides alternative approaches to teaching and assessment, which may aid in the development of metaliteracy abilities.

Based on the findings from this study, we know that *some* students do leave the course with metaliteracy abilities; however, these findings are not as pronounced as others. Student reflections indicate that students apply their metaliteracy abilities outside of class when using social media and accessing other multimedia information resources, as well as for their work in other classes. Although few in number, some student reflections demonstrate an ability to connect the strategies learned in class to future academic and professional goals as well as different formats of information. This ability to reflect on past experiences and strategies and adapt them to new information situations is an indicator of a metaliterate individual.

Student learning outcomes from this study indicate that IUSS students are developing metaliteracy abilities that strongly align with the first three goals of the metaliteracy model put forth by Mackey and Jacobson, and to a lesser extent the fourth goal.[76] This study implies, however, that in order to accomplish learning outcomes associated with metaliteracy, student learning must be developed over a period of time. As a semester-long course, IUSS has an advantage over one-shot sessions. Instructors of IUSS have the privilege of spending one hour per week for an entire semester with students (sixteeen class sessions total). Rather than throwing students directly into library and other information resources, we are able to devote time building upon the current technological competencies of students. This time allowance also provides us with the opportunity to engage in active and collaborative learning with students continuously over a period of time, which allows for self-reflection in the learning process. This approach to learning does not occur in one-shot instructional sessions.

One-shot instructional sessions do not provide enough time to teach information literacy learning outcomes nor metaliteracy abilities. As an instructional method created to teach tools, this approach is outdated. While the creation of a credit-bearing course may be unrealistic, there are alternatives, which may require that we reconceptualize the way we view our role as instructors or increase collaboration between librarians and faculty members to foster reflective, adaptable, and self-empowered learners.

To be truly information literate in this post–information age, students need to be actively engaged in the socially constructed multimedia environment in which we live. Metaliteracy requires "critical reflection about individual and collaborative learning and active engagement in the production of new knowledge,"[77] thereby demanding a shift in instructional methods. As Mackey and Jacobson state, "metaliteracy shifts the emphasis from a set of discrete skills one learns in an information session to an iterative process of reflection and interactivity."[78] Information literacy instruction has evolved with changes in the information environment and based on the needs and resources of faculty and librarians. In order to develop metaliterate learners, a more radical and overarching shift in instruction needs to occur.

NOTES

1. Association of College and Research Libraries (ACRL), *Information Literacy Competency Standards for Higher Education* (Chicago: American Library Association, 2000), www.ala.org/acrl/sites/ala.org.acrl/files/content/standards/standards.pdf.

2. Thomas P. Mackey and Trudi E. Jacobson, *Metaliteracy: Reinventing Information Literacy to Empower Learners* (Chicago: Neal-Schuman, 2014), 49.

3. Paul G. Zurkowski, "The Information Service Environment Relationships and Priorities" (Related Paper No. 5, National Commission on Libraries and Information Science, National Program for Library and Information Services, November 1974), http://files.eric.ed.gov/fulltext/ED100391.pdf; ACRL, *Information Literacy Competency Standards*.

4. Mackey and Jacobson, *Metaliteracy*.

5. Trudi E. Jacobson and Thomas P. Mackey, "Proposing a Metaliteracy Model to Redefine Information Literacy," *Communications in Information Literacy* 7, no. 2 (2013): 84–91.

6. Association of College and Research Libraries (ACRL), *Framework for Information Literacy for Higher Education* (Chicago: American Library Association, 2015), www.ala.org/acrl/standards/ilframework.

7. Zurkowski, "Information Service Environment," 23.

8. Mackey and Jacobson, *Metaliteracy*, 47.

9. 3G.co.uk, "Assisted-GPS Test Calls for 3G WCDMA Networks" (November 10, 2004), www.3g.co.uk/PR/November2004/8641.htm; Phys.org, "First Modernized GPS Satellite Built by Lockheed Martin Launched," *Space Daily*, September 26, 2005, http://phys.org/news6762.html.

10. Mackey and Jacobson, *Metaliteracy*.

11. Ibid., 14.

12. Ibid., 15.

13. Ibid.

14. Ibid.

15. Melissa Gross and Don Latham, "Attaining Information Literacy: An Investigation of the Relationship between Skill Level, Self-Estimates of Skill, and Library Anxiety," *Library and Information Science Research* 29, no. 3 (2007): 332–53.

16. Paul L. Hrycaj, "An Analysis of Online Syllabi for Credit-Bearing Library Skills Courses," *College and Research Libraries* 67, no. 6 (2006): 525–35; Gross and Latham, "Attaining Information Literacy"; Amanda L. Folk, "How Well Are We Preparing Them? An Assessment of First-Year Library Student Assistants' Information Literacy Skills," *College and Undergraduate Libraries* 20, no. 2 (2014): 177–92; Wendy Holliday et al., "An Information Literacy Snapshot: Authentic Assessment across the Curriculum," *College and Research Libraries* 76, no. 2 (2015): 170–87.

17. Mackey and Jacobson, *Metaliteracy*, 47.

18. Folk, "How Well Are We Preparing Them?"

19. US Department of State, *A Test of Leadership: Charting the Future of U.S. Higher Education* (Washington, DC: US Department of Education, 2006), www2.ed.gov/about/bdscomm/list/hiedfuture/reports/final-report.pdf.

20. Anna Zilberberg et al., "American College Students' Attitudes toward Institutional Accountability Testing: Developing Measures," *Educational Assessment* 18, no. 3 (2013): 213.

21. Ibid.

22. Ibid., 208.

23. Christine Bruce, *Seven Faces of Information Literacy,* (Blackwood, South Australia: Auslib Press, 1997).

24. Susie Andretta, "Phenomenography: A Conceptual Framework for Information Literacy Education," *Aslib Proceedings: New Information Perspectives* 59, no. 2 (2007): 152–68.

25. Christine Bruce, Sylvia Edwards, and Mandy Lupton, "Six Frames for Information Literacy Education: A Conceptual Framework for Interpreting the Relationships between Theory and Practice," *Innovation in Teaching*

and Learning in Information and Computer Sciences 5, no. 1 (2006): 1–18.

26. Mackey and Jacobson, *Metaliteracy*, 2; Trudi E. Jacobson and Emer O'Keefe, "Authentic Inquiry Models for Our Evolving Information Landscape," *Knowledge Quest* 43, no. 2 (2014): 26–33.

27. ACRL, *Information Literacy Competency Standards*, para. 13.

28. ACRL, *Framework for Information Literacy*.

29. Kristine N. Stewart and John M. Budd, "Investigating the Use of ACRL Standards in Instruction Programs," in *Worldwide Commonalities and Challenges in Information Literacy Research and Practice*, Communications in Computer and Information Science 397, ed. S. Kurbanoglu et al. (Heidelberg, Germany: Springer), 386–93.

30. Dane Ward, "Revisioning Information Literacy for Lifelong Learning," *The Journal of Academic Librarianship* 32, no. 4 (2006): 396–402.

31. Mackey and Jacobson, *Metaliteracy*, 84.

32. Barbara Fister, "The Information Literacy Standards/Framework Debate," *Library Babel Fish* (blog), January 22, 2015, www.insidehighered.com/blogs/library-babel-fish/information-literacy-standardsframework-debate; Cara Berg et al., "An Open Letter Regarding the Framework for Information Literacy for Higher Education," *ACRLog* (blog), January 7, 2015, http://acrlog.org/2015/01/07/an-open-letter-regarding-the-framework-for-information-literacy-for-higher-education.

33. Berg et al., "Open Letter Regarding the Framework," para. 7.

34. Ibid.

35. ACRL, *Framework for Information Literacy*, Introduction, para. 2.

36. Char Booth, *Reflective Teaching, Effective Learning: Instructional Literacy for Library Educators* (Chicago: American Library Association, 2011).

37. Mackey and Jacobson, *Metaliteracy*, 2.

38. Mackey and Jacobson, *Metaliteracy*.

39. Stewart and Budd, "Investigating Use of ACRL Standards."

40. Mackey and Jacobson, *Metaliteracy*, 84.

41. Ibid.

42. Ian Beilin and Nancy Foasberg, "Moving Beyond Standards: A Response to the Open Letter Regarding the Framework for Information Literacy for Higher Education," *ACRLog* (blog), January 15, 2015, http://acrlog.org/2015/01/15/moving-beyond-standards-a-response-to-the-open-letter-regarding-the-framework-for-information-literacy-for-higher-education.

43. University of Missouri, "About Mizzou" (accessed August 13, 2015), http://missouri.edu/about/index.php.

44. Ibid.

45. University of Missouri, "MU Facts" (accessed August 13, 2015), http://missouri.edu/about/facts.php.

46. Ibid.

47. ACRL, *Framework for Information Literacy*, Information Has Value, para. 1.
48. Mackey and Jacobson, *Metaliteracy*.
49. Jacobson and Mackey, "Proposing a Metaliteracy Model."
50. American Press Institute, "How Millennials Use and Control Social Media" (published March 16, 2015), www.americanpressinstitute.org/publications/reports/survey-research/millennials-social-media.
51. Joanna M. Burkhardt, Mary C. Macdonald, and Andree J. Rathemacher, *Teaching Information Literacy: 50 Standards-Based Exercises for College Students* (Chicago: American Library Association, 2010).
52. John Flavell, "Metacognition and Cognitive Monitoring: A New Area of Cognitive-Developmental Inquiry," *American Psychologist* 34, no. 10 (1979): 906–11.
53. Mackey and Jacobson, *Metaliteracy*.
54. Ibid.
55. Ibid., 66.
56. Ibid., 87.
57. Norman K. Denzin and Yvonna S. Lincoln, *Collecting and Interpreting Qualitative Materials* (Thousand Oaks, CA: SAGE Publications, 1998).
58. Klaus Krippendorff, *Content Analysis: An Introduction to Its Methodology* (Thousand Oaks, CA: SAGE Publications, 2004).
59. Mackey and Jacobson, *Metaliteracy*.
60. Krippendorff, *Content Analysis*.
61. Ibid.
62. Mackey and Jacobson, *Metaliteracy*, 87, 88, 90.
63. Ibid., 87.
64. Ibid.
65. Jacobson and Mackey, "Proposing a Metaliteracy Model," 89.
66. Jacobson and O'Keefe, "Authentic Inquiry Models."
67. Mackey and Jacobson, *Metaliteracy*.
68. Frank Menchaca, "The Future Is in Doubt: Librarians, Publishers, and Networked Learning in the 21st Century," *Journal of Library Administration* 52, no. 5 (2012): 396–410.
69. Mackey and Jacobson, *Metaliteracy*, 89.
70. Ibid.
71. Ibid., 90.
72. Ibid.
73. Ibid.
74. Ibid.
75. Valeria E. Molteni and Emily K. Chan, "Student Confidence/Overconfidence in the Research Process," *The Journal of Academic Librarianship* 41, no. 1 (2015): 2–8.
76. Mackey and Jacobson, *Metaliteracy*.
77. Ibid., 93.
78. Ibid.

BIBLIOGRAPHY

American Press Institute. "How Millennials Use and Control Social Media." Published March 16, 2015. www.americanpressinstitute.org/publications/reports/survey -research/millennials-social-media.

Andretta, Susie. "Phenomenography: A Conceptual Framework for Information Literacy Education." *Aslib Proceedings: New Information Perspectives* 59, no. 2 (2007): 152–68.

Association of College and Research Libraries (ACRL). *Framework for Information Literacy for Higher Education*. Chicago: American Library Association, 2015. www.ala.org/acrl/standards/ilframework.

———. *Information Literacy Competency Standards for Higher Education*. Chicago: American Library Association, 2000. www.ala.org/acrl/sites/ala.org.acrl/files/ content/standards/standards.pdf.

Beilin, Ian, and Nancy Foasberg. "Moving Beyond Standards: A Response to the Open Letter Regarding the Framework for Information Literacy for Higher Education," *ACRLog* (blog), January 15, 2015. http://acrlog.org/2015/01/15/moving- beyond-standards-a-response-to-the-open-letter-regarding-the-framework-for -information-literacy-for-higher-education.

Berg, Cara, Leslin Charles, Steve Chudnick, Heather Cook, Heather Dalal, Megan Dempsey, Eleonora Dubicki, et al. 2015. "An Open Letter Regarding the Framework for Information Literacy for Higher Education," *ACRLog* (blog), January 7, 2015. http://acrlog.org/2015/01/07/ an-open-letter-regarding-the -framework-for-information-literacy-for-higher-education.

Booth, Char. *Reflective Teaching, Effective Learning: Instructional Literacy for Library Educators*. Chicago: American Library Association, 2011.

Bruce, Christine. *Seven Faces of Information Literacy*. Blackwood, South Australia: Auslib Press, 1997.

Bruce, Christine, Sylvia Edwards, and Mandy Lupton. "Six Frames for Information Literacy Education: A Conceptual Framework for Interpreting the Relationships between Theory and Practice." *Innovation in Teaching and Learning in Information and Computer Sciences* 5, no. 1 (2006): 1–18.

Burkhardt, Joanna M., Mary C. Macdonald, and Andree J. Rathemacher. *Teaching Information Literacy: 50 Standards-Based Exercises for College Students*. Chicago: American Library Association, 2010.

Denzin, Norman K., and Yvonna S. Lincoln. *Collecting and Interpreting Qualitative Materials*. Thousand Oaks, CA: SAGE Publications, 1998.

Fister, Barbara. "The Information Literacy Standards/Framework Debate." *Library Babel Fish* (blog), January 22, 2015. www.insidehighered.com/blogs/library -babel-fish/information-literacy-standardsframework-debate.

Flavell, John. "Metacognition and Cognitive Monitoring: A New Area of Cognitive- Developmental Inquiry." *American Psychologist* 34, no. 10 (1979): 906–11.

Folk, Amanda L. "How Well Are We Preparing Them? An Assessment of First-Year Library Student Assistants' Information Literacy Skills." *College and Undergraduate Libraries* 20, no. 2 (2014): 177–92.

Gross, Melissa, and Don Latham. "Attaining Information Literacy: An Investigation of the Relationship between Skill Level, Self-Estimates of Skill, and Library Anxiety." *Library and Information Science Research* 29, no. 3 (2007): 332–53.

Holliday, Wendy, Betty Dance, Erin Davis, Britt Fagerheim, Anne Hedrich, Kacy Lundstrom, and Pamela Martin. "An Information Literacy Snapshot: Authentic Assessment across the Curriculum." *College and Research Libraries* 76, no. 2 (2015): 170–87.

Hrycaj, Paul L. "An Analysis of Online Syllabi for Credit-Bearing Library Skills Courses." *College and Research Libraries* 67, no. 6 (2006): 525–35.

Jacobson, Trudi E., and Thomas P. Mackey. "Proposing a Metaliteracy Model to Redefine Information Literacy." *Communications in Information Literacy* 7, no. 2 (2013): 84–91.

Jacobson, Trudi E., and Emer O'Keefe. "Authentic Inquiry Models for Our Evolving Information Landscape." *Knowledge Quest* 43, no. 2 (2014): 26–33.

Krippendorff, Klaus. *Content Analysis: An Introduction to Its Methodology*. Thousand Oaks, CA: SAGE Publications, 2004.

Mackey, Thomas P., and Trudi E. Jacobson. *Metaliteracy: Reinventing Information Literacy to Empower Learners*. Chicago: Neal-Schuman, 2014.

Menchaca, Frank. "The Future Is in Doubt: Librarians, Publishers, and Networked Learning in the 21st Century." *Journal of Library Administration* 52, no. 5 (2012): 396–410.

Molteni, Valeria E., and Emily K. Chan. "Student Confidence/Overconfidence in the Research Process." *The Journal of Academic Librarianship* 41, no. 1 (2015): 2–8.

Phys.org. "First Modernized GPS Satellite Built by Lockheed Martin Launched." *Space Daily*, September 26, 2005. http://phys.org/news6762.html.

Stewart, Kristine N., and John M. Budd. "Investigating the Use of ACRL Standards in Instruction Programs." In *Worldwide Commonalities and Challenges in Information Literacy Research and Practice*, Communications in Computer and Information Science 397, edited by S. Kurbanoglu, E. Grassian, D. Mizrachi, R. Catts, and S. Spiranec, 386–93. Heidelberg, Germany: Springer, 2013.

3G.co.uk. "Assisted-GPS Test Calls for 3G WCDMA Networks." November 10, 2004. www.3g.co.uk/PR/November2004/8641.htm.

University of Missouri. "About Mizzou." Accessed August 13, 2015. http://missouri.edu/about/index.php.

———. "MU Facts." Accessed August 13, 2015. http://missouri.edu/about/facts.php.

US Department of State. *A Test of Leadership: Charting the Future of U.S. Higher Education*. Washington, DC: US Department of Education, 2006.

Ward, Dane. "Revisioning Information Literacy for Lifelong Learning." *The Journal of Academic Librarianship* 32, no. 4 (2006): 396–402.

Zilberberg, Anna, Robin D. Anderson, Sara J. Finney, and Kimberly R. Marsh. "American College Students' Attitudes toward Institutional Accountability Testing: Developing Measures." *Educational Assessment* 18, no. 3 (2013): 208–34.

Zurkowski, Paul G. "The Information Service Environment Relationships and Priorities." Related Paper No. 5. National Commission on Libraries and Information Science, National Program for Library and Information Services, November 1974. http://files.eric.ed.gov/fulltext/ED100391.pdf.

IRENE McGARRITY

8

Developing Agency in Metaliterate Learners

Empowerment through Digital Identity and Participation

TRENDS IN HIGHER EDUCATION HAVE BEEN MOVING TOWARD pedagogical practices that encourage student agency by trading lectures for discussions, flipping classes, and decentralizing the classroom through collaborative learning models. In academic libraries, the movement toward metaliteracy mirrors this transformation. According to Thomas Mackey and Trudi Jacobson's seminal article "Reframing Information Literacy as a Metaliteracy," the concept of metaliteracy "promotes active engagement with emerging technologies and learner-centered production of information."[1] In addition to collaborative information production, metaliteracy emphasizes student empowerment and agency by decentralizing the class and reaching out beyond the classroom into online communities.

Although library faculty at Keene State College lead one-shot and two-shot sessions, as do most academic librarians, we also have the benefit of teaching full courses. Highly influenced by the scholarship on metaliteracy and participatory models of pedagogy, two library instructors, Irene McGarrity and Jennifer Ditkoff, designed and taught the four-credit course II 399: Digital Identity and Participatory Culture. In designing the course, the instructors decided that students would lead the content and create the assignments.

Students would also engage with participatory communities and social networks outside of the classroom. In this chapter, I provide background on student-centered learning, collaborative learning, participatory culture, and metaliteracy in higher education. I discuss the challenges and implications of II 399: Digital Identity and Participatory Culture and suggest ways that academic librarians and disciplinary faculty might experiment with student-led content and student-created assignments in their attempt to empower and instill a sense of agency in metaliterate learners.

STUDENT-CENTERED LEARNING

Student-centered or learner-centered education has become a dominant mode of pedagogy over the past twenty years. In their 1995 article "From Teaching to Learning—A New Paradigm for Undergraduate Education," Barr and Tagg state, "A paradigm shift is taking hold in American Higher Education."[2] The *Greenwood Dictionary of Education* defines student-centered instruction as a model in which students influence the "contents, activities, materials, and pace of learning. This pedagogical model places the learner in the center of the learning process."[3] Student-centered learning is rooted in a constructivist philosophy of education founded by developmental psychologist Jean Piaget.[4] According to constructivism, knowledge is created through an interaction between a learner's previous experiences and new information. The learner is active rather than passive, constructing meaning rather than accepting it. Although much constructivist scholarship is focused on early education, constructivism is applied widely to college teaching as well. Barr and Tagg make the important distinction between "providing instruction," a traditional role of higher education institutions, and "producing learning," a new and preferred role; the traditional approach is the "Instruction Paradigm" and the new approach is the "Learning Paradigm." Barr and Tagg state:

> For many of us, the Learning Paradigm has always lived in our hearts. As teachers, we want above all else for our students to learn and succeed. But the heart's feeling has not lived clearly and powerfully in our heads. Now, as the elements of the Learning Paradigm permeate the air, our heads are beginning to understand what our hearts have known.[5]

In the Learning Paradigm, rather than charging instructors with transferring their knowledge to students, a college's role is to "create environments and experiences that bring students to discover and construct knowledge for themselves, to make students members of communities of learners that make discoveries and solve problems."[6] This represents a radical departure from traditional lecture-style, content-focused college learning experiences.

In his book *Becoming a Critically Reflective Teacher*, Stephen Brookfield emphasizes the importance of challenging assumptions that we, as teachers, carry into the classroom and into our interactions with students. What we take for granted as best practice or in the best interest of the student may simply be an assumption that serves neither the student nor the teacher.[7] In her text *Learner-Centered Teaching: Five Key Changes to Practice*, Maryellen Weimer identifies five areas in which traditional pedagogical practice needs to change: the balance of power, the function of content, the role of the teacher, the responsibility for learning, and the purpose and process of evaluation.[8] In her discussion about the balance of power, Weimer reflects on the political implications of a learner-centered versus teacher-centered classroom. The connection between education and politics was primarily initiated by Paulo Freire's seminal work *Pedagogy of the Oppressed*, first published in 1968, which brought attention to the power dynamics at play in the classroom.[9] Freire pointed out that the "banking model of education" treats students as empty receptacles to be filled by the all-knowing instructor. The banking model of education does not treat the learner as an agent, but as a passive recipient of facts, information, assignments, directions, and, finally, grades. Learner-centered approaches treat students as cocreators of knowledge. Freire challenged a method of pedagogy in which "knowledge is a gift bestowed by those who consider themselves knowledgeable upon those who [sic] they consider to know nothing."[10]

About power dynamics in the classroom, Weimer suggests that "to be truly learner-centered, we must begin with greater insight into the role of power in our classrooms: who exerts it, why, and with what effects and what benefits."[11] Weimer notes that although students do need a certain amount of structure and direction from teachers, the particular ways in which teachers control the classroom often benefit the teacher, not the learner. As an alternative power structure, Weiner offers a shared model: "When teaching is learner centered, power is shared rather than transferred wholesale. Faculty still make key decisions about learning, but they no longer make all decisions and not always without student input."[12]

In learner-centered practices, the instructor is recast as a facilitator rather than as an all-knowing professor. In her article "Sage on the Stage to Guide on the Side," Alison King describes the shift from instructor to facilitator: "The professor is still responsible for presenting the course material, but he or she presents that material in ways that make the student do something with the information—interact with it—manipulate the ideas and relate them to what they already know."[13] Students' knowledge, insight, and experience should be central to the learning situation rather than peripheral or left out altogether. Weimer notes that despite our best efforts, instructors are still often disseminating rather than facilitating. This is most easily observed in the kinds of questions students often ask us: What do you want in this assignment? How do you want me to do this? After a K–12 experience in which students' own experiences, insights, and judgments were often not part of the educational process, they have difficulty making the shift to an environment in which success hinges upon those very experiences, insights, and judgments.

Another shift in learner-centered pedagogy is reflected in the changing role of a student's peers or classmates. Rather than being fellow passive recipients of knowledge instilled by the professor, peers have become cocreators of knowledge and, potentially, teachers. In Lev Vygotsky's social constructivism, there is an inherent social nature to learning. Meaning is constructed through a process of collaborative inquiry.[14] People in a collaborative learning situation are accountable to, and responsible for, one another. The collaboration can take place between two students or between a student and an instructor. Connectivism, a learning theory developed by George Siemens, recognizes that "technology has reorganized how we live, how we communicate, and how we learn."[15] The Internet is inherently a collaborative space where people can meet virtually and participate in activities, conversations, and knowledge creation synchronously or asynchronously. The static roles of creator and consumer, expert and novice have become more fluid. The learning environment has expanded well beyond the classroom. In connectivism, the individual is just the starting point for learning. Networks and communities are integral to the learning process. Similarly, participatory culture, a concept that has grown out of new media scholarship, "shifts the focus of literacy from one of individual expression to community involvement"[16]; participatory culture scholars aim to take an "ecological approach, thinking about the interrelationship among all these different communication technologies, the cultural communities that grow up around them, and the activities they support."[17] Henry Jenkins defines a participatory culture as one with low barriers to artistic expression and civic engagement, strong support for creating and sharing one's creations, and a process of informal membership whereby knowledge is passed from the most experienced to novices. Members should also believe that their contributions matter and they should care, at least somewhat, what others in the group think about their contributions.[18] Applying these criteria to a classroom setting facilitates an environment that is supportive of all members and relatively flat in terms of power structure. The instructors who designed and taught II 399: Digital Identity and Participatory Culture were greatly influenced by participatory culture, connectivism, and social constructivism in the conception of the course.

INFORMATION LITERACY TO METALITERACY

The shift from information literacy to metaliteracy in academic libraries runs parallel to the evolution of learner-centered, collaborative, and participatory models of education. The concept of information literacy has undergone much revision and evolution in the past forty years due largely to the drastic changes in the information and technology landscape. New technologies that make it possible to transmit data to millions of people with the click of a button, along with the ease with which people are able to connect, collaborate, and publish online, have caused scholars and theorists from all disciplines to rethink the concept of information literacy and identify a multiplicity of other literacy types—media literacy, visual literacy, and cyberliteracy are just a few examples.

Greg Bobish's constructivist approach to integrating information literacy and Web 2.0 tools shows the connection between learner-centered and participatory pedagogy.[19] Bobish notes that Web 2.0 tools, "if used thoughtfully in information literacy instruction, are not simply the latest flashy trend, but can have a solid pedagogical basis that enhances student learning while at the same time making connections with technologies that are already being used for research purposes and in daily life outside of the classroom."[20] Bobish's and other approaches to information literacy instruction that acknowledge and make use of online networks mark a clear paradigm shift. Although traditional information literacy instruction certainly acknowledges the Web, for example, in a website evaluation session or in a session that explores the authority of online sources, the instruction is still based heavily on the values of print culture. Students are either implicitly or explicitly told not to use *Wikipedia*, not to trust Web sources, and to privilege traditionally published academic books and peer-reviewed articles over all other types of sources. The importance of collaboration and shared responsibility for the end product is also a notable departure from information literacy sessions centered around individual students' research papers.

When Mackey and Jacobson published "Reframing Information Literacy as a Metaliteracy," academic librarians found a language, and a framework, with which to understand the shift in thinking about instruction and social technologies. In addition to using learner-centered pedagogy and asking instructors to facilitate rather than teach, metaliteracy incorporates the emergence of social media and social models of knowledge creation: "Within this context, information is not a static object that is simply accessed and retrieved. It is a dynamic entity that is produced and shared collaboratively."[21] Metaliteracy considers information literacy in a collaborative, participatory, digital environment. Metaliteracy also moves beyond the skills-based approach of information literacy and encourages an inquiry-based model of learning. In this context, learners can "take control of their lives and their own learning to become active agents, asking and answering questions that matter to them and to the world around them."[22]

The paradigm shift from information literacy to metaliteracy has inspired librarians to make changes at the macro level in their information literacy programs and on the micro level in their lesson plans and classroom activities. The librarians at Keene State College have transformed how we work with disciplinary faculty and our role on campus as a whole. The movement toward metaliteracy has been the primary inspiration for these changes.

INSTITUTIONAL CONTEXT

The approach to information literacy instruction at academic libraries has undergone a tremendous transformation over the past several years, and the library at Keene State College is no exception. Like many other academic librarians, the library faculty at Keene State College decided to move toward a train-the-trainer model of information literacy instruction. Hartman, Newhouse, and Perry describe the process of transitioning to this model in their work with an introductory biology lab.[23] The librarians in this study found that a model of one-shots was not sustainable, which is similar to the predicament that many other academic librarians face. There is a growing sense among librarians that they do not need to, and indeed should not, own information literacy instruction. Mackey and Jacobson note that the transition from information literacy to metaliteracy "challenges us to think beyond the library as the sole provider for information literacy instruction and instead to envision metaliteracy as embedded through the curriculum and supported by the entire institution."[24]

This is a difficult shift, particularly for academic librarians who only five or ten years ago pushed for required one-shots, two-shots, or embedded models of information literacy in their institutions. The work those librarians did to institute programs is valuable in that it brought to light the necessity of information literacy and made it an integral part of instruction. Nonetheless, continuing to function in that model does a disservice both to students and to librarians. Librarians often cannot sustain teaching so many one- or two-shot sessions, and the pedagogical implications of teaching the same session twenty or even forty times in one semester are dire. Functioning under the requests of faculty members who may want only skills-based information sessions that provide students with basic database demos and information about the library is stifling to many librarians. Just as students need to be empowered, so do librarians. Furthermore, continuing in this model enforces the idea that information literacy is a skill that can be taught in one or two sessions. Exposing students to repeated library sessions conflates research skills and information literacy. It can also turn students against the library because of the seemingly needless repetition of sessions. A colleague of mine once received a student evaluation from an information literacy session with the comment "I'm so sick of these database sessions. I HATE the library!"

Our attempts at Keene State College to move to a train-the-trainer model and to shift from teaching information literacy skills to integrating metaliteracy across campus have taken several different forms. Library faculty discontinued required, course-integrated information literacy sessions within the Integrative Thinking and Writing (ITW) program. Before that change, library faculty conducted two or three sessions in each ITW class. Those sessions focused on concept mapping, identifying scholarly sources, and database search strategy. The overall impression from several years of doing these course-integrated sessions is that they were ineffectual. Because research is a recursive process requiring metacognition, it cannot be addressed in a few compartmentalized library sessions. The timing of the sessions would often be inadequately aligned with course assignments to actually benefit the student. Collaborating with disciplinary faculty was often challenging for a variety of reasons. Some faculty members were resistant to working with the library at all because they didn't want to relinquish valuable time in their classes. Others wanted to limit their class's interactions with the library to basic database tutorials, rather than allowing for lessons that created opportunity for critical thinking about information. Some faculty wanted information sessions about the library itself, focusing on services like interlibrary loan, logging in from off campus, checking out laptops, and hours of operation, rather than cognitive and affective aspects of researching and interacting with information. The timing of the sessions was often an issue. Faculty would schedule sessions too early or too late in the research process, making the content of the sessions not applicable or beside the point. Finally, and most important, these sessions often did not result in the desired outcome, namely, for students to use more scholarly, in-depth sources for their research papers.

This embedded model used too much of the library faculty's time and energy without benefiting the students, the faculty, or the institution. Currently, the information literacy librarian provides instructional consultations and workshops for ITW faculty so that they can incorporate lesson plans related to information evaluation and database search strategy into their own courses. In addition, we maintain a "Faculty DIY" page of resources on the Keene Info Lit Bank that instructors can mine for activities that support research skills acquisition and higher level abilities to evaluate and contextualize information.[25] Instead of conducting sessions in ITW, library faculty now teach sections of the credit course. This gives library faculty time and space to develop metaliteracy with students throughout the semester.

Other collaborative ventures are also attempting to address the changed model. Two library faculty members recently started a Research and Technology Fellows program in which students are intensively trained to provide in-class research assistance and basic database demonstrations. We have also begun to design online modules in the Canvas course management system that are based on the new ACRL (Association of College and Research Libraries) *Framework for Information Literacy for Higher Education* as well as basic research skills outcomes.[26] The goal is to eventually replace one-shots with the online modules. We also hope to use the modules in conjunction with face-to-face teaching in a blended or flipped model.

Another exciting initiative is the development of the Information Studies minor, which is slated to begin in fall 2015. Because Keene State College allows faculty to design and teach experimental courses for one semester before the course is required to be officially approved, we were able to offer II 399: Digital Identity and Participatory Culture, one of the courses in our Information Studies minor, in the fall of 2014 as an upper-level, experimental, interdisciplinary course.

METALITERACY CASE STUDY

The instructors planned II 399: Digital Identity and Participatory Culture to focus students' attention on digital identity creation along with social and ethical implications of living and interacting online. The instructors wanted to encourage students to critically analyze the online worlds where they interact daily. From a pedagogical perspective, we determined to embody the core components of metaliteracy: collaboration, technology-enhanced learning environments, and learner-centered teaching. We wanted students not only to think about and consume technology but also to engage and create with it. Finally, we wanted to facilitate a sense of agency in students by giving them more control and decision-making power over course content and assignments. Mackey and Jacobson note, "This shift from a linear instruction mode to a decentered learning style focuses on the choices made by the student and reflects the nonlinear format of online spaces."[27]

The idea to experiment with student-led content and student-created assignments evolved as we conceptualized the class. The two instructors had attended a campus event in which a graphic design professor described his experience teaching a student-run course. At the beginning of the semester, the students generated a series of projects that required the utilization of technology like Vine, a video-making platform that creates six-second videos, and mapping apps that would track their route through the town of Keene. In addition to experimenting with technology, students reflected upon their experiences using the technology and the self-directed nature of the course. One of the library faculty members, Jennifer Ditkoff, had also been previously inspired by Jim Groom's DS106: Digital Storytelling course, which he describes as "part storytelling workshop, part technology training, and, most importantly, part critical interrogation of the digital landscape that is ever increasingly mediating how we communicate with one another."[28] Metaliteracy scholarship along with collaborative models of learning, such as team-based and inquiry-based learning, motivated the other library faculty member, Irene McGarrity, to envision a new approach to the course. Influenced and inspired in multiple ways, these two instructors embarked upon the course.

In 2009, Tyma described his experience leading a media literacy course that provided insight into the process of seeking student input while maintaining some control in the class.[29] He notes that one of the challenges with trying to change from a top-down to a shared power structure is that grades are due at the end of the semester, and the instructor is the one responsible for determining those grades. Because of this, "the truly egalitarian classroom . . . may not be possible, at least not until a cultural shift occurs within the educational structure as a whole."[30] This tension between student-led content and assignments and instructor-determined grades was one of the major challenges the two instructors faced with designing and teaching this course.

Another challenge of implementing a learner-centered pedagogy is student resistance. The two instructors were both well aware that students may not easily embrace learner-centered approaches. Maryellen Weimer describes how students' lack of confidence can create an obstacle to learner-centered practices:

> The [students] in my classes are hopeful but generally anxious and tentative. They want all classes to be easy but expect that most will be hard. They wish their major (whatever it might be) did not require math, science, or English courses. A good number will not speak in class unless called on. Most like, want, indeed need, teachers who tell them exactly what to do. Education is something done unto them. It frequently involves stress, anxiety, and other forms of discomfort.[31]

Agency is about empowerment, but it's also about responsibility. For those students who are trained as passive recipients of knowledge and learning, the prospect of making decisions about their learning can be paralyzing. The instructors believed that facilitating students' ability to transcend these fears and become more self-directed was one of the most important outcomes of the course.

After reflecting on how best to facilitate the student task creation, the instructors developed an assignment to create an assignment. It included two sample rubrics to encourage students to design their own. The instructors wanted students to become more aware of their own learning through the construction of the activities, rather than rote completion of activities as in a traditional class. The instructors felt it was important that students take responsibility for how assignments would be evaluated, which would address some of the top-down power dynamics inherent in the traditional instructor-generated grading system. Once the students had submitted their assignments, the instructors taped them up around the classroom. Students reviewed each assignment and voted on their favorites with sticky notes. This process gave students insight into the thought processes and creativity of their peers. The instructors selected the assignments with the highest number of votes and built those into the rest of the course. Before the voting took place, students assumed that everyone would vote for their own assignment, but because students were so engaged in the work of their peers, they ultimately voted for the assignment that they found most interesting. The assignments that students created were quite diverse. Four are described here:

A Vine contest: Vine is a short-form video-sharing service. Videos are six seconds long and they loop, displaying the same six-second clip repeatedly. In groups, students create vines based on the theme "Man I'm glad I went to Keene State." The group responsible for the vine voted best in the class would be exempt from one assignment.

Spotify playlists: Spotify is a streaming music service that allows users to create playlists. Students created Spotify playlists that represented different aspects of their digital identities and shared them on their blogs. Students were instructed to comment on one another's playlists.

Meaningful blog post: Students all kept blogs as part of the Digital Identity and Participatory Cultures course. Some used Tumblr and others used WordPress. For this assignment, students wrote a post about a particular cause or social movement that they were passionate about and that has been widely discussed on social media.

Social media friend analysis: In this assignment, students looked at their social media accounts and analyzed the virtual friendships in comparison to their analog friendships. The assignment required them to describe in blog posts the depth of those relationships.

The other student-led portion of the course consisted of students working in teams that planned and led three days' worth of classes with content and activities related to a particular theme. The instructors taught the first five weeks of the course to lay the conceptual foundations: participatory culture, digital identity, privacy, online anonymity, and information ethics. During these weeks, the instructors provided the students with some examples for how they might convey their own content and lead the class.

Students brainstormed topics in small groups during class and through a threaded discussion. The instructors analyzed all of the topics and developed six key themes: psychology of Internet use, law and the Internet, creativity and the Internet, education and the Internet, online activism, and online careers. Once the themes were identified, students were put into groups based around their first, second, and third choices of theme, and the groups were given an assignment for developing course material. The assignment provided some structure about how to focus the content and offered suggestions for teaching methods.

The student-led content and student-created assignments, including the assignment to make an assignment, counted for 50 percent of the grade. This raised some concerns for the two instructors, particularly because the assignments and the content were all developed ad hoc during the course. The instructors didn't know what those assignments would be or what content the students would choose to present until a few weeks into the semester. Nevertheless, because both instructors felt strongly about empowering students and working with a shared power structure, it seemed important to dedicate a large percentage of class points to assignments and content of the students' choosing.

APPLICATION OF METALITERACY LEARNING OBJECTIVES

The instructors understood that empowering students would require more than just the development of creative assignments and a bit of intentional class design. The instructors anticipated that teaching the course would require trial and error, constant reinforcement, and, of course, some failures along the way; however, both were excited to encourage students to engage in self-directed learning that would ultimately empower them. The metaliteracy learning objectives on the Metaliteracy.org website provided much assistance in the instructors' ability to conceptualize how to embed agency as a learning goal into the course.[32]

Metaliterate learning falls into four major domains: behavioral, cognitive, affective, and metacognitive. There are four broad metaliteracy goals, and each of those has five to eleven more specific learning objectives enumerated beneath it. The instructors of II 399 had goals for all four domains. Although most interested in the affective and metacognitive areas, the instructors also hoped for growth at the behavioral and cognitive levels. For example, on the behavioral level, the instructors wanted students to become more proficient with online tools, including blogging platforms, social media, and the Canvas course management system. Many of the behavioral expectations of the course had to do with students' ability to engage with technology and use it to complete assignments and activities successfully.

The instructors also expected that as students developed the content for the class, they would use their cognitive abilities to comprehend, evaluate, and organize their sources. Since the instructors didn't require or restrict types of information sources, students needed to use their own judgment to critically evaluate the information and decide about issues like scope and authority. In addition, the instructors wanted students to think critically about issues of information ethics, privacy, online identity, and anonymity. Virtually every lecture, class discussion, and class activity asked students to do this in some way. For example, one student writes in her blog, "I think that everyone deserves freedom of speech but the line needs to be drawn somewhere when things like child pornography are being posted onto popular websites. That is where cyber ethics should come in."[33] Another student makes an interesting observation about the images people portray on Facebook and how those often show only the "highlights" of one's actual life, a curated set of memories and experiences: "For instance, on my Facebook, I may only upload pictures that give off the idea that I am doing things with my life like hiking, swimming, traveling, etc. No one posts pictures of them sitting at home watching Netflix, or crying about something tragic that has happened in our lives."[34]

As the semester progressed, students became more aware of their own thinking about digital identity, which falls into the metacognitive domain. In class and on assignments, the instructors often asked for students to reflect upon their own attitudes and thought patterns. For instance, in one activity, the instructors asked students to create a profile using the social network of their choice. The profile could be true to who they were in "real life" or completely fabricated. Students were then asked to write a blog post in which they reflected on the choices they had made in constructing that online identity.

Students met the objectives and outcomes articulated at the beginning of the semester in many of the class assignments. For example, during the semester there were two "open blog" assignments in which students could choose their topics. Students almost always used these assignments for opportunities to be reflective about either their own thinking or behavior around social media or their own changing attitudes toward social media and learning in general, even though the instructors hadn't specifically asked them to be reflective in those assignments. It seemed as though having the freedom to choose what they did in assignments led many students in more metacognitive and affective directions. In reflecting upon her use of social media, one student asks this question: "Do we control our social media by sharing our experiences, or do we have experiences only to be able to post them on our social media?"[35]

Because students generated much of the content for the second half of the semester, they were constantly evaluating the information they encountered, which addresses metaliteracy goal 1: "Evaluate content critically, including dynamic, online content that changes and evolves, such as article preprints, blogs, and wikis."[36] Since the instructors hadn't provided any specific instruction about which types of information sources students should use, there was quite a range that students could consider. Some student groups used sources from theoretical to legal to pop culture in order to look at the issue holistically, while contextualizing the sources appropriately. Other groups used mainly Web articles and videos and did not do much contextualizing. All student groups did, however, display an understanding of the limitations and potential biases of their information sources during discussions and activities. Although not all students were necessarily able to "distinguish between editorial commentary and information presented from a more research-based perspective" on their own, when they were prompted after presenting the material, students were able to recognize "that values and beliefs are embedded in all information" (metaliteracy goal 1.2).[37] Often, the instructors used time left over after the groups had led the sessions to tease out some of the nuances and potential biases of their information sources.

Much of the course content addressed metaliteracy goal 2, "Understand personal privacy, information ethics, and intellectual property issues in changing technology environments," in the content, activities, and class discussions.[38] The topic of online anonymity generated many lively class discussions and diverse opinions from students. For example, we discussed Anonymous, the loosely connected network of hacktivists. This group is well-known through a series of cyber terrorist attacks on religious and government organizations.[39] Some students thought that members of Anonymous were heroic because they rebelled against hate groups like the Westboro Baptist Church. Other students, however, found Anonymous too extreme. As one student noted in a class discussion, the ends didn't justify the means.

One student group explored the theme of law and the Internet. The students addressed a variety of interesting topics, including the NSA (National Security Agency) and Edward Snowden, GPS (Global Positioning System) tracking, and online information collection. Students were particularly drawn in by the Edward Snowden interview.[40] The class content and discussion led students to "recognize the ethical considerations of sharing information" (metaliteracy goal 2.5).[41] For example, during the GPS class, the students leading that day's content and discussion divided the class into two groups: one was to argue for GPS technology, and the other was to argue against it. This allowed students to approach the ethical considerations of sharing information from a relevant perspective. Almost all students relied upon GPS technology daily. Considering the potentially negative impacts of GPS on privacy made students think differently about their trusted devices, although almost all said they would continue to use GPS just as much as they had before.

Although the instructors did not specify any outcomes for the student-created assignments, they all addressed metaliteracy goal 3: "Share information and collaborate in a variety of participatory environments."[42] In the Vine contest, students shared information in a video format. In several of the other assignments, students shared information on their blogs. On Spotify, students shared information on a social network based on musical tastes and interest. Only the Vine contest, however, included a direct process of collaboration. The other assignments required that students create, write, or analyze something on their own and then share the results with the instructors and their classmates. All assignments involved some form of commenting or feedback.

The student blogs, assignments, and class discussions reflected metaliteracy goal 4: "Demonstrate ability to connect learning and research strategies with lifelong learning processes and personal, academic, and professional goals."[43] Students naturally connected what they were doing in class with their lives outside of class. One student observes:

> When learning about our online identities and how we want people to perceive us, it turned into real life material that exists in our everyday life and I then began to love this class. I didn't realize how much time and effort people put into their profiles to make them seem a certain

> way. . . . How attached we become to our technology and the effects that it has on us such as loneliness and depression. After learning about this I noticed it in myself and becoming aware of it was pretty cool.[44]

One student notes in an anonymous evaluation "the way that we talk about online relationships and the sometimes drastic impacts that technology has on our lives, in some cases not in the best way. This class has made me more conscious about how and when I use technology and has in a way made me use it less."

We asked students to "use self-reflection to assess one's own learning and knowledge of the learning process" (metaliteracy goal 4.4) at several points during the semester in self-evaluations and reflective blog posts.[45] Students expressed throughout the semester that they felt comfortable sharing their opinions and that they enjoyed hearing different viewpoints from their peers (metaliteracy goal 4.7). Students also expressed that because they were responsible for teaching the content to their peers, they took more time and energy to find information, evaluate it, and synthesize it. They also retained the information much more than they normally would have in a class where they were completing an instructor-determined assignment or memorizing information for a test (metaliteracy goals 4.9 and 4.10).

Throughout the semester, it was challenging for the instructors to avoid giving more direction when students became anxious about creating assignments and leading content. Although the instructors wanted to encourage students to develop a sense of agency, it was difficult to remain firm in the face of students' anxiety. This was especially true at the beginning of the semester. Students would often ask us, the instructors, what we wanted them to do or how they were supposed to complete a given task. The instructors responded by supporting them and clarifying details, but not giving instructions. Often, given time and space, students were able to work through their anxieties and make decisions. Sometimes those decisions did not work out, but for the most part, students took that in stride and made adjustments, which was reflective of metaliteracy goal 4.8: "Recognize that learning is a process and that reflecting on errors and mistakes leads to new insights and discoveries."[46]

ASSESSMENT OF INSTRUCTION ENDEAVOR

The instructors assessed the students' learning experiences in informal and formal course evaluations. At the midpoint of the semester, students submitted anonymous answers to three questions. Out of twenty-two students in the class, only eight responded. The instructors found this troubling in a course so focused on student input. When asked directly why they hadn't filled out the evaluation, students said they were busy or they had forgotten. Of the students who did respond, several expressed that they had been challenged by the open, self-directed nature of many of the assignments. One student notes, "I personally have a hard time with creative things like 'Open Blogs' just because I'm not sure what to post about or where to start. I tend to enjoy/learn more when I have more structure." This reflects Maryellen Weimer's point that students are often lacking the confidence to be self-directed and thus seek out structure and direction from the instructor.[47] It was interesting that the student expressed the ability to learn more with structure, and the instructors questioned whether this was actually true, or if the student was simply expressing that he or she was more comfortable with structure.

For end-of-semester evaluations, the instructors assigned students a wrap-up blog post in which students responded to the following prompts:

- Your expectations versus the actual course
- What you learned
- What opinions/beliefs of yours were challenged
- Most effective versus most challenging aspect of the class
- If this class ran again, what you would change and what you would keep

Formal course evaluations were also conducted. Both evaluations yielded commentary about the student-created assignments and the student-led content aspects of the course.

In general, students found it challenging to generate their own assignments for the class, but they found the process of doing so to be a good learning experience. In her wrap-up blog, one student notes, "I would say making up assignments for the class was the most challenging part, but was also the most effective."[48] Grading, however, was an issue for the instructors in terms of the student-created assignments. Most students attached some form of rubric to their assignments. Some of the rubrics, though, did not fit the assignment so they were difficult to use. In future iterations of the course, the instructors would reimagine how grading and evaluation should happen for the student-created assignments. See the following Discussion/Lessons Learned section for additional details.

In terms of the student-led content development, the instructors identified a mixture of responses from students. Some found the student-led portion of class empowering and engaging. Others found it problematic. Many had initially found it uncomfortable but ultimately enjoyed the process. One student notes:

> The first day I was intrigued by the topic but when our professors described to us that we would be making up our classes halfway through the semester, I wanted to bail. As the semester went on I ended up liking the students teaching the class more. . . . I thought it made us really have to learn about our subject instead of just listening to our teachers talk about it.[49]

Another student commented that at first he thought the student-led content was "lazy teaching." However, he felt he learned much more knowing he was the one responsible for presenting it. Another student notes: "Breaking the class into small groups and giving them each a topic with three days to present was a great way to get everyone involved. . . . I thought that was a very effective way of learning."[50] In an anonymous evaluation, one student comments, "I really enjoyed the class. I learned a lot more than I had expected to. I enjoyed how the content of the course was in the hands of the students." In his wrap-up blog, one student expressed that the student-led content had challenged him to define his own goals and direct his own learning. He found it to be a powerful learning experience. Another student noted in her post that she appreciated the bottom-up structure of the class.

On the other hand, some students disliked being taught by their peers. One student notes on the anonymous course evaluation: "The course itself was interesting, fun, and interactive. However, I feel it lacked in structure. It was hard to stay motivated to learn and come to class when most of the class was designed and led by peers." In their final blog posts, many students expressed that the student-led portion of the class felt more like student presentations than students teaching the class. Many felt they were being presented with information but not given an opportunity to apply it. Others felt that the student-led portions of the class went on for too long and should have been either reduced or broken up. The majority of responses in the wrap-up blogs critiqued the execution of student-led classes, yet they felt the experience had been useful or powerful in some way. Almost all responses indicated that the students had enjoyed leading their classes and had learned a lot from the process but did not particularly enjoy sitting through the classes led by their peers.

The instructors also had mixed feelings about the effectiveness of the student-led portion of the course. Many students approached this project as they would a presentation. Despite the attempts at designing the assignment to give students a lot of choice, they seemed hesitant to venture out with any unconventional teaching activities or approaches. Although all groups at least attempted some form of interactivity in the classes they led, not all groups were successful in their attempts to engage their peers. Also, because the instructors did not specify a time frame for the student-led portions, there was great variety in the length of student-led classes. One student took only fifteen minutes of class time to present her content. Other students took the entire class period, which is an hour and forty-five minutes at Keene State College. After reviewing the evaluations, the instructors developed a list of ideas for revision to the next iteration of this course, which will run in the fall 2015 semester:

- Make student-led content a collaboration between instructors and students.

- Require conferencing before students present so instructors can assist students with pedagogy and innovative presentation of content.
- Have a clear, agreed-upon time frame for student-led content.
- Emphasize that students need to tie their content back into larger course themes.
- Include at least one class worth of content, activities, and assignments about effective educational practices as well as ideas for how to stimulate critical thinking and engagement in others.
- Formalize some method of engagement for groups that are not leading the class that day.

DISCUSSION/LESSONS LEARNED

Five words sum up teaching Digital Identity and Participatory Culture: messy, exciting, engaging, empowering, and challenging. Messy may sound negative, but as an instructor, I embrace mess. In her 2015 article, Mahrya Carncross discusses the pitfalls of working within a neat, unambiguous framework when teaching. Carncross notes that one of the things that made her uncomfortable about teaching with the ACRL *Information Literacy Competency Standards for Higher Education* was "how tidy IL seemed under its prescription. The document describes a universe where one can 'determine the extent of an information need' where search strategies are 'designed,' and useful information is 'extracted.'"[51] At its core, metaliteracy is about thinking beyond linear instructional models, engaging in metacognition, and cocreating knowledge. This means that we often walk into the classroom with some objectives, some questions, and many unknowns. The visual representation of the metaliteracy model illustrates the recursive, nonlinear ways in which abilities, concepts, creation, and metacognition all converge in the student's learning experience.[52] Reframing of information literacy as metaliteracy "places all of the essential characteristics in a nonlinear, circular, and transparent framework. This integrated design recognizes that users approach information from multiple perspectives and may start and end an information process . . . from any point and not necessarily in sequential order."[53] Thus, the squirming and rebooting the II 399 instructors and students did throughout the semester struck me as appropriate and powerful. Many of the students were empowered through the class experience. I also felt empowered as an instructor to let go. Educators want to do everything they can to make sure students are getting all the tools they need from our classes to go on and be successful. This can sometimes lead us to overstructure or be too prescriptive when a more appropriate reaction would be to sit back and say, "You figure it out." Throughout this class, I felt empowered to do just that. That being said, there are several things I will do differently the next time I teach the course. It is my hope that these four suggestions will assist instructors who are designing a similar course or who simply desire to use student-led content and student-created assignments in an existing course or lesson.

1. Be clear about what you, as the instructor, are responsible for and what the students are responsible for, and maintain that distinction. Remember, in student-centered learning pedagogy, the instructor is a facilitator. Understand what type of structure you need to provide in order for students to be successful, and remain as consistent as you can in that role. Also, be firm about making sure students are consistent in their roles.

2. Consider assessment—carefully. One of the major challenges with this course was determining how to assess and evaluate the student learning. Many of the assignments were open ended, and although they came with a rubric, the instructors struggled with grading. Several self-assessment measures were used successfully. Many of the students graded themselves at or near where the instructors would have graded them. The instructors considered involving the students in the grading of one another's projects, something the instructors might consider for a future iteration of the course. Perhaps a collaborative grade based on instructor, peer, and self-assessments would be the best approach.

3. Coteach if possible. One of the greatest things about teaching this course was that the two instructors were able to do it together. The instructors wanted to embody the collaborative, participatory concepts being taught. For both instructors, this was the first experience coteaching, and contrary to expectations that it would mean less work, it often meant more. However, the outcome of that work was richer and more diverse than what either instructor would have been able to accomplish on her own. Coteaching is often not a possibility due to the financial constraints of institutions not willing to pay two instructors for teaching a course. Hopefully, institutions and faculty will continue to strategize about making cotaught courses a staple, particularly in courses where collaborative learning models are used.

4. Don't be afraid to try something new—and fail. The instructors often tell students that learning is a process, and that mistakes are a part of that process, but sometimes this is forgotten in the instructors' own practice. One of the biggest obstacles to innovative teaching may be fear. What if it doesn't work? What if no one learns anything and it turns into chaos? These are all legitimate fears. Of course the instructors don't want to fail and don't want the students to fail. But failure often gives birth to success. Don't be afraid to have a class that is difficult in some way. Discomfort often gives birth to some new strength

or idea that can be applied in future classes. In my mind, the only real failure in teaching is to not try something because you're afraid. Instructor agency is an important precursor to student agency.

CONCLUSION: EMPOWERMENT, AGENCY, AND METALITERACY

In February 2015, the *Framework for Information Literacy for Higher Education* was filed by the ACRL. The Introduction states:

> Students have a greater role and responsibility in creating new knowledge, in understanding the contours and the changing dynamics of the world of information, and in using information, data, and scholarship ethically. Teaching faculty have a greater responsibility in designing curricula and assignments that foster enhanced engagement with the core ideas about information and scholarship within their disciplines.[54]

The flexible threshold concepts around which the *Framework* is centered represent an opportunity for teaching librarians to move away from the traditional skills-based approach to information literacy and create dynamic classroom opportunities that facilitate critical thinking, metacognition, and, more broadly, metaliteracy. Nonetheless, the threshold concepts present challenges similar to those experienced by the students in II 399. Teaching librarians are used to the highly structured *Information Literacy Competency Standards for Higher Education*, which delineate in a clear and linear manner what exactly library instructors are supposed to do with students and what exactly students should be able to do after that instruction activity.[55] The *Framework* is composed of six frames, each of which contains a threshold concept. Although the frames are listed in an order, it is simply alphabetical. It is clear from the way they are presented that the process of moving through those frames is not linear. The recursive nature of learning is embedded in the recursive nature of the six frames. The *Framework* allows the space for both librarians and students to collaborate and define the scope, trajectory, and challenges in any given teaching situation. The *Framework* and metaliteracy both allow space for students to be involved in the process of thinking about their own learning and making decisions based on those thoughts. This will likely be challenging and uncomfortable, both for students and instructors. Experimentation and trial and error, as well as failure, will be steps in the process of transitioning from a model of information literacy instruction to a model of facilitating metaliteracy. We felt the discomfort and excitement that comes from making a difficult but necessary change while teaching II 399. The students in the course felt it too.

In the fall 2015 semester, II 399: Digital Identity and Participatory Culture will run again, this time as II INFO 320: Participatory Cultures. Both the threshold concepts from the ACRL *Framework* and the metaliteracy learning outcomes will continue to guide the development of the course, as will the instructors' unwavering pedagogical dedication to student agency and empowerment.

NOTES

1. Thomas P. Mackey and Trudi E. Jacobson, "Reframing Information Literacy as a Metaliteracy," *College and Research Libraries* 72, no. 1 (2011): 68, doi:10.5860/crl-76r1.

2. Robert Barr and John Tagg, "From Teaching to Learning—A New Paradigm in Undergraduate Education," *Change* 27, no. 6 (1995): 13.

3. John W. Collins and Nancy Patricia O'Brien, eds., *Greenwood Dictionary of Education* (Westport, CT: Greenwood, 2003), 446.

4. Constance Kamii and Yasuhiko Kato, "Constructivism," in *Early Childhood Education: An International Encyclopedia*, ed. Rebecca S. New and Moncrieff Cochran (Santa Barbara, CA: Praeger, 2007), http://search.credoreference .com/content/entry/abceceduc/constructivism/0.

5. Barr and Tagg, "From Teaching to Learning," 14.

6. Ibid.

7. Stephen D. Brookfield, *Becoming a Critically Reflective Teacher* (San Francisco: Jossey-Bass, 1995).

8. Maryellen Weimer, *Learner-Centered Teaching: Five Key Changes to Practice* (San Francisco: Jossey-Bass, 2013).

9. Paulo Freire, *Pedagogy of the Oppressed*, trans. Myra Ramos, 30th Anniversary Edition (New York; London: Continuum, [1968] 2005).

10. Ibid, 72.

11. Weimer, *Learner-Centered Teaching*, 28.

12. Ibid.

13. Alison King, "From Sage on the Stage to Guide on the Side," *College Teaching* 41, no. 1 (1993): 30.

14. Carol D. Lee and Peter Smagorinsky, eds., *Vygotskian Perspectives on Literacy Research: Constructing Meaning through Collaborative Inquiry* (Cambridge, England: Cambridge University Press, 2000).

15. George Siemens, "Connectivism: A Learning Theory for the Digital Age," *International Journal of Instructional Technology and Distance Learning* 2, no. 1 (2005): 3.

16. Henry Jenkins, *Confronting the Challenges of Participatory Culture: Media Education for the 21st Century* (Chicago: The MacArthur Foundation, 2006), 4, www.macfound.org/media/article_pdfs/JENKINS_WHITE_PAPER.PDF.

17. Ibid., 8.

18. Ibid.

19. Greg Bobish, "Participation and Pedagogy: Connecting the Social Web to ACRL Learning Outcomes," *Journal of Academic Librarianship* 37, no. 1 (2011): 54–63.

20. Ibid., 63.

21. Mackey and Jacobson, "Reframing Information Literacy," 62.

22. Quoted in ibid., 67.

23. Patricia Hartman, Renae Newhouse, and Valerie Perry, "Building a Sustainable Life Science and Information Literacy Program Using the Train-the-Trainer Model," *Issues in Science and Technology Librarianship* (Summer 2014), www.istl.org/14-summer/refereed1.html, doi:10.5062/F4G15XTM.

24. Thomas P. Mackey and Trudi E. Jacobson, *Metaliteracy: Reinventing Information Literacy to Empower Learners* (Chicago: Neal-Schuman, 2014), 34.

25. Keen Info Lit Bank, "Faculty DIY Information Literacy Modules and Resources" (accessed April 22, 2015), http://infolit.keene.edu/faculty-diy-modules/.

26. Association of College and Research Libraries (ACRL), *Framework for Information Literacy for Higher Education* (Chicago: American Library Association, 2015), www.ala.org/acrl/standards/ilframework.

27. Mackey and Jacobson, *Metaliteracy*, 21.

28. Jim Groom, "Welcome to ds106," DS106 (accessed April 21, 2015), http://ds106.us/.

29. Adam W. Tyma, "Pushing Past the Walls: Media Literacy, the 'Emancipated' Classroom, and a Really Severe Learning Curve," *International Journal of Communication* 3 (2009): 891–900, http://ijoc.org/index.php/ijoc/article/view/633/364.

30. Ibid., 896.

31. Weimer, *Learner-Centered Teaching*, 23.

32. Metaliteracy.org, "Goals and Learning Objectives," updated September 11, 2014, http://metaliteracy.org/learning-objectives/.

33. Kelsey Marscher, "Open Blog: Anonymity," *Kelsey Marscher* (blog), September 18, 2014, https://kelseymarscher16.tumblr.com.

34. Sam Provencher, "Internet Persona," *Sam Provencher* (blog), September 8, 2014, https://samprovencher94.wordpress.com.

35. Ibid.

36. Metaliteracy.org, "Goals and Learning Objectives."

37. Ibid.

38. Ibid.

39. David Kushner, "An Inside Look at Anonymous, the Radical Hacking Collective," *The New Yorker*, September 8, 2014, www.newyorker.com/magazine/2014/09/08/masked-avengers.

40. Kevin M. Gallagher, *NSA Whistleblower Edward Snowden: "I Don't Want to Live in a Society That Does These Sort of Things"* (Praxis Films, Freedom of the Press Foundation, 2013), accessed February 16, 2015, http://youtu.be/5yB3n9fu-rM.

41. Metaliteracy.org, "Goals and Learning Objectives."

42. Ibid.

43. Ibid.

44. Sam Provencher, "Wrapping Up the Semester," *Sam Provencher* (blog), December 8, 2014, https://samprovencher94.wordpress.com.
45. Metaliteracy.org, "Goals and Learning Objectives."
46. Ibid.
47. Weimer, *Learner-Centered Teaching.*
48. Victoria Folk, "Wrapping Up the Semester: Open Blog," *torifolk18* (blog), December 3, 2014, https://torifolk18wordpress.com.
49. Provencher, "Wrapping Up the Semester."
50. Kelsey Marscher, "Open Blog: Wrapping Up the Semester," *Kelsey Marscher* (blog), December 12, 2014, https://kelseymarscher16.tumblr.com.
51. Association of College and Research Libraries (ACRL), *Information Literacy Competency Standards for Higher Education* (Chicago: American Library Association, 2000); Mahrya Carncross, "Redeveloping a Course with the Framework for Information Literacy for Higher Education from Skills to Process," *College and Research Libraries News* 76, no. 5 (2015): 248–49.
52. Mackey and Jacobson, "Reframing Information Literacy," 23.
53. Ibid., 25.
54. ACRL, *Framework for Information Literacy.*
55. ACRL, *Information Literacy Competency Standards.*

BIBLIOGRAPHY

Association of College and Research Libraries (ACRL). *Framework for Information Literacy for Higher Education.* Chicago: American Library Association, 2015. www.ala.org/acrl/standards/ilframework.

———. *Information Literacy Competency Standards for Higher Education.* Chicago: American Library Association, 2000. www.ala.org/acrl/standards/informationliteracycompetency.

Barr, Robert, and John Tagg. "From Teaching to Learning—A New Paradigm in Undergraduate Education." *Change* 27, no. 6 (1995): 12–25.

Bobish, Greg. "Participation and Pedagogy: Connecting the Social Web to ACRL Learning Outcomes." *Journal of Academic Librarianship* 37, no. 1 (2011): 54–63.

Brookfield, Stephen D. *Becoming a Critically Reflective Teacher.* San Francisco: Jossey-Bass, 1995.

Carncross, Mahrya. "Redeveloping a Course with the Framework for Information Literacy for Higher Education from Skills to Process." *College and Research Libraries News* 76, no. 5 (2015): 248–73. http://crln.acrl.org/content/76/5/248.

Collins, John W., and Nancy Patricia O'Brien, eds. *Greenwood Dictionary of Education.* Westport, CT: Greenwood, 2003.

Elmborg, James. "Critical Information Literacy: Implications for Instructional Practice." *Journal of Academic Librarianship* 32, no. 2 (2006): 192–99.

Folk, Victoria. "Wrapping up the Semester: Open Blog." *torifolk18* (blog), December 3, 2014. https://torifolk18wordpress.com.

Freire, Paulo. *Pedagogy of the Oppressed.* Translated by Myra Ramos. 30th Anniversary Edition. New York; London: Continuum, 2005. https://libcom.org/files/FreirePedagogyoftheOppressed.pdf.

Gallagher, Kevin M. *NSA Whistleblower Edward Snowden: "I Don't Want to Live in a Society That Does These Sort of Things."* Praxis Films, Freedom of the Press Foundation, 2013. Accessed February 16, 2015. http://youtu.be/5yB3n9fu-rM.

Groom, Jim. "Welcome to ds106." DS106. Accessed April 21, 2015. http://ds106.us/.

Hartman, Patricia, Renae Newhouse, and Valerie Perry. "Building a Sustainable Life Science and Information Literacy Program Using the Train-the-Trainer Model." *Issues in Science and Technology Librarianship* (Summer 2014). www.istl.org/14-summer/refereed1.html. doi:10.5062/F4G15XTM.

Jenkins, Henry. *Confronting the Challenges of Participatory Culture: Media Education for the 21st Century.* Chicago: The MacArthur Foundation, 2006. www.macfound.org/media/article_pdfs/JENKINS_WHITE_PAPER.PDF.

Kamii, Constance, and Yasuhiko Kato. "Constructivism." In *Early Childhood Education: An International Encyclopedia*, edited by Rebecca S. New and Moncrieff Cochran. Santa Barbara, CA: Praeger. http://search.credoreference.com/content/entry/abceceduc/constructivism/0.

Keene Info Lit Bank. "Faculty DIY Information Literacy Modules and Resources." Accessed April 22, 2015. http://infolit.keene.edu/faculty-diy-modules/.

King, Alison. "From Sage on the Stage to Guide on the Side." *College Teaching* 41, no. 1 (1993): 30–35.

Kuhlthau, Carol Collier. "Information Skills for an Information Society: A Review of Research." An ERIC Information Analysis Product. Information Resources Publications, 1987. http://eric.ed.gov/?id=ED297740.

Kushner, David. "An Inside Look at Anonymous, the Radical Hacking Collective." *The New Yorker*, September 8, 2014. www.newyorker.com/magazine/2014/09/08/masked-avengers.

Lee, Carol D., and Peter Smagorinsky, eds. *Vygotskian Perspectives on Literacy Research: Constructing Meaning through Collaborative Inquiry.* Cambridge, England: Cambridge University Press, 2000.

Mackey, Thomas P., and Trudi E. Jacobson. *Metaliteracy: Reinventing Information Literacy to Empower Learners.* Chicago: Neal-Schuman, 2014.

———. "Reframing Information Literacy as a Metaliteracy." *College and Research Libraries* 72, no. 1 (2011): 62–78. doi:10.5860/crl-76r1.

Marscher, Kelsey. "Open Blog: Anonymity." *Kelsey Marscher* (blog), September 18, 2014. https://kelseymarscher16.tumblr.com.

———. 2014. "Open Blog: Wrapping Up the Semester." *Kelsey Marscher* (blog), December 12 2014. https://kelseymarscher16.tumblr.com.

Metaliteracy.org. "Goals and Learning Objectives." Updated September 11, 2014. http://metaliteracy.org/learning-objectives/.

Provencher, Sam. "Internet Persona." *Sam Provencher* (blog), September 8, 2014. https://samprovencher94.wordpress.com.

———. "Wrapping Up the Semester." *Sam Provencher* (blog), December 8, 2014. https://samprovencher94.wordpress.com.

Rheingold, Howard. "Digital Storytelling 106: Open, Participatory, Student-Centric, Social . . . the Future?" *dmlcentral: Digital Media + Learning: The Power of Participation*, September 9, 2013. http://dmlcentral.net/blog/howard-rheingold/digital-storytelling-106-open-participatory-student-centric-socialthe-future.

Siemens, George. "Connectivism: A Learning Theory for the Digital Age." *International Journal of Instructional Technology and Distance Learning* 2, no. 1 (2005): 3–10.

Tyma, Adam W. "Pushing Past the Walls: Media Literacy, the 'Emancipated' Classroom, and a Really Severe Learning Curve." *International Journal of Communication* 3 (2009): 891–900. http://ijoc.org/index.php/ijoc/article/view/633/364.

Weimer, Maryellen. *Learner-Centered Teaching: Five Key Changes to Practice.* San Francisco: Jossey-Bass, 2013.

PAUL PRINSLOO

9
Metaliteracy, Networks, Agency, and Praxis

An Exploration

I N THIS CHAPTER I PROPOSE THE NEED TO LOCATE *AGENCY* AS A critical foundation for understanding metaliteracy as "reading the world,"[1] a world characterized by the changing nature of knowledge and the production of knowledge,[2] rising inequalities,[3] as well as a variety of networks that not only include but also exclude.[4] Using Bourdieu's concepts of field, habitus, and capital,[5] I propose the notion of *performing metaliteracy* using the broad tenets of actor-network theory (ANT).[6]

Performing metaliteracy involves an embodied and agentic understanding[7] of the cognitive, technological, social, affective, and metacognitive dimensions of metaliteracy. I conclude by proposing *metaliteracy-as-agency* in the service of hope,[8] moving from "a rhetoric of conclusions towards a rhetoric of contentions"[9] in a time "when the old is dying and the new cannot be born."[10]

INTRODUCTION: LOOKING FOR A CENTER THAT HOLDS

> The critic is not the one who debunks, but the one who assembles. The critic is not the one who lifts the rugs from under the feet of the naive believers, but the one who offers participants arenas in which to gather.

> The critic is not the one who alternates haphazardly between anti-
> fetishism and positivism like the drunk iconoclast drawn by Goya, but
> the one for whom, if something is constructed, then it means it is fragile,
> and thus in great need of care and caution.[11]

In this closing chapter I engage critically with the discourses on literacy, and this chapter attempts to create a space that brings together a somewhat eclectic gathering of voices. I propose, among the certainty of new definitions and frameworks mapping literacy or different literacies, that literacy is and should remain a fragile concept, "in need of care and caution."[12] In verbalizing a counternarrative to the existing dominant voices regarding literacy informed by neoliberal[13] and human capital theory,[14] my critique *does not want* to take a stand or claim a unique and not-to-be-compromised standpoint. In my counternarrative I destabilize, open up, and keep open some of the controversies surrounding the notion of literacy and slow down the processes of getting to a consensus position of what literacy is and should be.[15] I point to the fact that our frameworks, definitions, and taxonomies are negotiated processes in the entanglement between different materialities, and nonmaterialities, subjectivities, ideas, and epistemologies.

I acknowledge the specific disciplinary contexts of the debates on information literacy as well as the "autonomous" and "ideological" models of literacy,[16] but I hope that this chapter opens up new possibilities to broaden our understanding and praxis of literacy.

Each of the chapters in this book discusses metaliteracy with a specific lens of critical praxis, and I aim to locate this chapter in the context of higher education's response to the current age, defined as a "risk society"[17] and an age of increasing uncertainty and liquidity.[18] Despite the fact that the different views of literacy and metaliteracy may contain contesting claims, I hope that these different views and approaches allow an understanding to emerge, fragile and uncertain, of what it means to be human in the twenty-first century. What does it mean to "live a fully human dignified life [and] what education contributes to this, and how [do] we assess its contribution"?[19]

The current age can be described through many lenses, but I situate this chapter in the context of increasing uncertainty and a realization that our ontologies and epistemologies of the past do not provide us with a fixed set of skills and literacies to navigate an "unknown future"[20] and an "age of supercomplexity."[21] Without clear guiding metanarratives, individuals are left to make choices—while the consequences of making a wrong choice may be irreversible: "At no other time has the necessity to make choices been so deeply felt and has choosing become so poignantly self-conscious, conducted under conditions of painful yet incurable uncertainty, of a constant threat of 'being left behind' and of being excluded from the game, with return barred for failure to live up to the new demands."[22] As we define lists of different literacies and skills to address the challenges and opportunities of living in the twenty-first century, we are like the three little pigs that are constantly on the run from the big bad wolf that destroys our latest efforts to ensure safety and stability: "We no longer possess a home; we are repeatedly called upon to build and then rebuild one, like the three little pigs of the fairy tale, or we have to carry it along with us on our backs like snails."[23]

Possibly underlying our anxious search for redefining "literacy" is an unease that the knowledge maps of the past have, to a large extent, been proven to be fragile[24] and (possibly) the illegitimate offspring of unsavory liaisons between ideology, context, and humanity's gullibility in believing in promises of unconstrained scientific progress.[25] Literacy has become our hope for creating a center that holds. As such, we experience a "crisis of proposals and a crisis of utopias."[26]

The discourses on literacies often claim distinctiveness based on a specific lens such as the twenty-first century, a current issue such as employability or sustainability, or a defining description such as digital. For instance, there are ample examples of authors using the "twenty-first century"[27] as a criterion and mostly coming to the conclusion that previous typologies and taxonomies have become outdated in the context of what is necessary for this new age. There are also authors who use a particular lens in a specific time period to reflect on the literacies needed, for example, the aspect of the "digital age,"[28] or "employability,"[29] or "sustainability."[30] We should also not forget the stakes various stakeholders, for example, employers, accrediting and quality assurance regimes, national governments, and global networks of inclusion and exclusion,[31] have in defining literacies.[32]

Amid the changing higher education landscape,[33] the current discourse in higher education is flooded with notions of different types of literacies,[34] meta-literacies,[35] fluencies,[36] intelligences,[37] and, of course, skills and attributes needed by students[38] and staff.[39] In responding to the tensions and anxieties of, but not limited to, the increasing inequalities of the twenty-first century[40] and the increasing number of claims and counterclaims by a range of stakeholders,[41] we increasingly scrutinize and reflect on the *purpose* of higher education and definitions of graduateness. Each new day therefore sees yet another set of literacies, skills, or propositions being introduced, replacing the lists received last month and acclaimed yesterday. Our continuous search for definitions, frameworks, and taxonomies of literacy has become our hope for creating a center that holds.

The current debates regarding literacy also need to be understood against the backdrop of the earlier contrasts between "autonomous" and "ideological" models of literacy.[42]

In the context of this book, dedicated specifically to the *application* of metaliteracy as framework in fields and contexts as diverse as faculty, curriculum developers, and librarians, I do not position my exploration in the context of what literacies are needed to ensure economic growth or employability or competency in a digital age as represented by human capital theorists[43] but, rather, propose that *literacy-as-agency* is a prerequisite to living a fully human, dignified life.[44] My take on literacies and metaliteracies is therefore informed by my position that social justice is an essential focus for thinking about literacy.[45] Social justice as focus speaks not only to the notion of access, as provided in the notion of metaliteracy, but also to the agentic qualities of understanding, evaluation, and determination.[46]

LITERACY, AGENCY, AND *BEING* AGENTIC

How do we think about literacy in terms of *agency*? What are the possibilities that are unlocked when we think of literacy, not as a list of skills or dispositions to be acquired and acted upon, but rather as *literacy-as-agency*? How do we translate literacy-as-agency into *praxis*? I realize by attempting to map literacy-as-agency I potentially open up a Pandora's box of different claims regarding the relationship between structure and agency—a relationship filled with tension and possibility. The notion of agency is "slippery"[47] and "stuck" between claims that agency refers to the capacity of individuals to act independently of their contexts and claims that agency cannot, and should not, be understood as something separate from its shaping conditions.[48] In this section I map and share a personal understanding of agency and being agentic and, specifically, understanding *literacy-as-agency*.

A possible starting point for reflecting on literacy-as-agency is the capacity to "read the world"[49]—described as a critical consciousness. "To be illiterate, for Freire, was not only the lack of skills of reading or writing; it was to feel powerless and dependent in a much more general way."[50] In order to read the world, individuals need to be able to map who shapes/shaped their world, the reasons for it, how the shape influences where they have been and where they currently are and the choices they had and have, the rules and metanarratives that govern their worlds, who benefits from those rules (and individuals' adherence to these rules), and, importantly, how to disrupt and formulate alternative narratives, for themselves and for others.

To "read the world" is, among many other elements, the ability of individuals to understand the shape of the world in which they find themselves, the factors and actors that shape the world, the way the shape of the world impacts on their choices and shapes their dispositions, the respective positions and roles of other players on the field, and the rules according to which the game is played. Such an understanding of "reading the world"[51] resembles the notion of "the field" in the work of Bourdieu.[52] Bourdieu's "the field" does not refer to a peaceful, pastoral English meadow. On the contrary, Bourdieu uses the notion of "the field" as resembling a battlefield where different armies and individuals battle it out for space and victory.[53]

Bourdieu tried to explain how society works—who determine the rules, what determines who becomes successful and so forth. Some of the central concepts in the work of Bourdieu are the notions of habitus, the field, and capital. Bourdieu emphasized that we cannot (and should not) disregard the identity of the players and how they grew up: the skills they acquired, the support they had, their training and their inborn and developed talents and dispositions, and how all of these allowed them to play on a specific field. He called this collection of identity traits, dispositions and skills, *habitus*.

Important elements in an individual's habitus are the amount and nature of the capital he or she has. Bourdieu therefore distinguishes between symbolic, social, and cultural capital.[54] While it falls outside the scope of this chapter to explore in detail these forms of capital and their relationship with *literacy-as-agency*, it suffices to state that these forms of capital shape, interact with, flow from, and sustain individuals' skills and literacies—an aspect that is often not taken into account in literacy frameworks. Not only is the dynamic relationship between literacies and capital absent in many of the frameworks, taxonomies, and typologies, but most of these frameworks of lists of literacies focus on the dispositions of the individual, separated from his or her context—past, present, and future. These frameworks are defined from the perspective of the *individual* who responds, as a separate entity, *to* the world. We mostly define capabilities, literacies, knowledges, resources, and tools as different types of capital and emphasize the choices of individuals as if they are not embodied and entangled in the sociomateriality of their contexts. Thinking in terms of a Cartesian dualism—individual *versus* the world—results in thinking that either individuals have the ability to make free choices or individuals' choices and identities are being constituted by external forces.[55] Key to understanding metaliteracy not only as agency but as praxis is to disrupt this binary and to understand and evaluate being agentic while being entangled and embodied *in* the world. *Being* agentic in the world therefore needs to be understood as "an embodied, entangled, relational, networked, mediated and mediating context-specific capability and choice."[56] We therefore need to think about "a chiaroscuro of agentic capacities as these emerge imperfectly within an *inter-corporeal* world."[57] Such an approach emphasizes that individuals are not only cognitive and rational but acting as carnal bodies-in-the-world,[58] making surprisingly many irrational decisions from within various relations and entanglements with other human beings, nonhuman beings, and material objects in a network-of-things. Our responses are, on the one hand, mediated by various, often interdependent and mutually constitutive variables and, on the other hand, mediating, in the sense that the choices I make impact exponentially on the unfolding of my agency and choices in the future. The main tenets of metaliteracy, namely, metacognition and acts of producing, participating, and sharing information using emerging technologies, take place in a specific context that is, in itself, a mediated and mediating environment—including and excluding choices.[59]

Social cognitive theory proposes, "People do not operate as autonomous agents. Nor is their behavior determined by situational influences. Rather, human functioning is a product of a reciprocal interplay of intrapersonal, behavioural, and environmental determinants. The triadic interaction includes the exercise of self-influence as part of the causal structure."[60] Bandura therefore proposes three modes of agency, namely, individual, proxy, and collective. It is important to note that these three modes do not function independent of one another but, rather, as a "blend."[61]

While individual agency and collective agency speak for themselves, proxy agency refers to situations when "people do not have direct control over conditions that affect their lives. . . . They do so by influencing others who have the resources, knowledge, and means *to act on their behalf* to secure the outcomes they desire."[62] Individuals are therefore "producers and products of their life circumstances, they are partial authors of the past conditions that developed them, as well as the future courses their lives take."[63]

The entanglement of individual agency in mediated and mediating contexts and circumstances is described as the "agentic management of fortuity" where "people are often inaugurated into new life trajectories, marriages, and careers through fortuitous circumstances."[64] Individuals have some control over the frequency and relative quality of these fortuitous events by "pursuing an active life that increases the number and type of fortuitous encounters they will experience."[65] As Maton states, "where we are in life in any one moment [is] . . . the result of numberless events in the past that shaped our past."[66]

A crucial aspect of being agentic (whether individual, collective, and fortuitous) is to understand the field/context in which one is acting or being acted upon. Though the individual and his or her being agentic can be described and explored, it is important to note that although distinct, individuals are not separate from their environments but are entangled. Being agentic is continuously generated from webs of relations within which individuals are located and are formed in the nexus between "social and natural, between the material and cultural, the human and the non-human, and between the technical and social."[67] As such, being agentic constitutes assemblies of a myriad of things, assemblages that are continuously made and unmade.[68]

Individuals-as-assemblages therefore need to understand the location on specific fields or in specific contexts, not as something outside of themselves, but as something that mediates their choices and being, but also, reciprocally, is mediated in return. The field, in the Bourdieusian sense, is a boundaried site where players have set and often predetermined positions. Players' roles should be understood in relation to the size and shape of the field and the positions and roles (predetermined and dynamic) of other players on the field.[69] The field, in all of its entanglements, is not a benign, pastoral space but rather *le champ*—"a battle field"[70]—where their personal dispositions (habitus) and various forms of capital interact with the (state, shape, and condition of the) field and other players' positions, roles, and habitus (and being agentic).

In the nexus of these entangled positionalities we find individuals acting out of their agency.[71] We therefore have to recognize the dialectical, constitutive relationship between individuals and their contexts, individuals as agents "as efficacious but constrained and structures as relatively open but constraining."[72] Context or networks, whether seen as local, global, or intertwined and ideological,[73] are fundamental to understanding literacy-as-agency. Referring to the work of Latour, Fenwick and Edwards state that "networks are not flat linear chains, but webs of associations among heterogeneous things and forces that grow and become extended as more connections are added."[74] Literacy-as-agency is therefore a sociomaterial practice: "Knowing [and literacy] is not separate from doing but emerges from the very matter-ings in which we engage."[75]

I therefore propose that *being agentic* can be defined as an embodied, entangled, relational, networked, mediated and mediating, context specific capability and choice.

METALITERACY-AS-AGENCY

The rest of the chapters in the book explore different conceptual and practical engagements with the notion of metaliteracy as not only an overarching framework but also a proposal that the "meta" in metaliteracy may actually indicate a state of "beta"—literacy as constantly being redefined and emerging. Should we accept, for a moment, that literacy-as-agency means being agentic, as described earlier, what are the implications for metaliteracy?

Mackey and Jacobson state that "metaliteracy provides the foundation for media literacy, digital literacy, ICT [information and communication technology] literacy, and visual literacy" and "provides a conceptual framework for information literacy that diminishes theoretical differences, builds practical connections, and reinforces central lifelong learning goals among different literacy types."[76] Though metaliteracy as proposed by Mackey and Jacobson[77] is an integrated framework for engaging with and through different literacies, the "meta" aspect does not necessarily embed literacies within the need to "read the world" as proposed by Freire[78] as embodied, entangled, relational, networked, mediated and mediating, context-specific capabilities and choices.

In this chapter I have proposed that we consider enriching the notion of metaliteracy by situating it within the broader discourses of structure and agency. We cannot, and should not, disembody and disentangle metaliteracy from being-and-acting-in-the-world, a state of perpetual flux and beta, a state of being agentic. In the next section I propose some considerations and pointers for metaliteracy as *praxis*.

CONSIDERATIONS AND POINTERS
FOR METALITERACY *PRAXIS*

In the context of critical consciousness as proposed by Freire[79] and praxis as "reflection and action directed at the structures to be transformed,"[80] it is clear that we have to consider metaliteracy praxis in the nexus between practitioners, practices, and context.[81] Mackey and Jacobson refer to a number of essential practices such as sharing, using, incorporating, and producing.[82] Metaliteracy therefore involves a combination of cognitive, behavioral, procedural, discursive, motivational, and physical practices that are coordinated and adapted to construct particular context-specific and context-appropriate practices.[83] As such, individuals' agency is shaped by not only *who* they are but also *how* they act and the *resources* they have or don't have at their disposal: "They derive agency through their use of the practices—ways of behaving, thinking, emoting, knowing and acting—prevalent within their society, combining, coordinating and adapting them to their needs in order to act within and influence that society."[84] In stark contrast to many of the taxonomies and typologies of decontextualized skills, intelligences, literacies, and graduate attributes, metaliteracy praxis is a situated and critical practice.[85]

It is, however, in the work of Bishop that one gets glimpses of metaliteracy as praxis. If one considers metaliteracy through a critical lens (among other possible lenses) and sees "literacy as political battleground,"[86] metaliteracy as praxis flows from and results in an interrogation of the "historical and contemporaneous privileging of and exclusion of groups of people and ideas from mainstream narratives."[87] Bishop therefore proposes that literacy-as-praxis should (1) mobilize learners as "social actors with knowledge and skills to disrupt the commonplace"; (2) conduct analysis and research and interrogate a variety of viewpoints on an issue; (3) identify "issues focused on socio-political realities in the context of the lives of the learners"; (4) design and undertake "actions focused on social justice outside of the classroom"; and (5) reflect upon the impact or a lack of impact of these actions and create "vision(s) for future project(s)."[88]

Bishop refers to the 2006 work of Behrman, who lists some common practices informed by a critical literacy approach. The practices include "(a) reading supplementary texts; (b) reading multiple texts; (c) reading from a resistant perspective; (d) producing counter-texts; (e) conducting student-choice research projects; and (f) taking social action."[89]

As such metaliteracy praxis is a "boundary activity" that no longer assigns "privilege to one tightly focused kind of information" but continuously crosses and encourages the crossing of boundaries.[90] As "boundary activity" metaliteracy praxis is and should remain fragile, "in need of care and caution."[91] We cannot, and should not, allow metaliteracy to become complacent, disembodied, and decontextualized from literacy-as-social-practice, "patterned by institutions and power relationships, and embedded in particular socio-historical and cultural contexts."[92]

Literacy-as-social-practice is and should resemble a noisy kennel,[93] with input from practice, different contexts, and, above all, different disciplines. There is a danger that metaliteracy as concept and practice will become an ossified, grand, unified and unifying theory[94] that is overly protective of its historical roots in information literacy and not open to the richness of sense-making from other disciplines and practices. While disciplines should remain vigilant to "intellectual voyeurism"[95] and amateurish interdisciplinarity, metaliteracy-as-praxis can benefit from creating and being a space for different voices from different disciplinary backgrounds who question, engage, critique, and make sense of what it means to be human, participate in the discourses of the day, and live dignified lives.

(IN)CONCLUSIONS

Amid the proliferation of frameworks, typologies, taxonomies, and various descriptions of literacies, this chapter attempted to destabilize, open up, and keep open some of the controversies surrounding the notion of literacy and to slow down the processes of getting to a consensus position of what literacy is and should be.[96]

My purpose in this chapter was not to debunk different approaches to and frameworks of metaliteracy but, rather, to assemble a number of critical voices in order to destabilize, however temporarily, some of our taken-for-granted assumptions and claims. I hope that the chapter offered an arena for discourse and for reconsideration, accepting that our frameworks and definitions are and should be fragile and in need of care and caution.[97]

I propose that we need to embed literacies within the broader necessity to "read the world" as proposed by Freire[98] as embodied, entangled, relational, networked, mediated and mediating, context-specific capabilities and choices. This chapter was informed and shaped by questions such as these: How do we think about literacy in terms of *agency*? What are the possibilities that are unlocked when we think of literacy not as a list of skills or dispositions to be acquired and acted upon but, rather, as *literacy-as-agency*? How do we translate literacy-as-agency into *praxis*?

By bringing together a number of disparate voices, such as social cognitive theory,[99] field theory,[100] and actor-network theory,[101] I considered metaliteracy-as-agency and metaliteracy-as-praxis. Considering the notion of metaliteracy in the context of networks, agency, and praxis (possibly) opened up metaliteracy as a "boundary activity"[102] where our praxis is found in the nexus of embodied, entangled, relational, networked, mediated and mediating, context-specific capabilities and choices.

NOTES

1. Paulo Freire, *Learning to Question: A Pedagogy of Liberation* (New York: Continuum, 1989), xvii.

2. Ronald Barnett, "Supercomplexity and the Curriculum," *Studies in Higher Education* 25, no. 3 (2000): 255–65; Ronald Barnett, "Learning for an Unknown Future," *Higher Education Research and Development* 23, no. 3 (2004): 247–60, doi:10.1080/0729436042000235382; Ronald Barnett, "Knowing and Becoming in the Higher Education Curriculum," *Studies in Higher Education* 34, no. 4 (2009): 429–40, doi:10.1080/03075070902771978.

3. Zygmunt Bauman, *Globalization: The Human Consequences* (Cambridge, UK: Polity Press, 1998); Zygmunt Bauman, *Collateral Damage: Social Inequalities in a Global Age* (Cambridge, UK: Polity Press, 2011); Thomas Piketty, *Capital in the Twenty-First Century*, trans. Arthur Goldhammer (Cambridge, MA: Belknap Press, 2014); Guy Standing, *The Precariat: The New Dangerous Class* (London: Bloomsbury, 2011).

4. Manuel Castells, *Communication Power* (Oxford, UK: Oxford University Press, 2009).

5. Michael Grenfell, ed., *Pierre Bourdieu: Key Concepts*, 2nd ed. (Durham, UK: Acumen, 2012).

6. Tara Fenwick and Richard Edwards, *Actor-Network Theory in Education* (London, UK: Routledge, 2010); Tara Fenwick and Richard Edwards, "Networks of Knowledge, Matters of Learning, and Criticality in Higher Education," *Higher Education* 67, no. 1 (2014): 35–50.

7. Margaret S. Archer, *Structure, Agency and the Internal Conversation* (Cambridge, UK: Cambridge University Press, 2003); Matt Dawson, "Optimism and Agency in the Sociology of Zygmunt Bauman," *European Journal of Social Theory* 15, no. 4 (2012): 555–70; Mustafa Emirbayer and Anne Mische, "What Is Agency?," *American Journal of Sociology* 103, no. 4 (1998): 962–1023; Chris Shilling, "Towards an Embodied Understanding of the Structure/Agency Relationship," *British Journal of Sociology* 50, no. 4 (1999): 543–62.

8. Darren Webb, "Pedagogies of Hope," *Studies in Philosophy and Education* 32, no. 4 (2013): 397–414. doi:10.1007/s11217-012-9336-1, 2013.

9. Renee-Marie Fountain, "Socio-scientific Issues via Actor Network Theory," *Journal of Curriculum Studies* 31, no. 3 (1999): 339.

10. Antonio Gramsci, *Selections from the Prison Notebooks of Antonio Gramsci*, ed. Q. Hoare and G. N. Smith (New York: International Publishers, 1971), 110.

11. Richard Edwards and Tara Fenwick, "Critique and Politics: A Sociomaterialist Intervention," *Educational Philosophy and Theory*, article preprint (2014): 9.

12. Ibid.

13. Henry A. Giroux, "Selling Out Higher Education," *Policy Futures in Education* 1, no. 1 (2003): 179–311; Paul Prinsloo, "Graduateness as

Counter-Narrative: Gazing Back at Medusa," in *Developing Graduateness and Employability: Issues, Provocations, Theory and Practical Guidelines*, ed. Melinde Coetzee, Jo-Anne Botha, Neil Eccles, Nicolene Holtzhausen, and Hester Nienaber (Randburg, South Africa: Knowres Publishing, 2012), 89–102.

14. Ian Baptiste, "Educating Lone Wolves: Pedagogical Implications of Human Capital Theory," *Adult Education Quarterly* 51, no. 3 (2001): 184–201.

15. See Edwards and Fenwick, "Critique and Politics."

16. Stephen Reder and Erica Davila, "Context and Literacy Practices," *Annual Review of Applied Linguistics* 25 (March 2005): 170–87, doi:10.1017/S0267190505000097.

17. Ulrich Beck, "Living in the World Risk Society," *Economy and Society* 35, no. 3 (2006): 329–45, doi:10.1080/03085140600844902.

18. Bauman, *Globalization*; Zygmunt Bauman, *Wasted Lives: Modernity and Its Outcasts* (Cambridge, UK: Polity Press, 2004); Bauman, *Collateral Damage*.

19. Melanie Walker, "A Capital or Capabilities Education Narrative in a World of Staggering Inequalities?," *International Journal of Educational Development* 32, no. 3 (2012): 384, doi:10.1016/j.ijedudev.2011.09.003.

20. Barnett, "Knowing and Becoming in Higher Education."

21. Barnett, "Supercomplexity and the Curriculum."

22. Zygmunt Bauman, *On Education: Conversations with Riccardo Mazzeo* (Cambridge, UK: Polity Press, 2012), 21.

23. Ibid., quoting Melucci, 22.

24. Barnett, "Supercomplexity and the Curriculum."

25. John Gray, *Heresies: Against Progress and Other Illusions* (London: Granta Books, 2004); John Gray, "The Truth about Evil," *The Long Read* (blog), October 21, 2014, www.theguardian.com/news/2014/oct/21/-sp-the-truth-about-evil-john-gray.

26. Manfred Max-Neef, Antonio Elizalde, and Martin Hopenhayn, "Development and Human Needs," In *Real-Life Economics: Understanding Wealth Creation*, ed. Paul Ekins and Manfred Max-Neef (London: Routledge, 1992), 1.

27. Chris Dede, "Comparing Frameworks for 21st Century Skills," in *21st Century Skills: Rethinking How Students Learn*, ed. James Bellanca and Ron Brandt (Bloomington, IN: Solution Tree Press, 2010), 51–76, with an earlier version (Harvard Graduate School of Education, July 2009) available online at http://watertown.k12.ma.us/dept/ed_tech/research/pdf/ChrisDede.pdf; John Martin, *The Meaning of the 21st Century: A Vital Blueprint for Ensuring the Future* (London: Transworld Publishers, 2007).

28. David Bawden, "Information and Digital Literacies: A Review of Concepts," *Journal of Documentation* 57, no. 2 (2001): 218–59, doi:10.1108/EUM0000000007083; Allison Littlejohn, Helen Beetham, and Kathryn L. McGill, "Learning at the Digital Frontier: A Review of Digital Literacies in Theory and Practice," *Journal of Computer Assisted Learning* 28, no. 6 (2012): 547–56, doi:10.1111/j.1365-2729.2011.00474.x.

29. Mel Fugate, Angelo J. Kinicki, and Blake E. Ashforth, "Employability: A Psycho-social Construct, Its Dimensions, and Applications," *Journal of Vocational Behavior* 65, no. 1 (2004): 14–38, doi:10.1016/j.jvb.2003.10.005.

30. Bauman, *Collateral Damage*.

31. Castells, *Communication Power*.

32. Barnett, "Supercomplexity and the Curriculum."

33. See Jill Blackmore, "Universities in Crisis? Knowledge Economies, Emancipatory Pedagogies, and the Critical Intellectual," *Educational Theory* 51, no. 3 (2001): 353–70; see also Audrey Watters, "Unbundling and Unmooring: Technology and the Higher Ed Tsunami," *EDUCAUSE Review* 47, no. 4 (2012), www.educause.edu/ero/article/unbundling-and-unmooring-technology-and-higher-ed-tsunami.

34. Kamran Ahmadpour, "Developing a Framework for Understanding Information Literacy in the 21st Century: A Review of Literature" (master's thesis, University of Ontario Institute of Technology, 2014), http://faculty.uoit.ca/kay/files/capstones/Ahmadpour_%202014_FrameworkInformationLiteracy_Final.pdf.

35. Thomas P. Mackey and Trudi E. Jacobson, "Reframing Information Literacy as a Metaliteracy," *College and Research Libraries* 72, no. 1 (2011): 62–78, doi:10.5860/crl-76r1; Thomas P. Mackey and Trudi E. Jacobson, *Metaliteracy: Reinventing Information Literacy to Empower Learners* (Chicago: Neal-Schuman, 2014); Donna Witek and Teresa Grettano, "Teaching Metaliteracy: A New Paradigm in Action," *Reference Services Review* 42, no. 2 (2014): 188–208.

36. Jennifer Sharkey, "Establishing Twenty-First-Century Information Fluency," *Reference and User Services Quarterly* 53, no. 1 (2013): 33–39, doi:10.5860/rusq.53n1.33.

37. Howard Gardner, *Five Minds for the Future* (Boston: Harvard University Press, 2008); Howard Gardner, *Frames of Mind: The Theory of Multiple Intelligences* (New York: Basic Books, 2011); John White, "Howard Gardner: The Myth of Multiple Intelligences" (lecture-based paper, Institute of Education, University of London, 2005), http://eprints.ioe.ac.uk/1263/1/WhiteJ2005HowardGardner1.pdf.

38. Barnett, "Learning for an Unknown Future"; Carolin Kreber, "Rationalising the Nature of 'Graduateness' through Philosophical Accounts of Authenticity," *Teaching in Higher Education* 19, no. 1 (2014): 90–100, doi: 10.1080/13562517.2013.860114; Paul Prinsloo, "Metaliteracy in Beta: A Personal View from the South" (presentation, SUNY Metaliteracy MOOC, 2013), www.slideshare.net/prinsp/p-prinsloo-7-october2013-final.

39. Patricia B. Arinto, "A Framework for Developing Competencies in Open and Distance Learning," *International Review of Research in Open and Distributed Learning* 14, no. 1 (2013): 167–85; Sacha Kiffer and Guy Tchibozo, "Developing the Teaching Competencies of Novice Faculty Members:

A Review of International Literature," *Policy Futures in Education* 11, no. 3 (2013): 277–89.

40. Bauman, *Wasted Lives*; Piketty, *Capital in the Twenty-First Century*.

41. Michael W. Apple (ed.), *Global Crises, Social Justice, and Education* (New York: Routledge, 2010).

42. Reder and Davila, "Context and Literacy Practices."

43. See Baptiste, "Educating Lone Wolves."

44. Walker, "Capital or Capabilities Education Narrative."

45. Melanie Walker, "Framing Social Justice in Education: What Does the 'Capabilities' Approach Offer?" *British Journal of Educational Studies* 51, no. 2 (2003): 168–87; Leon Tikly and Angelene M. Barrett, "Social Justice, Capabilities and the Quality of Education in Low Income Countries," *International Journal of Educational Development* 31, no. 1 (2011): 3–14, doi:10.1016/j.ijedudev.2010.06.001.

46. Mackey and Jacobson, *Metaliteracy*.

47. Colin Campbell, "Distinguishing the Power of Agency from Agentic Power: A Note on Weber and the 'Black Box' of Personal Agency," *Sociological Theory* 27, no. 4 (2009): 407–18, referring to Hitlin and Elder, 2007.

48. Ibid.

49. Freire, *Learning to Question*, xvii.

50. Nicholas C. Burbules and Rupert Berk, "Critical Thinking and Critical Pedagogy: Relations, Differences and Limits," in *Critical Theories in Education: Changing the Terrains of Knowledge and Politics*, ed. Thomas S. Popkewitz and Lynn Fendler (New York: Routledge, 1999), 52.

51. Freire, *Learning to Question*, xvii.

52. Pat Thomson, "Field," in *Pierre Bourdieu: Key Concepts*, ed. Michael Grenfell (Durham, UK: Acumen Publishing, 2012), 65–82.

53. Ibid.

54. Nick Crossley, "Social Class," in *Pierre Bourdieu: Key Concepts*, ed. Michael Grenfell (Durham, UK: Acumen Publishing, 2012), 85–97.

55. Dianne Coole, "Rethinking Agency: A Phenomenological Approach to Embodiment and Agentic Capacities," *Political Studies* 53, no. 1 (2005): 124–42, doi:10.1111/j.1467-9248.2005.00520.x.

56. Paul Prinsloo, "Metaliteracy, Networks and Agency: An Exploration," (presentation, University of the Western Cape, November 24, 2014), www.slideshare.net/prinsp/metaliteracy-networks-and-agency-an-exploration.

57. Coole, "Rethinking Agency," 126; emphasis added.

58. Ibid.

59. See Mackey and Jacobson, *Metaliteracy*.

60. Alfred Bandura, "Toward a Psychology of Human *Agency*," *Perspectives on Psychological Science* 1, no. 2 (2006): 165.

61. Ibid.

62. Ibid.; emphasis added.

63. Ibid.

64. Ibid., 166.

65. Ibid.

66. Karl Maton, "Habitus," in *Pierre Bourdieu: Key Concepts*, ed. Michael Grenfell (Durham, UK: Acumen Publishing, 2012), 51.

67. Fenwick and Edwards, *Actor-Network Theory in Education*, 3.

68. Ibid.

69. Maton, "Habitus."

70. Thomson, "Field," 66.

71. Maton, "Habitus."

72. Coole, "Rethinking Agency," 135.

73. See Reder and Davila, "Context and Literacy Practices."

74. Fenwick and Edwards, "Networks of Knowledge," 38.

75. Ibid., 43.

76. Mackey and Jacobson, "Reframing Information Literacy," 29.

77. Ibid.

78. Freire, *Learning to Question*.

79. Ibid.

80. Paulo Freire, *Pedagogy of the Oppressed* (Harmondsworth, UK: Penguin, 1972), 120.

81. For example, Paula Jarzabkowski, Julia Balogun, and David Seidl, "Strategizing: The Challenges of a Practice Perspective," *Human Relations* 60, no. 1 (2007): 5–27.

82. Mackey and Jacobson, *Metaliteracy*.

83. For example, see Jarzabkowski, Balogun, and Seidl, "Strategizing."

84. Ibid., 10.

85. For example, Karen Nicholson, "CAIS Paper: Information Literacy as a Situated Practice in the Neoliberal University," *Proceedings of the Annual Conference of CAIS/Actes du congrès annuel de l'ACSI* (June 2014), www.cais-acsi.ca/ojs/index.php/cais/article/view/901/821.

86. Elizabeth Bishop, "Critical Literacy: Bringing Theory to Praxis," *Journal of Curriculum Theorising* 30, no. 1 (2014): 51.

87. Ibid., 53.

88. Ibid., 55.

89. Ibid., 57.

90. John M. Budd and Annemaree Lloyd, "Theoretical Foundations for Information Literacy: A Plan for Action," *Proceedings of the Annual Meeting of the Association for Information Science and Technology* 51 (2014), 4, www.asis.org/asist2014/proceedings/submissions/panels/32panel.pdf.

91. Edwards and Fenwick, "Critique and Politics," 9.

92. Nicholson, "Information Literacy as Situated Practice," 2.

93. For example, Lennard J. Davis, "A Grand Unified Theory of Interdisciplinarity," *The Chronicle of Higher Education* 53, no. 40 (2007), http://chronicle.com/article/A-Grand-Unified-Theory-of/13328.

94. See, for example, Dariusz Jemielniak and Davydd J. Greenwood, "Wake Up or Perish Neo-liberalism, the Social Sciences, and Salvaging the Public University," *Cultural Studies ↔ Critical Methodologies* 15, no. 1(2015): 72–82.
95. Davis, "Grand Unified Theory of Interdisciplinarity," para. 8.
96. For example, see Edwards and Fenwick, "Critique and Politics."
97. Ibid.
98. Freire, *Learning to Question.*
99. Bandura, "Toward a Psychology of Human Agency."
100. Coole, "Rethinking Agency"; Maton, "Habitus."
101. Edwards and Fenwick, "Critique and Politics."
102. Budd and Lloyd, "Theoretical Foundations for Information Literacy."

BIBLIOGRAPHY

Ahmadpour, Kamran. "Developing a Framework for Understanding Information Literacy in the 21st Century: A Review of Literature." Master's thesis, University of Ontario Institute of Technology, 2014. http://faculty.uoit.ca/kay/files/capstones/Ahmadpour_%202014_FrameworkInformationLiteracy_Final.pdf.

Apple, Michael W. (ed.). *Global Crises, Social Justice, and Education.* New York: Routledge, 2010.

Archer, Margaret S. *Structure, Agency and the Internal Conversation.* Cambridge, UK: Cambridge University Press, 2003.

Area, Manuel, and Teresa Pessoa. "From the Solid to the Liquid: New Literacies for the Cultural Changes of Web 2.0." *Communicar: Scientific Journal of Media Communication*, article preprint (2012). doi:10.3916/C38-2011-02-01. www.revistacomunicar.com/pdf/preprint/38/En-01-PRE-12378.pdf.

Arinto, Patricia B. "A Framework for Developing Competencies in Open and Distance Learning." *International Review of Research in Open and Distributed Learning* 14, no. 1 (2013): 167–85.

Bandura, Alfred. "Toward a Psychology of Human Agency." *Perspectives on Psychological Science* 1, no. 2 (2006): 164–80. doi:10.1111/j.1745-6916.2006.00011.x.

Baptiste, Ian. "Educating Lone Wolves: Pedagogical Implications of Human Capital Theory." *Adult Education Quarterly* 51, no. 3 (2001): 184–201.

Barnett, Ronald. "Knowing and Becoming in the Higher Education Curriculum." *Studies in Higher Education* 34, no. 4 (2009): 429–40. doi:10.1080/03075070902771978.

———. "Learning for an Unknown Future." *Higher Education Research and Development* 23, no. 3 (2004): 247–60. doi:10.1080/0729436042000235382.

———. "Supercomplexity and the Curriculum." *Studies in Higher Education* 25, no. 3 (2000): 255–65.

Bauman, Zygmunt. *Collateral Damage: Social Inequalities in a Global Age.* Cambridge, UK: Polity Press, 2011.

————. *Globalization: The Human Consequences*. Cambridge, UK: Polity Press, 1998.

————. *On Education: Conversations with Riccardo Mazzeo*. Cambridge, UK: Polity Press, 2012.

————. "Searching for a Centre That Holds." In *Global Modernities*, edited by Mike Featherstone, Scott Lash, and Roland Robertson, 140–54. London: SAGE Publications, 1995.

————. *Wasted Lives: Modernity and Its Outcasts*. Cambridge, UK: Polity Press, 2004.

Bawden, David. "Information and Digital Literacies: A Review of Concepts." *Journal of Documentation* 57, no. 2 (2001): 218–59. doi:10.1108/EUM0000000007083.

Beck, Ulrich."Living in the World Risk Society." *Economy and Society* 35, no. 3 (2006): 329–45. doi:10.1080/03085140600844902.

Bishop, Elizabeth. "Critical Literacy: Bringing Theory to Praxis." *Journal of Curriculum Theorising* 30, no. 1 (2014): 51–63.

Blackmore, Jill. "Universities in Crisis? Knowledge Economies, Emancipatory Pedagogies, and the Critical Intellectual." *Educational Theory* 51, no. 3(2001): 353–70.

Budd, John M., and Annemaree Lloyd. "Theoretical Foundations for Information Literacy: A Plan for Action." *Proceedings of the Annual Meeting of the Association for Information Science and Technology* 51 (2014). www.asis.org/asist2014/proceedings/submissions/panels/32panel.pdf.

Burbules, Nicholas C., and Rupert Berk. "Critical Thinking and Critical Pedagogy: Relations, Differences and Limits." In *Critical Theories in Education: Changing the Terrains of Knowledge and Politics*, edited by Thomas S. Popkewitz and Lynn Fendler, 45–66. New York: Routledge, 1999.

Campbell, Colin. "Distinguishing the Power of Agency from Agentic Power: A Note on Weber and the 'Black Box' of Personal Agency." *Sociological Theory* 27, no. 4 (2009): 407–18.

Castells, Manuel. *Communication Power*. Oxford, UK: Oxford University Press, 2009.

Coetzee, Melinde, Jo-Anne Botha, Neil Eccles, Nicolene Holtzhausen, and Hester Nienaber (eds.). *Developing Graduateness and Employability: Issues, Provocations, Theory and Practical Guidelines*. Randburg, South Africa: Knowres Publishing, 2012.

Coole, Dianne. "Rethinking Agency: A Phenomenological Approach to Embodiment and Agentic Capacities." *Political Studies* 53, no. 1 (2005): 124–42. doi:10.1111/j.1467-9248.2005.00520.x.

Crossley, Nick. "Social Class." In *Pierre Bourdieu: Key Concepts*, edited by Michael Grenfell, 85–97. Durham, UK: Acumen Publishing, 2012.

Davis, Lennard, J. "A Grand Unified Theory of Interdisciplinarity." *The Chronicle of Higher Education* 53, no. 40 (2007). http://chronicle.com/article/A-Grand-Unified-Theory-of/13328.

Dawson, Matt. "Optimism and Agency in the Sociology of Zygmunt Bauman." *European Journal of Social Theory* 15, no. 4 (2012): 555–70.

Dede, Chris. "Comparing Frameworks for 21st Century Skills." In *21st Century Skills: Rethinking How Students Learn*, edited by James Bellanca and Ron Brandt, 51–76. Bloomington, IN: Solution Tree Press, 2010. An earlier version (Harvard Graduate School of Education, July 2009) is available at http://watertown.k12 .ma.us/dept/ed_tech/research/pdf/ChrisDede.pdf.

Edwards, Richard, and Tara Fenwick. "Critique and Politics: A Sociomaterialist Intervention." *Educational Philosophy and Theory*, article preprint (2014): 1–20.

Emirbayer, Mustafa, and Anne Mische. "What Is Agency?" *American Journal of Sociology* 103, no. 4 (1998), 962–1023.

Fenwick, Tara, and Richard Edwards. *Actor-Network Theory in Education*. London: Routledge, 2010.

———. "Networks of Knowledge, Matters of Learning, and Criticality in Higher Education." *Higher Education* 67, no. 1 (2014): 35–50.

Fountain, Renee-Marie. "Socio-scientific Issues via Actor Network Theory." *Journal of Curriculum Studies* 31, no. 3 (1999): 339–58. doi:10.1080/002202799183160.

Freire, Paulo. *Learning to Question: A Pedagogy of Liberation*. New York: Continuum, 1989.

———. *Pedagogy of the Oppressed*. Harmondsworth, UK: Penguin, 1972.

Fugate, Mel, Angelo J. Kinicki, and Blake E. Ashforth. "Employability: A Psycho-social Construct, Its Dimensions, and Applications." *Journal of Vocational Behavior* 65, no. 1 (2004): 14–38. doi:10.1016/j.jvb.2003.10.005.

Gardner, Howard. *Five Minds for the Future*. Boston: Harvard University Press, 2008.

———. *Frames of Mind: The Theory of Multiple Intelligences*. New York: Basic Books, 2011.

Giroux, Henry A. "Selling Out Higher Education." *Policy Futures in Education* 1, no. 1 (2003): 179–311.

Gramsci, Antonio. *Selections from the Prison Notebooks of Antonio Gramsci*. Edited by Quintin Hoare and Geoffrey Nowell Smith. New York: International Publishers, 1971.

Gray, John. *Heresies: Against Progress and Other Illusions*. London: Granta Books, 2004.

———. "The Truth about Evil." *The Long Read* (blog), October 21, 2014. www .theguardian.com/news/2014/oct/21/-sp-the-truth-about-evil-john-gray.

Grenfell, Michael (ed.). *Pierre Bourdieu: Key Concepts*. 2nd ed. Durham, UK: Acumen, 2012.

Jarzabkowski, Paula, Julia Balogun, and David Seidl. "Strategizing: The Challenges of a Practice Perspective." *Human Relations* 60, no. 1 (2007): 5–27.

Jemielniak, Dariusz, and Davydd J. Greenwood. "Wake Up or Perish: Neo-liberalism, the Social Sciences, and Salvaging the Public University." *Cultural Studies ↔ Critical Methodologies* 15, no. 1 (2015): 72–82.

Kiffer, Sacha, and Guy Tchibozo. "Developing the Teaching Competencies of Novice Faculty Members: A Review of International Literature." *Policy Futures in Education* 11, no. 3 (2013): 277–89.

Knobel, Michele, and Colin Lankshear (eds.). *A New Literacies Sampler.* New Literacies and Digital Epistemologies, vol. 29. New York: Peter Lang, 2007. doi:10.1111/j.1467-8535.2008.00855_5.x. http://everydayliteracies.net/files/NewLiteraciesSampler_2007.pdf.

Kreber, Carolin. "Rationalising the Nature of 'Graduateness' through Philosophical Accounts of Authenticity." *Teaching in Higher Education* 19, no. 1 (2014): 90–100. doi:10.1080/13562517.2013.860114.

Littlejohn, Allison, Helen Beetham, and Kathryn L. McGill. "Learning at the Digital Frontier: A Review of Digital Literacies in Theory and Practice." *Journal of Computer Assisted Learning* 28, no. 6 (2012): 547–56. doi:10.1111/j.1365-2729 .2011.00474.x.

Mackey, Thomas P., and Trudi E. Jacobson. *Metaliteracy: Reinventing Information Literacy to Empower Learners.* Chicago: Neal-Schuman, 2014.

———. "Reframing Information Literacy as a Metaliteracy." *College and Research Libraries* 72, no. 1 (2011): 62–78. doi:10.5860crl-76r1.

Martin, John. *The Meaning of the 21st Century: A Vital Blueprint for Ensuring the Future.* London: Transworld, 2007.

Maton, Karl. "Habitus." In *Pierre Bourdieu: Key Concepts*, edited by Michael Grenfell, 48–64. Durham, UK: Acumen Publishing, 2012.

Max-Neef, Manfred, Antonio Elizalde, and Martin Hopenhayn. "Development and Human Needs." In *Real-Life Economics: Understanding Wealth Creation*, edited by Paul Ekins and Manfred Max-Neef, 197–213. New York: Routledge, 1992.

Nicholson, Karen. "Information Literacy as a Situated Practice in the Neoliberal University." *Proceedings of the Annual Conference of CAIS/Actes du congrès annuel de l'ACSI* (June 2014). www.cais-acsi.ca/ojs/index.php/cais/article/view/901.

Piketty, Thomas. *Capital in the Twenty-First Century.* Translated by Arthur Goldhammer. Cambridge, MA: Belknap Press, 2014.

Prinsloo, Paul. "Graduateness as Counter-narrative: Gazing Back at Medusa." In *Developing Graduateness and Employability: Issues, Provocations, Theory and Practical Guidelines*, edited by Melinde Coetzee, Jo-Anne Botha, Neil Eccles, Nicolene Holtzhausen, and Hester Nienaber, 89–102. Randburg, South Africa: Knowres Publishing, 2012.

———. "Metaliteracy, Networks and Agency: An Exploration." Presentation, University of the Western Cape, November 24, 2014. www.slideshare.net/prinsp/metaliteracy-networks-and-agency-an-exploration.

———. "Metaliteracy in Beta: A Personal View from the South." Presentation, SUNY Metaliteracy MOOC, 2013. www.slideshare.net/prinsp/p-prinsloo -7-october2013-final.

Reder, Stephen, and Erica Davila. "Context and Literacy Practices." *Annual Review of Applied Linguistics* 25 (March 2005): 170–187. doi:10.1017/ S0267190505000097.

Sharkey, Jennifer. "Establishing Twenty-First-Century Information Fluency." *Reference and User Services Quarterly* 53, no. 1 (2013): 33–39. doi:10.5860/ rusq.53n1.33.

Shilling, Chris. "Towards an Embodied Understanding of the Structure/Agency Relationship." *British Journal of Sociology* 50, no. 4 (1999): 543–62.

Standing, Guy. *The Precariat: The New Dangerous Class*. London: Bloomsbury, 2011.

Thomson, Pat. "Field." In *Pierre Bourdieu: Key Concepts*, edited by Michael Grenfell, 65–82. Durham, UK: Acumen Publishing, 2012.

Tikly, Leon, and Angelene M. Barrett. "Social Justice, Capabilities and the Quality of Education in Low Income Countries." *International Journal of Educational Development* 31, no. 1(2011): 3–14. doi:10.1016/j.ijedudev.2010.06.001.

Walker, Melanie. "A Capital or Capabilities Education Narrative in a World of Staggering Inequalities?" *International Journal of Educational Development* 32, no. 3 (2012): 384–93. doi:10.1016/j.ijedudev.2011.09.003.

———. "Framing Social Justice in Education: What Does the 'Capabilities' Approach Offer?" *British Journal of Educational Studies* 51, no. 2 (2003): 168–87. doi:10.1111/j.1467-8527.2003.00232.x.

Watters, Audrey. "Unbundling and Unmooring: Technology and the Higher Ed Tsunami." *EDUCAUSE Review* 47, no. 4 (2012). www.educause.edu/ero/article/ unbundling-and-unmooring-technology-and-higher-ed-tsunami.

Webb, Darren. "Pedagogies of Hope." *Studies in Philosophy and Education* 32, no. 4 (2013): 397–414. doi:10.1007/s11217-012-9336-1.

Wexelbaum, Rachel, and Plamen Miltenoff. "The Learning Curve: College Students, Social Media, and Metaliteracy." Paper presented at the Library Technology Conference, St. Cloud State University, St. Cloud, Minnesota, 2014. http:// digitalcommons.macalester.edu/cgi/viewcontent.cgi?article=1419&context =libtech_conf.

White, John. "Howard Gardner: The Myth of Multiple Intelligences." Lecture-based paper, Institute of Education, University of London, 2005. http://eprints.ioe .ac.uk/1263/1/WhiteJ2005HowardGardner1.pdf.

Witek, Donna, and Teresa Grettano. "Teaching Metaliteracy: A New Paradigm in Action." *Reference Services Review* 42, no. 2 (2014): 188–208.

About the Editors and Contributors

TRUDI E. JACOBSON, Distinguished Librarian, is Head of the Information Literacy Department at the University Libraries, University at Albany. Her professional interests focus on team-based and other forms of active learning, learner motivation, digital badging, and, of course, metaliteracy, a concept Tom Mackey and she developed in response to inadequate conceptions of information literacy in a rapidly changing information environment. She is thrilled to have the opportunity to work with members of the Metaliteracy Learning Collaborative and the authors of the chapters in this book, among others, to explore the breadth and depth of metaliteracy. Trudi can be reached at tjacobson@albany.edu. Her website is trudijacobson.com.

THOMAS P. MACKEY is Vice Provost for Academic Programs at SUNY Empire State College. His professional interests include open learning in innovative social spaces and critical engagement with emerging technologies. His collaborative work with Trudi Jacobson to originate the metaliteracy framework emphasizes the reflective learner as producer and participant in dynamic information environments. Tom appreciates all of their work together, especially the metaliteracy research, writing, editing, teaching, grant projects, and design of innovative learning spaces using competency-based digital badging and massive open online courses (MOOCs). Tom can be reached at Tom.Mackey@esc.edu and via LinkedIn at www.linkedin.com/in/thomasmackey.

Trudi and Tom's collaborative work: Trudi and Tom have been collaborating for over two decades, starting with jointly developed information literacy instruction for Tom's students in an innovative first-year experience program and an interdisciplinary information science program, to journal articles, books, and the conception of metaliteracy. Next came multiple keynote addresses and presentations, three MOOCs (working with some awesome colleagues), two SUNY Innovative Instruction Technology Grants (IITGs), the metaliteracy learning goals and objectives, and a partridge in a pear tree (sorry, make that a digital-badging system). And the adventures continue!

For readers interested in specific details, Trudi and Tom coedited four books published by Neal-Schuman that focus on faculty-librarian collaboration: *Teaching Information Literacy Online* (2011), *Collaborative Information Literacy Assessments: Strategies for Evaluating Teaching and Learning* (2009), *Using Technology to Teach Information Literacy* (2008), and *Information Literacy Collaborations That Work* (2007). They coauthored the book *Metaliteracy: Reinventing Information Literacy to Empower Learners* (Neal-Schuman, 2014). Key coauthored articles include "Reframing Information Literacy as a Metaliteracy" (*College and Research Libraries* 72, no. 1 [2011]: 62–78) and "Proposing a Metaliteracy Model to Redefine Information Literacy" (*Communications in Information Literacy* 7, no. 2 [2013]: 84–91).

ANDREW BATTISTA is Librarian for Geospatial Information Systems at New York University, where he facilitates GIS learning and develops geospatial data collections for the NYU community. After earning a PhD in English Literature, he has taught courses on information literacy, social media, art history, and the politics of information. In addition to geospatial literacy, he is interested in digital humanities, critical library pedagogy, social media, human attention, and games-based learning. His e-mail address is ab6137@nyu.edu.

DAVID M. BROUSSARD, BFA, MSLS, earned his MSLS from the University of Kentucky in 2011. He currently resides in Columbia, Missouri. He is a photographer, a painter, a sometimes poet, and hopes someday to be a librarian. He has been published in *The Christian Science Monitor*, *The Southwestern Review*, and *The Tulane Review*, among others.

SANDRA K. CIMBRICZ graduated from Indiana State University in 1985, with a Bachelor of Science in Elementary and Middle School Education. She earned her master's in English Education in 1992 and her PhD in Elementary/Interdisciplinary Studies in Education, K–12, from the SUNY University of Buffalo in 2001. Sandra's career in education currently spans twenty-eight-plus years. The teaching and learning of literacy, English language arts, and social studies at the secondary level are long-standing areas of expertise. This know-how has recently expanded to include literacy and learning important to mathematics and the sciences. She is currently Assistant Professor of Education at the SUNY College at Brockport, where she teaches adolescent literacy courses for undergraduate and graduate students seeking teacher certification in the academic core and/or B–12 literacy education. Sandra's e-mail is scimbric@brockport.edu.

BARBARA J. D'ANGELO is Clinical Associate Professor of Technical Communication at Arizona State University. She earned her MSLIS from the University of Illinois, Urbana-Champaign and her PhD from Texas Tech University. She teaches courses in technical communication, business communication, proposal writing, and health communication. She currently coordinates a multisection course on communication in health care. Barbara's work on information literacy spans two decades as both librarian and professor of technical communication, with a focus on the relationship between information literacy and writing. Her current research interests include information literacy, threshold concepts, writing assessment, and electronic portfolios. She has presented and published book chapters and articles on information literacy, writing assessment, and business communication. Her e-mail is bdangelo@asu.edu and her website is https://asu.digication.com/barbara_j_dangelo/Home.

TERESA GRETTANO is Assistant Professor and Director of First-Year Writing in the Department of English and Theatre at the University of Scranton in Pennsylvania. She teaches courses in writing, rhetoric, and public/political discourse. She earned her Bachelor's and Master's in English Literature from the University of South Alabama and her PhD in English Studies with a concentration in Rhetoric and Composition from Illinois State University. Her research interests include twenty-first-century literacies, critical pedagogy, interdisciplinarity, and post-9/11 discourses. She may be reached at teresa.grettano@scranton.edu or on Twitter @tgrett.

BARRY M. MAID is Professor, and for ten years was Program Head, of Technical Communication at Arizona State University. Previously, he taught at the University of Arkansas at Little Rock where, among other things, he helped in the creation of the Department of Rhetoric and Writing. For more than twenty years, he has been actively participating in online communities and using them as teaching/learning spaces. Along with numerous articles and chapters focusing on technology, outcomes assessment, information literacy, independent writing programs, and program administration, he is a coauthor, with Duane Roen and Greg Glau, of *The McGraw-Hill Guide: Writing for College, Writing for Life*. He can be reached at Barry.Maid@asu.edu.

IRENE MCGARRITY is Academic Technology Librarian at Keene State College in New Hampshire. Her research interests include innovative teaching practices, metaliteracy, and metafiction. She has taught writing and literature courses at various institutions in New York, Massachusetts, and New Hampshire. Irene has a Master of Arts in English Literature from SUNY New Paltz and a Master of Science in Information Studies from SUNY Albany. She is currently working toward a Master's in Fine Arts in Creative Writing at the New Hampshire Institute of Art. Read her blog at https://irenemcgarrity.wordpress.com/ and send her e-mail at imcgarrity@keene.edu.

KATHRYN M. MONCRIEF is Professor and Chair of English at Washington College in Chestertown, Maryland. She currently serves as coeditor of the Shakespeare Life and Times for the Internet Shakespeare Editions. She is coeditor, with Kathryn McPherson and Sarah Enloe, of *Shakespeare Expressed: Page, Stage and Classroom in Early Modern Drama* (Fairleigh Dickinson University Press, 2013). With McPherson, she is editor of *Performing Pedagogy in Early Modern England: Gender, Instruction and Performance* (Ashgate, 2011) and *Performing Maternity in Early Modern England* (Ashgate, 2007). She is the author of articles published in book collections and journals, including *Gender and Early Modern Constructions of Childhood*, *Renaissance Quarterly*, and others and is also author of *Competitive Figure Skating for Girls* (Rosen, 2001). Moncrief is the recipient of Washington College's Alumni Association Award for Distinguished Teaching and is Washington College's 2014 nominee for Carnegie–Case–Phi Beta Kappa US Professor of the Year.

PAUL PRINSLOO is Research Professor in Open Distance Learning in the College of Economic and Management Sciences, University of South Africa (Unisa). His academic background includes fields as diverse as theology, art history, business management, online learning, and religious studies. Paul is an established and recognized researcher and has published numerous articles and chapters in the fields of teaching and learning, student success in distance and distributed education contexts, learning analytics, (meta)literacies, curriculum development, and postgraduate supervision. He was awarded international fellowships to the Open University in 2007, 2009, and 2010 and received the Unisa Chancellor's Award for Outstanding Research in 2008. He received a South African National Research Foundation rating in 2013. His current research focuses on ethical and privacy considerations in the collection, analysis, and use of student data; changing roles of faculty in distributed learning contexts; and postgraduate supervisor identities and roles. Paul embraces social media and actively engages in digital scholarship through Twitter (@14prinsp), Facebook, LinkedIn, and a blog dedicated to open distance teaching and learning (www.opendistanceteachingandlearning.word press.com). His e-mail address is prinsp@unisa.ac.za.

LOGAN RATH is Associate Librarian at SUNY College at Brockport, where he focuses on information literacy instruction with teacher candidates and faculty in the Department of Education and Human Development as well as several other departments across campus. Logan graduated from SUNY Geneseo in 2005 with a Bachelor of Arts in Spanish-Adolescent Education Certification 7–12. Logan then obtained his Master of Library Science degree from the SUNY University at Buffalo in 2007 and a Master of Science in Information Design and Technology from SUNY Institute of Technology in 2012. Logan's research interests include effective collaboration, student perceptions of embedded librarianship, user design, and user experience in libraries. Logan can be reached at lrath@brockport.edu.

MICHELE R. SANTAMARIA is Assistant Professor and Learning Design Librarian at Millersville University in Pennsylvania. Michele coordinates information literacy instruction and assessment, with particular focus on the general education program. She also serves as liaison to the English, Latino/a Studies and foreign language departments. Michele earned her Master of Library and Information Science degree from Long Island University's Palmer School of Library and Information Science, her Master of Fine Arts degree in poetry from University of Oregon, and her master's in Anthropology from University of St. Andrews, Scotland. Her research interests include the role of metacognition in metaliteracy, the intersections between writing and research pedagogy, and the exploration of interdisciplinary approaches to library research, such as autoethnography. With her interest in autoethnography, Michele hopes to bridge her library and creative writing backgrounds. Michele would be happy to engage in further dialogue about any of these topics; she may be reached through e-mail at michele.santamaria@millersville.edu or @infolitmaven on Twitter.

AMANDA SCULL is Collection Development Librarian and Assistant Professor at Keene State College in New Hampshire, where she teaches information literacy sessions, freshman writing, and courses in the Information Studies minor. She is a graduate of Syracuse University's MLIS program and her background includes work in archives, international education, law libraries, and public libraries. Her areas of scholarly interest include online library instruction, collection assessment, the overlays between collections and library instruction, and library resource use by first-generation college students. She has recently published in *The Reference Librarian* and presented at The Digital Shift on these topics, and she is currently the cochair of the New England Library Instruction Group of ACRL New England. She may be contacted via e-mail at ascull@keene.edu.

KRISTINE N. STEWART received her PhD from the University of Missouri. She is currently Assistant Professor and Information Literacy Coordinator at Zayed University in the United Arab Emirates. Stewart's research interests focus on information literacy, with an emphasis on social and epistemological aspects of human information behavior. Her research explores information literacy in relation to issues such as public policy, multiculturalism, and social justice. Prior to Zayed University, she coordinated and taught information literacy courses at the University of Missouri. She has worked as an information professional in the United States, Egypt, Italy, Scotland, and the United Arab Emirates. She may be contacted via e-mail at Kristine.Stewart@zu.ac.ae.

LAUREN WALLIS is Assistant Instruction Librarian at Christopher Newport University. She received her MLIS and MA in English from the University of North Carolina at Greensboro. Her research and teaching interests include critical information literacy, metaliteracy, feminist pedagogy, and the tensions between open and closed systems of information. She may be contacted at lauren.wallis@cnu.edu.

DONNA WITEK is Associate Professor and Public Services Librarian in The University of Scranton's Weinberg Memorial Library. She provides research services and support through information literacy instruction and reference service to members of the university community and serves as liaison to the Theology/Religious Studies, English and Theatre, Sociology/Criminal Justice, and Women's Studies Departments, as well as the First-Year Writing Program. She earned her Master of Library and Information Science degree from Long Island University's Palmer School of Library and Information Science and her Master of Arts in Theology degree from the University of Scranton. Her research interests include social media and information literacy, metaliteracy, technology and critical pedagogy, and collaboration with faculty across disciplines. She may be reached at donna.witek@scranton.edu or on Twitter @ donnarosemary.

Index